SWEDENBORG'S DREAM DIARY

SWEDENBORG STUDIES

NO. 11

MONOGRAPHS

OF THE

SWEDENBORG FOUNDATION

SWEDENBORG'S DREAM DIARY

Lars Bergquist

TRANSLATED BY

Anders Hallengren

SWEDENBORG FOUNDATION PUBLISHERS
WEST CHESTER, PENNSYLVANIA

The original Swedish edition appeared in 1989 as
Swedenborgs drömbok: Glädjen och det stora kvalet,
published by Norstedts Förlag, Stockholm.

Swedenborg Studies is a scholarly series published by the
Swedenborg Foundation. The primary purpose of the series is to
make materials available for understanding the life and thought
of Emanuel Swedenborg (1688–1772) and the impact his thought
has had on others. The Foundation undertakes to publish original
studies and English translations of such studies and to republish
primary sources that are otherwise difficult to access.
Proposals should be sent to:
Senior Editor, Swedenborg Studies
Swedenborg Foundation
320 North Church Street
West Chester, Pennsylvania
19380

Library of Congress Cataloging-in-Publication Data
Bergquist, Lars, 1930–
[Swedenborgs drömbok. English]
Swedenborg's dream diary / Lars Bergquist ;
translated by Anders Hallengren.
p.   cm.   —   (Swedenborg studies ; 11)
Includes bibliographical references and index.
ISBN 0-87785-198-0 (hc)   —   0-87785-199-9 (pbk.)
1. Swedenborg, Emanuel, 1688–1772. Drèmboken.
2. Swedenborg, Emanuel, 1688–1772—Diaries.
3. Mystics—Sweden—Diaries.
4. Dreams—Early works to 1800.
I. Hallengren, Anders, 1950– .   II. Title.   III. Series

BX8712.D9949 B4713 2001
289'.4'092—dc21
[B]   00-049247

Edited by Mary Lou Bertucci
Designed by Alice Hyvonen, Philadelphia, Pennsylvania
Set in Weiss, Frutiger, and Footlight by Sans Serif, Inc.
Printed in the United States of America.

CONTENTS

ACKNOWLEDGMENTS

First of all, I would like to thank my wife Gunvor Bergquist for her help and advice. I also wish to express my gratitude to the Rev. Olle Hjern of The Lord's New Church in Stockholm. His generosity in sharing his knowledge and in lending me books from his library have been of great importance when writing this book.

For several years, the Bridgettine Sisters have kindly extended me the hospitality of their guest rooms in Vadstena Monastery during my stays in Sweden, in all respects an ideal work environment.

LARS BERGQUIST
Peking, China, 1987

PART ONE

An Introduction

An Introduction

THE PURPOSE OF THIS EDITION

The aim of this study is to offer a close examination of a possible meaning of the entries in Emanuel Swedenborg's posthumously published *Dream Diary*, which has also been published in other translations as *The Journal of Dreams*. The word *meaning* is confined to what these notes may have meant to Swedenborg and of what significance they are to an understanding of his religious development and his later theological works.

Since we cannot ask Swedenborg himself, we must penetrate the actual wording of the texts, especially since he never commented upon them and never intended them for publication. Nevertheless, this investigation is based on the belief that the diary notes contain keys both to his soul and to his mind and that an in-depth contextual analysis may prove particularly fruitful.

As will become evident through the course of this work, much of the notorious obscurity of the entries vanishes when we regard them as units or parts and look at the diary itself as a whole. One abstruse detail can be illuminated by another, more clearly formulated one. Swedenborg's dreams, interpretations, and reflections show a remarkable consistency and logic. His terminology and imagery cohere, recur, and develop.

But we must also study Swedenborg's other texts besides the diary and consult the work he was engaged in before, during and after the period covered by the diary. His "dream book" is part and parcel of his whole development and cannot be understood in isolation.

In these notes, we come across figures, phenomena, and books, all of which relate in one way or another to his work and his life. Insofar as it may increase our understanding to resuscitate them from relative oblivion, I have tried to identify and arrange these dream images in a context which may have been Swedenborg's own.

One particular area of reference deserves special mention: Swedenborg's relation to a Bohemian sect—the Moravian Brethren—and its thought and life. Probably he had already come under the influence of Nicolaus Ludwig von Zinzendorf's doctrines in Stockholm before the period covered by the diary and at The Hague, where Swedenborg first wrote down his experiences. During most of the time covered by the travel journal, his connection with the Moravians in London is beyond question. The Brethren he lodged with and his regular attendance at their meetings and services must have made him familiar with the Zinzendorfian religious atmosphere.

My analysis of text and "intertext" has its point of departure in Swedenborg's own interpretations. As we will see, these are often far from being immediately comprehensible. They serve as mirrors, sometimes clarifying but always important. Without entering into the theory of hermeneutics and the current discussion of the right *hermeneia*, I see my task as suggesting a reconstruction, an elucidation without claims to conclusiveness.[1] Possible exegeses, like possible approaches, are probably without end.

To the extent that historical-genetic data fall outside this framework, I have ignored them. Swedenborg's literary and philosophical roots have already been most ably traced by the Swedish literary historians Martin Lamm and Inge Jonsson.[2] These areas lie outside of both my subject and my expertise.

Regarding Swedenborg's psychology, I neither claim to interpret his diary in psychological terms nor try to fit his dreams into any psychological theory.[3] On the other hand, an attentive reading of a series of dreams like this—altogether about 150, including visions and interpretations—together with a knowledge of the author's background and subsequent life, creates an image of the underlying personality.

In dreams, commonplace matters and questions of vital importance run together in a continuous phantasmagoria and are at once both clear and obscure. For a modern reader of the dream book, it soon becomes obvious that the well-known thesis of Freud's *Interpretation of Dreams*—"dreams are absolutely egotistical"—to some extent applies here. Likewise applicable is Freud's basic view that dreams are expressions of "wish fulfillment" or that dream phenomena primarily "mean" just what they suggest to the dreamer. This is, to a large degree, Swedenborg's own thought—see further in this introduction under the heading "The Interpretation of Dreams." We can go further: "concentration," role changes, the merging of several figures into one "dream gestalt"—these and more Freudian key ideas confront us, without system or name, in the journal's accounts, discussions, and interpretations. This is also true of censure mechanisms—for example, Swedenborg's dreams on July 9/10, connected with attacks of illness, which can be studied from this point of view. An interpretation colored by Jungian views is likewise possible. The journal's controversies between a better and a worse "I" or self, the masculine and the feminine, can be seen as an individuation process, the struggle of the anima for its rightful place next to the animus.

There are many possible interpretations to be sure, but by no means one absolute. Numerous other ways of reading Swedenborg's dream diary are conceivable. The dreams are stratified, ambiguous, and phantasmagoric. The only certain thing is Swedenborg's striving, his will to give form, as if alchemically, to the solution, so that the "Great Work" could be born, the long series of texts where he was to note down what he had "heard and seen" in the other world.

DISCOVERY AND PUBLICATION
OF THE DIARY

The notebook in which Emanuel Swedenborg recorded his dreams and visions in 1743–1744, the so-called *Dream Diary*, was unknown for many years. After Swedenborg died in London in 1772, the heirs donated his correspondence and manuscripts to the Royal Academy of Science in Stockholm. The new owners shortly afterwards drew up a list of these documents, but it contains no mention of the diary.

We know nothing about the notebook's vicissitudes during the following seventy-seven years. It is possible that, in view of the private and sexual character of some entries, his heirs concealed it for a while. We do know the family tore out certain pages from an earlier travel diary that also mentioned his dreams, written during the years 1736–1740.[4] We may surmise that they thought some of the remarkably explicit erotic elements likely to harm him (or them) in the eyes of posterity.

In 1849, Reinhold Scheringson, an honorary professor and assistant headmaster, died at the age of ninety at Västerås.[5] As a young divinity student, he had publicly defended a thesis on Swedenborg's theology, which he dismissed as completely Neoplatonic.[6] When Scheringson died, his book collection was inherited by a Miss Littorin. It was then that Dean L. T. Boberg, also of Västerås, became aware of the journal's existence. It seems to have been in Scheringson's library all his life, at least since the 1780s. It is possible that he had received the diary from Bishop Lars Benzelstierna of Västerås, the son of Swedenborg's nephew, but this is mere guesswork. What we know for certain is that, in October 1858, the Royal Library in Stockholm bought the book for a sum of 250 dalers; and, according to a note on the inside front cover, the purchase was negotiated by Boberg.

The men behind this acquisition were the Royal Librarian G. E. Klemming, a well-known personality in Sweden, and one of his fellow librarians, J. E. R. Rydqvist.[7] One year later, Klemming published the book through P. A. Norstedt & Söner, in a limited edition of ninety-nine copies, under the title *Swedenborgs drömmar 1744* (Swedenborg's Dreams, 1744). In the preface, Klemming wrote:

> *Finally it only remains to mention and apologize for the small number of this edition. The fact is that its strange contents, which could easily bring it into conflict with the law, have not permitted its distribution unedited to the public; and it is for this reason that it is only now being passed on to enlightened thinkers, and those interested in the subject. So as not to exceed [the legal limit of] one hundred copies, we have stopped at ninety-nine, all numbered.*

But in the following year, 1860, a group of Swedenborgians published a new edition, this time of one thousand copies.[8] Here the crucial contribution was a fairly long preface, written by Anna Fredrika Ehrenborg. Speaking out on behalf of upset Swedenborgians, she tried to place the notes in their proper context, pointing out the personal crisis Swedenborg was going through at the time they were written and stressing the fact that the little book had never been intended for publication.

Over the years, German, English, and French translations have appeared—indeed, several in English. The linguistically most faithful of the English editions is that of Carl Theophilus Odhner, published at Bryn Athyn, Pennsylvania, in 1918.[9] Following Swedenborg's own custom of numbering paragraphs in his works, Odhner divided the *Dream Diary* into 286 numbered sections. For practical purposes, I have retained Odhner's numeration, adding one paragraph he omitted. Thus, the total number is 287.

Swedenborg's original dream diary, a little octavo volume, is bound in parchment, with pockets on the insides of the cover. A number of sheets have been torn out. Sixty-nine now remain, of which fifteen are blank: all in all, with the fifty-five pages with text, there are 139 pages. Swedenborg used black or sepia-colored ink. His handwriting is regular, compressed, sometimes very hard to make out. He abbreviates, obviously paying no particular heed to spelling or style. One has the impression of hasty jottings, done from memory and considered by the author to be strictly private.

They often seem to have been made by "a man in his nightshirt" (the expression is that of Anna Fredrika Ehrenborg in her preface). But in many cases, some period of time appears to have elapsed between a dream and its recording.

In this present edition, I have adhered to Klemming's reading of the manuscript, a reading scrutinized and approved at the time by a later royal librarian, the author and skilled linguist Fredrik August Dahlgren, famous for his comprehensive glossarium of archaisms in the Swedish language.

AN OUTLINE OF THE DIARY

Swedenborg's dream diary falls into two parts: a shorter section, describing a journey, and a longer one, detailing the writer's dreams.

The first part, his travel journal, begins on July 21, 1743. That day he leaves Stockholm by the post coach, on his way to Ystad, in the far south of Sweden, and the European continent. His ultimate destination is Leyden, Amsterdam, and The Hague, where he is to complete and send to the printer the first parts of his manuscript *Regnum Animale* (The Animal Kingdom). They will fill two volumes.

This section of his journal is reminiscent of similar ones Swedenborg usually kept when traveling on the continent: short, precise notes, obviously made as a personal memoir or to satisfy a general need to document his day-to-day existence. These first entries, apparently written down mostly as a matter of duty, bespeak hardly any pleasure from travel or discovery.

In his early notes of this kind, the listing of towns and sights is often interrupted by excerpts of books Swedenborg has read in public libraries or by technical descriptions relating to his profession as a mining expert. Few mines flank the road from Stralsund in Swedish Pomerania to The Hague, nor does the road pass by any library he finds worth halting at. Having traveled the

Ystad-Stralsund-Hamburg route several times, he is already quite familiar with its sights.

This part of the journal entries ends a day or two after August 20, 1743, when he says he is leaving "Harlingen, which is a large town." We may assume that from there he traveled directly to Leyden or Amsterdam, where there were large libraries. Later, perhaps at the turn of the year, he went on to The Hague to take his work to press. At the end of April and beginning of May 1744, he traveled to London.

Like a hinge between the first and second parts of the diary, some pages occur containing undated but for the most part numbered annotations. The numbered ones seem on the one hand to consist of dream themes, and on the other of changes he has been observing in his state of mind. Furthermore, some lines hint at a crisis in the progress of the scientific work he is engaged in. They seem to have been written after he had been in The Hague for a while. These changes in his state of mind are very significant. He observes: "I was not inclined toward sexual relations which I had been all my days." His self-love, too, has dwindled; no longer does he wish to write for the sake of his own honor. Further, he has found himself in "wakeful ecstasy almost continuously."

The unnumbered paragraphs seem, for reasons mentioned in the commentary, to be chronologically very near to the first "real" dream book annotation, i. e., the one for the night between March 24/25, 1744. Thematically, they are close to those that immediately follow: all truth comes from above, nothing is possible without God's help, true love calls for purity of intent.

The second part of the journal consists of a detailed record of his dreams and visions, interpretations and reflections, during the time before the night between March 24/25 (the "night between" is indicated by a cross), and October 26/27, 1744. In March and April, he makes notes on almost every night; in May, there are only two, perhaps three; in June, four. In July, the number rises to ten. In August, only four; in September, six. October, the last month covered by the diary, is well documented, with fourteen entries.

Thereafter follow two concluding notes, undated, together with two inserted memoranda about the amount of money, in florins and pounds, he has drawn in Amsterdam, at The Hague, and in London.

Regarding content, the entries—obviously often written down in haste, rarely punctuated, their syntax and spelling full of oddities—reflect the course of a religious crisis. Thanks to their continuity and candor, the picture we gain of this crisis is a remarkably clear one.

Their purpose is obvious. Swedenborg the scientist finds himself undergoing certain changes, a process he regards as part of his mission to report. The frequency and reality of his dreams and visions are the more significant since he had already come to realize that dreams are a form of knowledge and that dream images are a reflection of higher truths. The same applies to visions or things seen in waking or half-waking states.

The dreams of March 1744 center on his scientific work and his own personal moral qualities. In his *Regnum Animale*, the work he is now refining and finishing before sending it to the press at The Hague, Swedenborg tried, on the basis of available scientific data, to determine the human soul's seat and function. He investigated the body's mode of functioning, the brain, the nervous system, and the operation of the senses. All these data taken together would surely, he believed, point to conclusions of an incontrovertible nature.

Swedenborg lays deliberate stress on the analytical method, based on experience, realizing that, in his earlier works, he has relied too much on intuition. According to Swedenborg's theologically oriented theory of knowledge, intuition, or "inner sight," is a higher form of cognition that enables a human being who has been purified to have a part, through his or her soul, in divine insight. But, says Swedenborg, it is easy to go astray. And one risks not being believed. Skeptics wish to base their views solely on facts.

This analytical mode of proceeding implies a belief in human capacities: we can attain truth unaided. But egocentricity or self-love is always lurking nearby. His dreams are telling him that he has gotten stuck in the flesh.

Of the months covered by the diary, April 1744 is the most fully documented. Its annotations follow two main lines, which intersect each other. One line runs from an insight into his own sinfulness, to Christ as the source and Lord of all grace. The other line begins at one end with the question of "right" knowledge, while the task that lies ahead of him is at the other end. At the point of intersection of these two main courses of thought, we find his vision of Christ, on April 6–7, the night before the third day after Easter. By this time, he is crushed by the realization of his own unworthiness and the burden of sin. After an evening when he has pondered the relationship between belief and knowledge, he is overcome with fits of shuddering and audio hallucinations, and is flung down "on his face" to the floor. He finds his hands are forcibly being pressed together and words are being put into his mouth. Awake, or half-awake, he finds himself sitting in the Savior's lap. A conversation follows, consisting of three rejoinders. Christ asks whether he has a "health certificate" (*sundhetspass*, a "soundness passport"). To this Swedenborg replies that Christ himself knows best, for which he is reprimanded, "Well then, do!" Thereupon, he wakes up.

We can presume that this vision derived much of its intensity from the Lutheran doctrine of Christ as bearing the sins of humanity. Immediately upon wakening, Swedenborg interprets his soul-shaking experience as a special act of grace; and for the rest of the month, his own state of mind and his relationship to this grace remain an important theme.

Along the second line of his April dreams, we find his science and the epistemology problem. Swedenborg is progressively becoming convinced that "right" knowledge is exclusively of divine origin. But to participate in such knowledge, one must be pure, free from "the fires of the senses." His vision of Christ implied an assurance that his sins have been forgiven. Now arises the question how he, a human being born in sin, shall attain and remain within a state of purity. He oscillates between hope and despair. Very soon after this revelation, we encounter an idea typical to Swedenborg, that of a mission, a feeling of having been chosen, although this feeling is almost one of being elected to a task beyond his understanding.

At the same time as he experienced these nocturnal events, it seems—to judge at least by his diary entries the week after the vision—that he must have been going through his *Animal Kingdom* manuscript for the last time. By mid-April, he is apparently busy with the epilogue to its second part. This postscript is, in all essentials, a homage to that pure, divinely inspired knowledge he calls intuition.

Around the turn of April and May, Swedenborg left Holland to settle down in London. During the crossing, he was in the company of a Moravian craftsman and, on his arrival in London, immediately took lodgings with one of his fellow-traveler's brothers in faith.

The few entries for May bear witness to the intensity of his association with the Herrnhutist congregation, the Moravian Brethren. Questions of grace and sin and of faith and knowledge begin to be colored by these London brothers' mode of thought. Christ has forgiven his sins. Yet Christ must be invoked in the right way: a person's soul must be animated by Christ's spirit. Only if his worship is "pure" in this way will Swedenborg find himself in touch with the Divine. In this, he expressly refers to the Herrnhutists as his authority: "They are conscious of the operation of the Holy Spirit" (May 19/20, entry 202).

In the question of faith and knowledge, too, Swedenborg's thinking is developing along lines close to that of the Moravians. Self-surrender must be unconditional. Everything "selfish" must be laid aside like old clothes. Having acquired this insight, he is preoccupied with the implications of his calling: what the Christ figure had meant by exhorting him, "Well then, do!" Something altogether new, he intimates, awaits him, "something that will be committed to me after my work is finished; that perhaps I am going to do it at some other place, and perhaps to some other cause" (entry 196).

In June, his conviction of the importance of total self-surrender is further strengthened. And his Moravian connections continue, for, according to his journal entry of June 20/21, he has dreamed that the leaders of the congregation are discussing whether he is to be accepted into their community.

"Come as you are!" was one of the Brethren's passwords given them by their bishop and spiritual leader Count Zinzendorf. No penitent struggle, no anxiety-laden efforts at self-improvement were needed. Through Christ's sufferings, our sins have already been forgiven us. This point may have a bearing on the last entry of June 1744. Swedenborg dreams of tremendous battles between Swedes and Danes and of the enemy's finally being overcome after hand-to-hand fighting. Yet he does not himself participate in this struggle, but is protected by a screen, perhaps a Moravian screen of certitude, where spiritual struggle is deemed plethoric.

During the summer of 1744, Swedenborg continued with his scientific work, to which his dreams also refer. His achievements during this time were enormous. On July 9, however, he fell ill, probably from overwork. According to his landlord's account—let me here refer to the section below entitled "Swedenborg's Health"—we know the course of the illness and can follow what his dreams made of it. In view of his development during the period covered by the diary, we should note that, regarding his dreams during the night following the outbreak of this illness, he says he has told "the king" that he had been "modest in amour and veneration" (entry 215). This reiterates, significant for the months to follow, the emphasis that, in his May entry, he had laid on the importance of the love of God in forms filled by "the spirit of Jesus."

It is also in connection with this illness that he changes his lodgings, once more living with a Herrnhutist craftsman. The Brethren continue to play an important part in his mental world. Once again, he dreams of wishing to join them. In his annotations, we come across a series of unmistakably Moravian elements: Jan Hus, the importance of a childlike relation to God, purification before taking communion, and the ceremony of washing the feet.

Simultaneously, he continues to work on his writing. Notes relating to his book in progress are interwoven with questions as to whether his science may be evil, may be taking him away from "what is more urgent," although what this latter can be, he still does not know.

In August, too, his dreams concern his own sins and their consequences for his research. Although he now reacts against some Moravian customs, his whole mode of thinking is still colored by the Brethren's ideology.

Of the four August entries, the one for the night of August 27/28 deserves special attention. Here, for the third time, Swedenborg touches on the theme that will be the climax of the journal: God's guiding love and the calling and task of humanity in relation thereto. From his dream, it seems that Swedenborg envisages the Divine as a guide and a helmsman. It is the dreamer's task to "sweep clean," so that the divine power and love can flow freely through him. In this way, he is transformed into an instrument of the higher power.

His assiduous labor on what would later become a third part of *The Animal Kingdom* continues during September 1744. Now he is working harder than ever, so hard that, in a vision, he thinks he has been warned not to work at night. He feels as if he is on the right path. His satisfaction emerges in dream images—girl is singing, he fancies he is standing in front of a lovely palace.

The link to the Moravian congregation is apparently still as strong as ever. He feels he has been advised not to leave their circle. It is in their church he ought to take communion; otherwise, he is in danger of "once more becoming spiritually dead." He dreams a third time that he is accepted into the congregation, this time as an "immortal" member. No one had ever been that before, he writes, except "one who had been dead and lived" (entry 243). It may be added that this dream of a special status—which I discuss later in this introduction—will later find important expression in his works.

In his October dreams, visions, and reflections, earlier scattered and often enigmatic entries seem to be tied up and fit into a general pattern, the main idea of the journal: the connection with the Moravians has sharpened the realization of his own unworthiness and of the forgiveness of his sins through the merit of Christ. Seen from this angle, a person's task is prayer and invocation. Each person must approach the Divinity in adoration and thus become filled with Christ's love.

Christ's exhortation to Swedenborg that Easter night, "Well then, do!" refers precisely to such adoration. In worship, the act is what matters. In April, Swedenborg had stressed the fact that "faith without works is not true faith." During the "Moravian period," this aspect of sanctification slipped into the background; but now, toward the end of the diary, the theme reappears. The Moravians had rejected works as the means of justification: the decisive thing was faith. At the beginning of the month, his association with the Bretheren came to an abrupt end—he was refused admission to their society. Now, he was falling back into a belief in the efficacy of action, a belief he inherited from his father.

"I should not draw upon others' notions," he writes in one of the last entries, "but of my mine, as it was in the parlor I rented." Worship consists of "charity" (*caritas*), treating one's neighbor in a Christian way, "works of charity under the obedience of faith," as he wrote in the entry of April 20/21. This concept of worship is not developed further in the journal, except by implication, but it is to become one of the foundation stones of his theology, appearing again and again.

The person's worship must be guided by love to God. He or she must follow the *spiritus Dei*, learn how to "distinguish between the spirits"—this is yet another leitmotif in the October entries. Worship is meaningless if Christ is absent from our thoughts. In this contemplation, the Christian must try to find a childlike, unconditional faith, a "condition that I know nothing except that Christ should be all in all" (entry 266, October 12/13). In this freedom, we read in the penultimate entry, "the king"—God, Christ—comes toward him in all simplicity. Moreover, he receives *sapientia*, wisdom, which is free of all pride.

The result is a determination to document the insights that have now become clear. On October 26/27, he lays aside science, in order to undertake a work of quite a different nature. It is to be concerned with the worship of God and the love between God and humankind. His "head is thoroughly cleaned and rinsed from all that might obstruct these thoughts." The way to the Divine is open.

We may assume that Swedenborg immediately began writing this new book. Like most of his works, it was probably designed on a grand scale, first paraphrasing the biblical story of Creation, then describing Adam and Eve before the Fall. However, he never got as far as the emergence of sin into the world, and this epic, although extensive, was never finished.

His break with the past was probably facilitated by his increasing distance from the Moravians. In his entry for October 10/11, Swedenborg notes that the question of his adoption into the congregation has been turned down, a decision presumably made by a drawing of lots. In this way, his relationship to God was liberated from institutional ties, to become increasingly a matter of individualism.

Thus, to summarize, the vision of Christ is the dream journal's culmination but also a turning point. The writer is at a crossroads, through which are passing notions and ideas gathered from childhood and up to the present in ecstatic states and dreams, urging to be uttered and to be reconciled with the supernatural reality he has encountered. These disparate ideas are expressed by opposites. Swedenborg's thoughts readily take form in dialectic patterns governed by an "either/or"—the world of sin or the kingdom of grace, egotism or the love of God, exposure or protection, faith or knowledge, empirical analysis or theological synthesis, exclusion or absorption, purity or impurity.

The dream diary is a chronicle showing how all these lines of thought, intersecting the vision of Christ, gradually approach each other and finally merge into a single axis. Swedenborg describes this process himself toward the end of the volume: "in the name of God, first of all *de cultu Dei*, on the side *de amore*." Everything is to proceed under this symbol of hope, love, and faith, the old categories having crumbled away.

The Christ vision, the gradually emerging awareness, is the

manifestation of a special Swedenborg *unio mystica*, a mystical union with God. For he is already a mystic in the diary, and he becomes ever more one the longer he lives. The lonely state of absorption becomes his own special sphere, wherein he seems to find the source of his action.

THE CONTEXT OF 1743

In the spring of 1743, Sweden was going through its worst crisis since the death of Charles XII, twenty-five years earlier.[10] The war with Russia, which had been an attempt to avenge Sweden's losses under the treaty of Nystad in 1721, had ended in catastrophe. Peace negotiations had been going on at Åbo since January. It was even a question of whether Sweden would now lose Finland, which for nearly five centuries had been an integrated part of the kingdom, to Russia. The Swedes had only one card left to play: a promise to choose, as successor to an old and debauched King Fredrik I, a prince who could be regarded as a Russophile and thus be acceptable in St. Petersburg.

That spring the Swedish Parliament met. One of the candidates acceptable to the Russians was Adolf Fredrik of Holstein-Gottorp, Prince-Bishop of Lübeck and a relative of the Empress Elizabeth of Russia. But the choice was controversial. Behind what afterwards was called "the Dalesmen's Dance" lay resistance to this candidacy and widespread discontent with the way in which the country was being governed. Five thousand Dalesmen marched down to Stockholm, demanding a Danish heir to the throne, instead of the prince-bishop. In mid-June, they entered Stockholm and camped on the large square opposite to the royal palace, the present-day Gustav Adolfs Torg.

Despite protests, the peace negotiations continued over the heads of the Dalecarlians. On June 16, the Swedish delegates signed the peace treaty. All that was lost, against a promise to elect Adolf Fredrik, were certain territories in eastern Finland.

The election took place on June 23, 1743. The war was over, and the Dalesmen were dispersed by armed force.

Emanuel Swedenborg, an assessor in the Royal College of Mines and an expert on mineralogy, an inventor, a philosopher in line with Descartes, Locke, and Leibniz, had been more than an eyewitness to the spring's dramatic events. As head of a noble family, he had a seat in the House of Nobles, whose representatives, together with those of the clergy, the burghers and the peasants, constituted Sweden's parliament. In Sweden, the era between the death of Charles XII in 1718 and Gustaf III's coup d'état in 1772, the year Swedenborg died, is traditionally known as the Age of Freedom. In reaction against the absolute monarchy of the Carolinian Age, the king's functions had been reduced to little more than representative status. All power lay with the Council, with the parliament representing the four estates of the realm. Swedenborg strongly supported these constitutional principles.

In the spring of 1743, Swedenborg had probably been more than usually taken up with political affairs. We may assume that, participating in the parliamentary discussions and votes, his sympathies in foreign policy, without openly taking sides for either extreme, lay with the political faction later known as the Caps, the opponents of the policy of revenge that, with such disastrous results, had been carried through by the Hat party then dominating parliament. On the other hand, it transpires from the dream diary that he had close personal and economic connections with Count Fredrik Gyllenborg, one of the leading Hats.

A few days before the peace was signed, Swedenborg applied to the College of Mines for leave of absence to travel abroad. In a document dated June 17, 1743, he stresses that the purpose of his proposed journey is to publish a work he has just completed. But before he can do so, he must consult certain foreign libraries. In these troublesome times, he says, he would much prefer to stay at home, work for the common good, and administer his own property. This journey will be no pleasure trip. "I am obliged," he writes,

> to put myself to considerable dangers and discomforts, especially
> in these unquiet times, headache and indescribable labor, and

yet, in the end, to expect therefrom harsh criticism from many quarters, rather than mild. Yet, despite all this, I am driven by an inward desire and longing to bring to the light of day, during my lifetime, something real, which, in accordance with my wish and my ability, can be of use to the learned world in general, and presumably contribute to the uses, the enjoyment, and, if I attain my desire, the honor of the Fatherland too.[11]

Permission was granted.

He entitled the work he wished to complete *Regnum Animale* (The Animal Kingdom). It was planned as a part of a series of seventeen volumes, comprising four-thousand quarto pages.

SCIENCE AND DREAMS

After the crisis, when Swedenborg wrote his religious works, he felt himself guided and inspired by God. By divine impulses, automatic writing[12] or writing from spiritual dictation, and admittance to the spiritual world, he felt he had knowledge of things that were concealed to others. But even by at the end of his scientific period, he had access to this divine insight. The dream diary exhibits an interplay between celestial inspiration and science. The scientific part of this process, which the diary reveals, is manifest in the three parts of *The Animal Kingdom* that were written contemporaneously and also in the manuscript on the five senses (*De sensu communi*), which was published posthumously.

In my description of the journal, I touch upon the obvious conflict between mundane analysis and divine synthesis. The dreams and visions of this period become parts of an inward discussion on particulars of his scientific work in progress, on which his thoughts are continuously centered.

In the first dated entry, of March 24/25, 1744, Swedenborg notes that he dreams about the lungs of a fetus, which he is going to write about. It was concerning their natural passivity, which seemed to him connected with the absolute sinlessness of the unborn. He also felt urged to begin an epilogue to the second part of *The Animal Kingdom*.

With this portentous annotation, we are introduced into a future main theme. To the theosophist who traverses the spiritual world, all seems to depend on a breathing technique that makes the necessary psychological screening possible. In the epilogue of *The Animal Kingdom* (II, §§456–457)[13], Swedenborg had stressed the importance of will for this isolation of the mind, this inward concentration. As in his former philosophic-scientific work, he points out in his account of breathing that bodily features lie heavy on the soul and pose obstacles to divine inspiration. The epilogue ends in a tribute to synthetic thinking. "The bodily fires" lead us astray—Swedenborg the scientist asks us to beware of science (*The Animal Kingdom* II, §463).

During the night between April 6 and 7, Swedenborg had his vision of Christ. Although he is both excited and anxious following this experience, he dreams a week afterwards on the mammary gland and of the purging power of the kidneys. He had discussed these matters in the second part of *The Animal Kingdom*. The significant connection here is that physiological purification is now grasped as a counterpart or correspondence of a cleansing of the mind—a refinement necessary for the reception of truth. The context of this reasoning is the religious crisis, where thoughts about purity recur. A little later, in the note on April 12/13, he jots down, as if by automatic writing, the theory of breathing that is also included in the epilogue. Presumably he then sent the concluding section to the printer.

On April 15/16, he dreams about a return to *res memoriae* and *imaginationes*, matters he had memorized and his thoughts about them. Nevertheless, after his return to London in the beginning of May 1744, we find him occupied not by remembrances but with preparations for the third part of *The Animal Kingdom*, which he later reworked and which was published posthumously as *The Five Senses*. The few entries from May and June, during the time he was absorbed by that work, are supplemented by notes on dreams and visions in the manuscript. When he leaves the sphere of facts and, contrary to his intentions, starts synthesizing concluding *imaginationes*, he feels that he is being corrected: "This matter . . . comes not before, parts of it being against *viam analyticam*, but all this and other things to the epilogue or later" (*The Five Senses* §592).[14]

It is obvious that, during the spring and summer of 1744, Swedenborg had no end of trouble sticking to science; time and again he slips into his inspirations. In a passage on sensory perception (*The Five Senses* §569), he apparently writes about his own. The interior person, he says, fights against the exterior person, and the soul fights against the senses. The particulars of this altercation, and how the good can win, must be treated separately, however— "yea, a temple must be built" with the acquired insights as building stones. He adds:

> *This was shown to me by the gold I was carrying. By means of that, I would, although with difficulty, be able to open a gate. Inside there was to be plenty of gold on a table. Which means that I would get entrance permit to spiritual things.* (*The Five Senses* §570)

In the beginning of July, Swedenborg intuits the solution of a fundamental problem in his theologically and philosophically tinted science: how do we tell the good from the bad? Living in the Age of Reason, Swedenborg found it necessary to find objective criteria for all kinds of values. According to his thinking at that time, this was basically a matter of psychology: reason and the senses provided the proof.

His fervent quest is reflected in his book of dreams. The night between July 1/2, his experiences seem as intense and vehement as they had been in his vision of Christ. He observes that he is lifted up, shivers, feels the back of a stranger, in a vision darkly perceives a face. He genuflects before someone whom he afterwards considers "a holy angel." This appears to him as an annunciation: he shall "perceive *veritates de sensationibus internis*" (the truths of internal sensations). However, this truth is only partially revealed, "from behind and obscurely on the front." We find the meaning in *The Five Senses*, where he refers many times to this dream and this vision. Thus, sensual perception gives rise to ideas, notions, the correct meaning of which emerges when they are put into a universal context. For Swedenborg, as for Immanuel Kant, "right" is what can be determined as a universal law. Swedenborg considers this law divine. Thinking, being associated with "darkness" or obscurity, can be supplemented by revelations to reach higher spiritual truths, unattainable to the intellect.

Swedenborg's theory is outlined in *The Five Senses* (§592, §616) the day after he has this dream, and he does so with explicit reference to the dream of July 1/2. After that, on the night of July 3/4, he is told in a dream that his account was incomprehensible. In the same entry, he notes down that he shall proceed to the cerebrum. Then, he refers probably to the following, concluding section of the manuscript, "On reason and its function" (*The Five Senses* §617ff). In the next dream, July 7/8, he describes how observation, analysis, and synthesis can lead to truth. Together, these stages comprise divine goodness. In this dream, he sees this process from the other side—how the Divine reaches the human being by means of tongues or rays.

> *I saw how everything in an elliptical sphere concentrated itself upwards in the highest part, since, in the lowest part, there was something like a tongue from which it spread out. This means, I think, that the innermost was* sanctuarium, *as a center of the globe above, and that such things indicated by the tongue shall be conceived. I believe I am destined to do this. . . . [dream entry 213]*

In *The Five Senses* §634, this same theme recurs:

> *Our understanding cannot reach beyond realizing that the spiritually good is the superior. It cannot grasp how this good thing shall befall us, since that is not a matter of sensations. Another, higher force is called for, which flows into the intellect by all means, making it discern the good as well as the true. The upper must flow into the lower, not the reverse.*

Swedenborg's hectic working pace and the spiritual strain of which the journal bears witness probably explain the illness that struck him about July 10; I explain this illness later in this introduction under the subhead "Swedenborg's Health."

In August 1744, Swedenborg seems to be busy with one of his central questions: the transformation of single exterior sensory data into apperceptions recognizable to the brain. He views this as a question of general importance: how the particular is related to the common and the individual to the Divine. From this point of view, he describes the stratum of jagged or ribbed cells under the outermost layer of epidermis, which is still today named for the seventeenth-century Italian anatomist Marcello Malphigi, *corpus reticulare Malphigi* (*The Animal Kingdom* III §495ff). They work as a relay and link in the continual movement back and forth in the human organism, a self-regulation by "influx" and "efflux," impulse and outflow (*The Animal Kingdom* III §499, §531ff., §547).

In his earlier philosophy, Swedenborg had seen this circular movement as a guiding principle of the universe; he now transfers it to the human anatomy.[15] On the night of April 5/6, he dreamt about "indescribable circumvolutions." Some nights later, on April 9/10, he saw how everything moved in circles:

> *Everything seemed in a consummate way to be fulfilled, flew upwards as it were, concealing itself in something infinite, as a center, where love itself was, and it seemed as if it issued thence round about and then down again, thus moving around in incomprehensible circles from a center that is love, and back.*
> *[dream entry 87]*

The propelling force is love, and the same principle rules the human body. This primary idea can already be found from 1734, in his work "On the Infinite and the Final Cause of Creation."[16] During the period he composed the dream diary, he also outlined this theory in the epilogue to the second part of *The Animal Kingdom* (§466):

> *The final aim, which is also the first one, is that our senses are transformed into vessels of knowledge and innocence forming a spiritual heaven or a holy society. In this, God can watch the end of creation, and see the ultimate aim of aims. From infinite*

wisdom and power, from the first unto the last, this eternal des-
tiny flows, which by intermediary objectives perpetually be-
speaks the divine glory.

This aim and direction of Swedenborg's thought are also manifest in the entries of September 1744, the second-to-last month of
the journal. On September 16, he dreams he is congratulated for
"the conclusion of the first chapter on *sensu tactus*" (*The Animal Kingdom* III, §568ff). Obviously, he had by then left the manuscript for
The Five Senses and was working on the third part of *The Animal Kingdom*, which was to be published in London in 1745. The conclusion
of the chapter in question deals with the interaction between soul
and body, how perception is influenced by the mental state. In the
next chapter, he develops this idea further: "a certain rational light
or life flows into the sensory organs from the soul . . . the innermost cause is in the outermost fibers, which are inspired by the
soul" (*The Animal Kingdom* III, §573). Here we are confronted with
one side of Swedenborg's theory of the harmony between the soul
and the body: we see and grasp what we want.

In the entry for September 29/30, Swedenborg makes a final
note that refers to *The Animal Kingdom*. The dream for that night
seems to indicate that what he has written on "organic forms in
general" has received divine approval. As in the former case, this
refers primarily to the conclusion (*The Animal Kingdom* III, §547).
The field of study is likewise connected with the former one: the
sensory registration of incoming data and their transformation as
they pass into the brain. In this section, Swedenborg the physiolo-
gist examines the separating and distinguishing functions of the
brain: anything considered evil or useless is swept away. The selected inflow is then put in action.

In the beginning of October 1744, he dwells upon the question
of discriminating between spirits, as can be seen from the diary.
The expression is taken from the first epistle of John, where the
apostle urges the congregations to "try the spirits" whether they are
of God or not. The spirit of God confesses "that Jesus Christ is
come in the flesh."

The question at issue is the one extensively treated before the period of illness in July—Swedenborg's work ethic. His scientific work is put on trial in a logically exclusive manner. Is his work from God or is it from "bodily fires"? In the last entries of the dream journal, we can see how he is moving away from ambiguity, solely seeking knowledge in the *regno innocentiae*, the domain of innocence, where divine inspiration reigns supreme. The entry for October 9/10 indicates that he has started writing a new book based on divine criteria, even as he continues to work on the third part of *The Animal Kingdom*. The question is whether this combination of the sacred and the profane is possible. He decides to abandon science, but soon changes his mind because in a dream he has become aware of how the sensations move upwards and downwards. In other words, his discovery of this cybernetic interplay is of great importance and must be described.

Swedenborg's gamut of values, as it is reflected in contemporary sections of his scientific work, appears remarkably Manichaean. "The spirits"—to use his terminology—were either good or evil. There were two lords but only one choice. When Swedenborg finally makes up his mind, the dream diary comes to a close, and so no doubt does *The Animal Kingdom*. The remaining notes describe an obviously painful purification, where the root of all evil, "the love of self, and pride," yield to divine love and wisdom. In the last entries, he feels the urge to concentrate on his new work, *The Worship and Love of God*. That title summarizes the direction of his life for its remaining twenty-eight years.

BETWEEN ORTHODOXY AND REVIVAL

In the dream diary, we can see impressions from the Lutheran confession of the Swedish State Church of Swedenborg's day, mingled with elements of eighteenth-century nonconformism. The stress Swedenborg lays on the importance of being like a child, on total surrender, and especially on the intensely personal relation to the Divine, are revivalist traits.

Basic to the official Swedish version of Christianity was—and still is—the belief in the Trinity. Human nature is evil; Christ came down to earth to take our sins upon himself. He suffered vicariously on our behalf and obtained forgiveness for us from the Father. Through belief and prayer, by living within the framework of the church and its services and sacraments, we are granted forgiveness and salvation. And when the Last Judgment comes, we shall be taken up into the congregation of saints, into heaven—or else consigned to the kingdom of death.

One important element in this official faith is the notion of original sin. From the idea that the human being is essentially evil follows an important corollary: so total is humanity's perdition that, on our own, we have no free will.

Swedenborg's childhood bore the imprint of a specific type of Protestant orthodoxy. His father Jesper Swedberg—a military chaplain, professor of theology, and bishop of Skara—had based his confession on Lutheran dogma. At the same time, Swedberg had gone further than most of his contemporaries in stressing the importance of a deeply felt personal relationship with God. This had brought him close to the Lutheran mysticism that, throughout his life, he had found in his regular reading of Johann Arndt's and Christian Scriver's devotional manuals. As has often been pointed out, the bishop had a certain Pietistic leaning. Again and again, he stressed in his many books that salvation is never to be gained by faith alone.[17] Works—action—are also needed. In Jesper Swedberg's view, "the great faith," the *sola fides* doctrine, posed a threat to the Church of Sweden. On this point he meant that the church had misunderstood Luther's reforms.

Another trait of Bishop Swedberg's character was that he seems to have lived Bible in hand, as it were, and to have known large parts of it by heart.[18] For him, it was the source of all knowledge.

In 1710, at the age of 22, Emanuel Swedenborg undertook the first of his long journeys abroad, from which did not return until 1714. Once home again, he was busy throughout the 1720s establishing and confirming his own status, in particular in the College of Mines, where he was an assessor, and in general in the mineral sciences. For a while, he seems to have been less interested in religious matters.

After Sweden's defeat by Russia and the peace treaty of 1721, three years after the death of King Charles XII, a Pietistic wave passed through certain Swedish religious circles. Returning home were men who had been prisoners of war in Russia, officers mostly, who had gone in their exile without chaplains or churches and had found consolation in a personally tinged Lutheranism. Thus, while the orthodox state church, dating from Sweden's period as a great power, survived and retained its position as a massive apparatus designed to preserve both heavenly and earthly power relationships, there came prompting for a more "existential" kind of Christianity.

During the period when Swedenborg was preoccupied with mineralogy, the well-known German Pietist and mystic J. C. Dippel visited Sweden.[19] During his sojourn in the country—he arrived in 1726 and after a year, as a result of pressure from the clergy, was ordered to leave—Dippel had come into close contact with the royal family and aristocratic circles in Stockholm. He stressed a personal relationship to the Divine and the importance of genuine conversion. Dippel seems to have aroused interest in mystics like Jacob Boehme and Mme. Guyon, and, in general, gave voice to attitudes closer to those of the Swedish soldiers returning from Russia than did the clergy. The religious line of thought represented by Dippel is usually known as Radical Pietism because of its demand not only for a heartfelt conversion but also for an ascetic way of life and for Christian charity. Swedenborg met Dippel in Stockholm and was well aware of his mission and ideas. Everyone in the capital Stockholm at the time discussed Dippel.

We get a picture of enthusiastic religiosity in Stockholm during the 1730s from the diary of the Swedish Pietist Sven Rosén (who later became a Moravian): incessant religious discussions, prayer meetings, and services of worship. Deeply involved in all this was a circle that included some of Swedenborg's colleagues at the College of Mines.[20] To put the matter schematically, these intensely religious individuals found themselves forced to choose between two kinds of religion.

On the one hand, there was Radical Pietism, which, in Dippel's manner, called not only for a radical change of heart, conversion, and spiritual rebirth, but also for an absorption into the Godhead, facilitated and conditioned by asceticism. On the other, there was a movement which, springing up during the later 1730s, would come into full bloom in the early 1740s, and which categorically rejected these Pietistic demands. This was the so-called Bohemian or Moravian influence, emanating from Count Ludwig Zinzendorf's estate at Berthelsdorf in Saxony. Swedenborg's links with Zinzendorf's adherents, which I have already alluded to, will be discussed in more detail in the next part of this introduction. Here, however, it is important to point out its strong Christocentric character.[21]

According to the Moravians, Christ's blood made full atonement for the sins of humankind. This doctrine of reconciliation and the suffering and blood of Christ were made elements of strongly sensual mysticism. No spiritual struggle to achieve conversion was needed. On the contrary "Come as you are!" was their motto.

Thus, official Swedish Christianity blends with nonconformist trends in Swedenborg's diary entries, where we also come across thoughts auguring the theology and theosophy that characterize his works in years to come, the last period of his life upon which his fame rests. But for the time being, Swedenborg is essentially anchored in Swedish official dogma and does not yet deviate in any radical way from it. Even the official image of the Godhead as a trinary being remains intact. Later, like many another mystic, Swedenborg comes to perceive the universe as a fundamental unity and emphatically opposes any division of the Divinity, where it is interpreted as three separate "persons."

The doctrine of Christ's vicarious suffering is often reflected in the dream journal, as in this example from entry 214 of July 7/8:

> *There came to me also the assuring thoughts that God's Son is love and that he took all sins of mankind upon himself and atoned for them up to the maximum penalty, since, if justice*

was to be done, there had to be misericordia per amorem
[compassion by love].

The Atonement will later be rejected by Swedenborg the
theosophist. His rewriting of the theological equation removes any
need for a *satisfactio vicaria*. According to his new dogmatics, the
human being possesses free will, and Christ is God.

Christian grace/mercy—the Swedish word *nåd* means equally
one and the other—is always present in Swedenborg's annotations.
To take part in it, one must have "love for God in Christ"; all goodness comes from above, none from the human being. Soon, when
the exaltation following his Easter experience has calmed down,
Swedenborg abandons this one-sided view and recalls the demand
for good works, the doctrine that had been ingrained in him from
childhood. Grace is imparted to the person who believes and who
follows his or her belief. This thought will run through all his later
works like a golden thread.

As for the significance of the church, services, and sacraments,
Swedenborg adheres essentially to the teachings and notions of
Swedish eighteenth-century society. During his spiritual crisis,
worship and communion play an important part, as they also do
later on. Swedenborg never broke with the Church of Sweden;
moreover, it was legally impossible for him to do so. But he was
convinced that his own work would, little by little, transform the
Christian church from within.

Nowhere in his notes does Swedenborg question Luther's doctrine about the afterlife. At this point, perhaps Swedenborg had no
inkling of his most radical divergence from classical theology—his
interpretation of the Last Judgment. Certainly, there was as yet no
forerunner of his later belief: that we judge ourselves, here in
worldly life, through our mental attitudes and our actions.

Thus, from a dogmatic point of view, the dream diary could indeed have been approved by contemporary inquisitors. Its emphasis on good works might, of course, have been subject to criticism;
but this was a matter still regarded as moot, at least to some point,
since the emphasis had a biblical basis; for example, it was the
theme of the first letter of James.

Despite their formal doctrinal orthodoxy, Swedenborg's notes show obvious traces of his having been influenced by the "revivalism" characteristic of Swedish and northern European Protestant religious movements of the 1730s and 1740s, a fact that will be further discussed in the next section.

WHAT THE BRETHREN OF HERRNHUT SAID

The religious confession of Nicolaus Ludvig Zinzendorf (1700–1760) should be seen against the background of the Pietist demand for a radical rebirth of the whole human being, a penitence in faith and deeds. Although Zinzendorf, too, "subjectivized" faith, as we have already seen, he placed no severe demands on the convert. Human salvation depended not upon the individual, but on God's infinite grace and mercy, as expressed in Christ's sufferings for our sake on the cross. The concrete image of this idea was Christ's wounds and blood.

To Zinzendorf, faith was revelation and visualization.[22] As the Swedish Moravians explained, the individual received a "feeling" or "sensation."[23] He or she saw Christ with the mind's eye, heard the Savior speaking, and after such an event, was changed, "awakened," converted. This awakening was a twofold insight: on the one hand, into the whole breadth of Christ's grace and mercy; on the other, into the depth of one's own sinfulness. This latter aspect was so important that a new concept was coined: to become a poor sinner became synonymous with being born again.

Zinzendorf's theology is based on the grace/sin antithesis. All Christian doctrine must be understood in this perspective. Dogmas, ritual, life within the congregation—all is essentially aimed at a realization of personal unworthiness and an actualization of divine love, which has called the individual to the Divine.

Zinzendorf saw his own confession as at once Lutheran in particular and Christian in general. His calling was universal: to strengthen and deepen the Christian faith and help people all over the world. The original center for the propagation of the count's ideas was his estate at Berthelsdorf in Saxony. One of the villages on his lands, called Herrnhut ("under the Lord's protection") had been built and occupied by Hussites who, at Zinzendorf's invitation, had immigrated from Moravia. Before long, the religious activities at Berthelsdorf and Herrnhut became known not merely in Germany but throughout northern Europe and North America.[24] As a preacher, author, and traveler, the count was immensely active, his ambition being to spread his interpretation of the Gospels throughout the known world. In Christian countries, he tried to bring about a spiritual renewal by sending out so-called diaspora workers. Brethren who had been trained at Herrnhut went abroad and settled wherever they found conditions favorable for a revival.

Knowledge of Zinzendorf's doctrine was also spread through his writings, sermons, and reflections; his tracts were printed and translated. In 1735, Zinzendorf visited Copenhagen, where he was accused of heresies. The Swedish government, informed that Zinzendorf intended to visit Sweden also, became concerned for orthodox, evangelical doctrine and hastened to inform the provincial governors that the king in council had decided to deny Zinzendorf entry.[25]

During that same year, therefore, Zinzendorf printed in Germany an open letter to King Fredrik of Sweden concerning the Moravian congregation's "faith and confession."[26] This document was disseminated, and we may assume that it soon came to be known in circles where Swedenborg moved.

Most widely read of all the count's writings was probably his "Berlinische Reden" printed in 1738, a collection of addresses on the second article of faith, i.e., "I believe in Jesus Christ, His only begotten son." This particular work seems to have been important to a well-known Stockholmer, Erland Fredrik Hjärne, leading to his adoption of Zinzendorf's doctrines. Hjärne, like Swedenborg, was an official in the College of Mines.[27]

In the summer of 1736, Swedenborg set out on a new journey. After stays in Germay, Holland, France, and Italy, he returned to

Stockholm in October 1740. In the unlikely event of his not having earlier made the acquaintance of Zinzendorf's revivalist movement, he must surely have become familiar with its ideas shortly upon his return. Several of his younger colleagues were deeply involved in Zinzendorf's movement; they all belonged to a circle surrounding the clergyman Thore Odhelius, the leading Stockholm Herrnhutist, whose sermons attracted large audiences of both laymen and clergy.

In the summer of 1741, Zinzendorf sent some of the leading representatives of his congregation to Stockholm.[28] One of them, a Swede named Arvid Gradin, had already been ordained a Brethren priest. Gradin, who had earlier studied at Uppsala and had contacts in academic and clerical circles, lent further strength to the Moravian revival both in Stockholm and the Swedish provinces. In the spring of 1743, Odhelius reported his successes in the capital to Gradin: "here . . . souls are being awakened in larger numbers."[29]

Gradin had a charismatic personality. Did Swedenborg meet him? Perhaps he had sat listening in a pew of the Storkyrkan, Stockholm's main cathedral, when Gradin, having been shown exceptional favor by the ecclesiastical authorities, preached there.

However this may be, we may assume that, when he set out on his journey in the summer of 1743, Swedenborg was familiar with Zinzendorf revivalism. We may also assume that religious questions in general were of interest to him just then, his scientific work having entered a phase where the divine factor was becoming ever more important. Explorations into the question of the human soul's function and seat—basic to *The Animal Kingdom*—required clarifying the relationship between God and humankind. And this, in turn, was dominated by another question: under what conditions will a person become receptive to the Divine? We meet the same question of an existential relationship in Pietist teaching. If God is love, purity, and omnipotence, human beings cannot approach him without realizing their own imperfection, on the one hand, and yet striving for union on the other.

Zinzendorf's grace/sinfulness dichotomy fit in well with the questions preoccupying Swedenborg around the year 1743, questions that incessantly confront us in his dream journal. For a considerable period, the question he primarily asks is how he, a scientist imprisoned in his own self-love, can obtain divine forgiveness and come closer to divine truth. Even if he did not leave his native country an adherent to Zinzendorf doctrines, his whole mode of solving this problem, as mirrored in the diary, has unmistakably Moravian characteristics.

Thus, a true feeling of sinfulness and imperfection was a condition for conversion. Yet, in order to understand one's own depravity, it was necessary to contrast it with Christ's grace, as expressed in his sufferings on humanity's behalf. Anyone desiring conversion had to strive to comprehend the events of Christ's great suffering, preferably in such an impassioned manner and with such personal involvement that the figure of Christ himself appeared to the convert's inner eye.[30] Only in this state of total absorption, Zinzendorf taught, would the individual receive a message suited to his or her own special circumstances: a particular sentence, a life-changing pronouncement.

Swedenborg's vision, however, was not of the crucified Christ; the Easter passion week, after all, was over. In his entry for April 6/7, 1744, he describes the risen Christ who appeared to him, with "a countenance of a holy mien:" "All was such that I cannot describe. He was smiling at me, and I was convinced that he looked like this when he was alive."

Of course, we do not need to see Moravian influence to understand Swedenborg's experience. Visions of this kind have occurred in all ages, without benefit of Zinzendorf's doctrine. What is crucial is the intensity of the visionary's longing for the Divine—an experience in all essentials a function of its own intensity. Even so, a comparison between the respective experiences of Zinzendorf and Swedenborg is interesting. For the German revivalist, intense empathy with Christ's sufferings is obligatory if the individual is to escape the usual state of distraction and approach the Divinity. The supplicant must mobilize all his or her senses—the whole body must be engaged.[31] Swedenborg's Easter vision possesses just such complete bodily involvement: he sees, hears, is flung onto the floor, finds his hands being pressed together, etc. Indeed, Swedenborg had long been interested in a sensually engaged relationship with the Divine. Several times in his travel notes he had remarks how the Catholic mass activates the senses of hearing, sight, feeling, and smell.[32]

From a broader perspective, too, the question of Swedenborg's relationship in March–April 1744 with the Moravians is worth studying. Yet it is not until Easter is over, during the three weeks he visited The Hague and during the summer in London, that his relation to the Brethren becomes truly important not only to our understanding of the diary, but also as a background to his later writings.

It seems probable that Swedenborg, immediately after his Easter vision, had direct contacts with the Evangelical Congregation of Brethren, yet another name for the Moravians. Zinzendorf had followers at The Hague: his ideas had been spreading in Holland.[33] As early as 1736, Zinzendorf's Dutch friends had purchased a property for the establishment of a new "Moravian Church" in Herrendyk in Ysselstein, south of Amsterdam. Here they would set up a congregation of Brethren, both for the pious Dutch and for immigrant followers. A Herrnhut society was also established that same year in Amsterdam, which was visited many times by Zinzendorf himself. The Amsterdam merchant Isaac de Long, who functioned as the Brethren's treasurer and commissioner, corresponded with the Stockholm priest Odhelius, to whom I have already referred, in November 1743.[34] Even in Leyden, a group of reformed professors and students was influenced by the movement.

Unfortunately, nothing is known of Swedenborg's possible relationship to these Dutch groups. Nevertheless, we find an annotation in the German congregation's register at The Hague, where he spent a great deal of the winter and spring of 1744, to the effect that Swedenborg attended communion in their church on Maundy Thursday, April 22, 1744. The society's pastor was Johann Gottlieb Pambo. Later on, when Swedenborg's crisis had reached an acute stage, Pastor Pambo was summoned to the residence of the

Swedish envoy Joakim Fredrik Preis to administer confession and communion to the anguish-ridden Swede. Pambo, whom we shall discuss in the commentary on dream diary entry 30, was probably a Herrnhuter.

One concrete element that seems to indicate Moravian influences is the strong emphasis Swedenborg lays, even as early as April 1744, on the importance of properly preparing oneself for the Eucharist. In later dreams, this becomes even more striking. Here we come across one of Zinzendorf's basic ideas: the supplicant must invoke God with his or her whole being.

Halfheartedness was neither possible nor permissible, least of all in regard to the Eucharist. The day before taking Holy Communion, the communicants, like the Swedish peasantry of those days, were to assemble together and confess their sins. In the Lutheran church, it was in the presence of the clergyman; in the Brethren, of the elders. For Zinzendorf, conscientious preparation, culminating in the intense emotion of the confessional, was a condition for the wholehearted self-involvement called for not only in the Sunday service but in the individual's entire relationship to the Divine.[35]

In London since the end of the 1730s, there had been a Moravian society, originally under the leadership of John Wesley and the bookseller/publisher James Hutton. In 1738, they established a Fetter Lane Society, named after the street where the movement's church was located. Following a split, Wesley broke away from the society in 1739; and in 1742, the little Herrnhutist group registered itself as the "Moravian Brethren, formerly of the English Communion." The society had seventy-two members at that time, mostly craftsmen, many of German origin. The leader was James Hutton. Zinzendorf's representative and the spiritual leader was Professor August Gottlieb Spangenberg.[36]

When Swedenborg moved to London at the turn April–May 1744, his contacts with the Moravians became intense. He lodged with one of their noted members, as we know from the diary. He attended services at their church in Fetter Lane, close to his quarters. During the summer months, we can discern how the Moravian sphere of thought gradually affects him. The need for careful preparation for communion has already been mentioned. Another characteristic emphasis for the Moravians was *pedilavium*, the washing of feet. In the New Testament, this ceremony is a gesture of humility; to the Brethren, it is a ceremonial spiritual ablution.[37] Swedenborg mentions this ritual on several occasions, especially in connection with his illness in July. His Moravian landlord has left us an account of that illness, which we will address later.

In the biblical excerpts that Swedenborg almost certainly jotted down simultaneously with his writing of the journal, we come across quotations of St. Paul's farewell to his fellow Christians: "greet the brethren with a holy kiss" (1 Thess. 5:26).[38] These notes should probably be seen in light of the brotherhood's habit of greeting each other in Pauline fashion, a custom that a man of Swedenborg's reserved nature may have found some difficulty in accepting. We also come across notes that refer to the question of whether he is to be adopted into the congregation, a question not formally resolved until October 1744.

Of greater importance is Swedenborg's attitude toward Moravian doctrine, with its dichotomy between sin and grace and its stress on the purified individual's duty to strive for conjunction with the Divine. These made a strong impression on him.

Thus, against this background, three salient points emerge:

(1) There can be no doubt about Swedenborg's sympathy for the Moravian emphasis on total adoration, involving the individual's whole being. In the German count, this had found mystical expression in contemplation of Christ's blood and absorption in his sufferings. Such mysticism was wholly foreign to Swedenborg's sober nature, however, and we find hardly a trace of it in the dream journal. What we do find is the fundamental notion that God is to be worshiped most deeply and wholeheartedly. As we see clearly from his notes of October 1744, this doctrine was to be one of the intended themes of his unfinished work *The Worship and Love of God.* In several places in his religious writings, Swedenborg stresses the importance of total surrender:

> He who worships the Lord and gives glory to the Lord is in humiliation; and what is his own . . . departs from the man who is

in humiliation; and insofar as this departs, so far the Divine is received; for what is man's own . . . is that which alone obstructs the Divine. (Arcana Coelestia §10646 [3])

(2) God cannot be properly invoked unless the worshiper has first purified him- or herself. Swedenborg was always to stress the relationship between divine worship and purification from sin and evil (for example, in *Arcana Coelestia* §10042). Such purification is in part dependent upon the individual:

> *Many believe that a person is purified from evils merely by believing what the church teaches; some, by doing good; others by . . . reading the Word and books of devotion. . . . And yet none of these things purifies man at all unless he examines himself, sees his sins, acknowledges them, condemns himself on account of them, and repents by desisting from them.* (Divine Providence §121)

But not until response is received through "divine virtue and operation meant by the Holy Spirit" does purification become a fact, he writes in *True Christian Religion* §142.

(3) It is in total and inward love that the individual participates in the Divine and experiences "bliss" or "enters into the spirit," again to use Swedenborg's terminology. There thus exists a personal relationship to the Divine, outside and independent of both church and sacraments.

Even before his diary period, Swedenborg stressed the importance of this relationship, but then as a condition for true knowledge. Now "the operation of the Holy Spirit" becomes for Swedenborg, as for the Brethren, a result of true worship, extended beyond the epistemological sphere, as we see from diary entry of May 19/20, 1744, in entries 199 and 202. Later on, he conceives of life within this relationship as one of the Christian's main tasks (for example, *True Christian Religion* §152).

To say that Swedenborg was "influenced" in these ways does not imply a mere cause-and-effect connection. The importance of a personal relationship with God had been emphasized to him in his childhood, as well as later in Stockholm's Pietist circles.

That grace comes to meet the pious worshiper in his or her adoration of the Divinity is a common Christian tenet. But the ground
had been prepared to make Swedenborg receptive to Zinzendorf's
ideas: they lay, as it were, in his path. Afterwards he would break—
bitterly—with the Moravians. In the criticism he would direct at
them at that time, as we find in the *Spiritual Diary* §§4763, 4816,
and 6043, the crux of the matter—Zinzendorf's doctrine of a direct
and strictly individual relationship with God—was hardly mentioned. Instead, Swedenborg concentrated on the Moravians' rejection of good deeds, living in accordance with faith, as a condition
for divine grace and salvation.

THE INTERPRETATION OF DREAMS

Swedenborg's dominant interest, overshadowing everything else in
his life, was his scientific work. His need to understand actualized
his Christian heritage and led him to an organic view of life, in
which everything fits together and contributes to the realization of
creation purposes. In his Easter vision of 1744, he believed that
God had exhorted him to subordinate himself in everything to the
divine will. As the months pass, Swedenborg, and his latter-day
reader, understands that capitulation has its reward: *la vision en Dieu*,
perception in God, through God. In "the real mystics," writes
Nathan Söderblom, "thought feels a need to penetrate God's wisdom and find a coherence, alien to the uninitiated, embracing the
whole of existence."[39] These words might have been written of
Swedenborg.

Swedenborg generally sees his dreams and visions in relation to
this "wisdom in God"; it is theosophy, in the original sense of the
word. Implicit in having a part in divine knowledge is the notion
that dreams are inspired from above and constitute a form of
knowledge. Later, in 1745, Swedenborg formulated his general
theory of dreams—in *The Word Explained* and just about at the same
time in his *Spiritual Experiences* (*Diarium Spirituale*). The basic idea is

that dreams are inspired by God or the spiritual world and, thus, by departed souls, whether good and evil, according to the view expressed by Swedenborg some time after the dream journal:

> As regards dreams in particular, I wish at present to say merely that they are induced on man by spirits, dreams wherein are revealed future events, and also truths, being induced by the spirits of God Messiah, and all other dreams by spirits who are not spirits of God Messiah. But dreams whereby men are deceived are induced by evil spirits, and thus by the crew of the devil, and this either by living voices, [or] for the most part, by representations and their innumerable species. One who is ignorant of these representations can never know what representative dreams signify. Representations of things in heaven are effected by means of the same kind of things existing on earth, especially by such as are seen; and thus by things natural. Sometimes they are so compounded that unless one knows the several species of representations, they can hardly be disentangled. That they are of such a nature, is most clearly apparent from Joseph's dream, and also from Pharaoh's. It is especially apparent in the prophets, where much is said of dreams; not to mention visions when the men are wide awake, and which also are exactly like dreams, being similar representations, effected quite vividly, as though in clear day. (The Word Explained §1893)

The way that the dream's message is presented depends upon human circumstances, more specifically, by our individual memories and state of mind:

> I again had a dream, but an ordinary one like those of other people. A certain person spoke with me, and upon awakening I related the whole matter from beginning to end. The angels said that it coincided entirely with those things which they had spoken among themselves; not that the things seen in the dream were really the same, being in fact altogether different, but yet they were such that the thoughts of their speech were capable of being turned into them, so that they were representatives and

correspondences; nay, this so extended to single things, that there was nothing which did not coincide. I spoke with them concerning influx, and the manner in which such things were turned into things quite different and not recognizable as coming from such an origin, and indeed flowing into ideas variously conceived, and how each particular with them excited something agreeing with it in the idea; as, for example, the person seen in the dream was one of whom I had the idea that he was in natural truth, and this only from the actions and speech of his life; while with the angels, in the meantime, there was a discourse concerning natural truth, wherefore that person was represented, together with what he had spoken and done, all which followed in order. (The Spiritual Diary §4404)

The knowledge Swedenborg obtained relates to his everyday life. The elements of the message consist of court gossip, reminiscences of meetings, indisposition after opulent dinners, an attack of illness, Bible reading, scientific work, and morally compromising situations. All these diverse elements blended together coordinate with the question of his divine calling and, toward the end of the journal, of his new book and its contents. In certain instances, we come across events that have etched themselves deeply into his consciousness, but whose special nature is an obstacle to this integrational process. In Swedenborg's reports—undoubtedly faithful and exact of what he can recall of his dreams—these enigmatic fragments crop up, like odd pieces in a jigsaw puzzle.

In the passage just quoted from *The Word Explained*, Swedenborg writes that one must be acquainted with the various elements of dream language, especially when in regard to more complicated dreams. There is a connection here with past experiences. Around 1740, Swedenborg developed his doctrine of correspondences or interrelations.[40] Swedenborg the scientist discovered that he lives in a world of mirrors, where even the most insignificant thing points to something above itself. Everything flows from God; everything could be regarded both as a thing in itself and as a symbol. In this ordered universe, everything coheres through analogies. The always systematic Swedenborg, some years before the dream journal, had attempted to sort out what he realized were important correspondences or interrelations. His classification is found in a posthumously published manuscript entitled *Clavis hieroglyphica* (The Hieroglyphic Key) portending the colossal list of biblical symbolism he would record a few years after he stopped keeping his dream journal.[41]

Swedenborg's struggle in the journal with correspondences, symbols, and analogies is not an exercise in lexical gymnastics. The "inner," "essential" meaning of the Word goes hand in hand with other issues he confronted at various times. In the dream diary, the approach is most often from the point of view of his call. When he later studies the Old Testament, his interpretation relates to the advent of Christ and how this historical event, which far postdated the prophets' chronicles, is prefigured in their ideas and utterances.

Thus, the syntax varies, while the basic elements recur, both in the diary and in the later biblical commentaries. Words and word groups reappear, and Swedenborg treats them as symbols with definite, consistent meanings.

For this dreamer, who had grown up under the absolute monarchy of the Carolinian period, the word *king* is synonymous with God. Swedenborg's king of preference is Sweden's Charles XII, although there are others. In the same royalist manner, *queen* suggests wisdom, and *princes*, angels. Swedenborg often dreams of women. On this subject, he is never indifferent; on the contrary, a dream's meaning is conditioned by his relation to the women who appear in it. He loves them with varying degrees of intensity: remains passive, rejects them, associates with them, is guided by them, or is led astray. These dream relationships have a logic of their own. He dreams of intercourse in April; in an October dream, the same woman is pregnant.

To both Swedenborg and his reader alike, it is clear that these women stand for his love. They are objectifications of his passion for knowledge, his science: images of work and tasks that lie ahead for him. In the diary's last, undated entry, *virgins* are apparently synonymous with truth. This applies to all women in the journal, but the quality of the truth is related to the dreamer's spiritual progress.

"The Great Work" is to emanate from his relationship with
Divinity and truth. To Swedenborg, it appears as a palace, with
wings, and a sunlit gable. His labors in writing it, his own thoughts
and plans, are but a minor part of this grand building, its chambers,
rooms, and hall.

Recurrent symbols relate to this overriding task. In the palace
and his particular chamber, the window stands for cognitive theory. It signifies his own view of the world and the influence of the
world upon him. The window's curtains are drawn: the dreamer
finds himself protected from outside influences; instead, he receives his knowledge from above.

Innocence and purity are prerequisites to higher knowledge.
The children encountered in Swedenborg's dreams usually represent that desirable quality. Indeed, in the realm of innocence, insight is imparted to the dreamer like milk or bread in beautiful
vessels. The symbols are usually connected with his projects. His
ongoing and progressing work appears in the diary as horses and
carriages, sometimes in long processions.

The dreamer himself and the modern reader are able to penetrate the symbolic language without great difficulty. Viewing the
document as a whole and being aware of the problems Swedenborg was grappling with before, during, and after the diary period,
they are about as clear as the biblical sheaves that bowed down to
Joseph.

A knowledge of the semantics and grammar of dream language
is important and not only for the interpretation of the journal.
Swedenborg later made use of the same interpretative criteria when
revealing, in several voluminous works, the "inner meaning" of the
Old Testament texts. The language of the prophets is also that of
Swedenborg—dreams of a message.

We also encounter the symbolic language of the diary in accounts of conversations he later claimed to have had with spirits
and angels, as the following example from *Divine Providence* §36
illustrates:

> *I have spoken at times about wisdom with angels who said that
> wisdom is conjunction with the Lord because he is wisdom itself,*

*and that the man who rejects hell comes into this conjunction
and comes into it so far as he rejects hell. They said that they
picture wisdom to themselves as a magnificent and highly or-
nate palace into which one mounts by twelve steps. No one arrives at even the first step, they said, except from the Lord by
conjunction with him; and according to the measure of conjunction one ascends; also as one ascends, one perceives that no
man is wise from himself but from the Lord. Furthermore, they
said that the things in which one is wise are to those in which
one is not wise like a few drops of water to a large lake. By the
twelve steps into the palace of wisdom are meant goods united to
truths and truths united to goods.*

Swedenborg's phrasing here is consonant with a common religious phenomenon. Mystics express themselves in analogies, because their experiences are "ineffable" and can only be reproduced
in the form of a parable.

VISIONS AND ECSTASY

Dreams can be described as a series of images appearing during
sleep, occurring from the time we fail asleep to the time we
awaken, sometimes followed by an awareness of the unreal nature
of these autonomous film sequences shown to us on our inward
screen. It is worth noting that, in his dream journal, Swedenborg
never uses the word *dream* (*dröm*). Probably the word was superfluous to him in this context, since he no doubt knew what kind of
notes he was taking down. The entries are brief reports, often introduced with expressions like "It seemed to me," "I saw," "There
was," or something to the same effect. To define these experiences, he uses the word *representationer*, that is, images, expostula-
tions, reflections.

Along with these "representations," there are reports of other
experiences: "visions" or "ecstasies." One year later, in *The Word Explained* §1351 and §1353, he provides an account of his singularly

dreamy or hallucinatory experiences. Then he explains a passage in Genesis 32, in which Jacob is met by angels on his way to Canaan. Swedenborg observes that Jacob "saw angels with eyes wide open. This sight is vouchsafed the inner congregation alone. They can see angels almost as they see humans. This ability is also granted many other persons mentioned in the Word of God." This faculty or particular spiritual state is thus reserved for a selected few, "the inner congregation" or "the inner church." As can be seen from his comment, that capacity is beyond his personal powers.

The second form of sight that is mentioned in this context is of another kind, taking place when "we are awake, and our internal senses appear to be distinguished from our external senses. In this case the perception is clear too, but not comparable to that of Jacob, Abram, and others." This kind of perception occurs "rather often," Swedenborg says.

The same can be said of a third form of vision that Swedenborg mentions. According to him, a state where we are "almost awake, and believe we are awake, but are not. In this state angels can be seen as if in daylight, or images of various apparitions." He contends that this kind of vision is also common.

Even more frequent are inward visions while awake, but with eyes closed. The fifth and final form of vision enumerated is dreams.

All these different kinds of visions, except the first, appear in Swedenborg's dream journal. In telling a dream from a vision, the crucial criterion is sleep. Visions, in their turn, seem to be distinguished by various degrees of vacancy. The second level—when we are awake and our internal senses appear to be distinguished from our external senses—seems to be the kind Swedenborg experienced in his Easter vision. In this instance, it is as if the soul has distanced itself from the body, and the connections between body and soul are broken.[42] The body appears to be insensible, but still there are tactile perceptions. "The inner life and the power of thought" are unchanged, he states in *Heaven and Hell* §169. The breath is bated. Before, during, and after he has such an experience, he is shivering and trembling. Still, a particular sense of joy is connected with this kind of experience, "indescribable delight, so intense that, had it been increased, the body would have been, as it were, dissolved from delight alone" (dream entry 48).

The third form of vision obviously refers to the "hypnagogic" state, the precise moment that we awaken, when we are neither asleep nor awake. This is a sphere of everyday experience—at best, we fall asleep and wake up "with a smile on our lips"—yet in that transitory state, we appear to be particularly suggestible.

Regarding the contents of Swedenborg's dreams, there are images, occurrences, and certain verbal messages. Often there are experiences of illumination. Colors are notably often mentioned.

In the visionary states, he is "inspirited," that is, through his soul in connection to the Divine. "The spiritual is heavenly," he writes, "almost ecstatic." A person who has once experienced this state longs to go back, and "in the same measure, he disregards bodily pleasures."

Swedenborg often describes the message he receives as "indescribable," "heavenly," or "unexplainable." He wakes up in joy, feels himself purified and his mind "cleared." This is certainly true of his vision of Christ on April 6/7, 1744. In his later works, there are many examples of similar visual experiences.

Swedenborg's description of his experiences has been discussed by scholars. The distinguished theologian Ernst Arbman, in particular, has pointed out that what Swedenborg terms a "vision" often is equivalent to "trance" or "ecstasy" among Christian and non-Christian mystics. These states are likewise characterized by a vacancy of the mind and insusceptibility to exterior impressions. The entranced subject concentrates on one single internal object, focused on a thought or a sphere of ideas. This is accompanied by intense bliss.

Certainly, *ecstasy* is the right word for many of Swedenborg's visionary states. Probably he would have agreed with Professor Arbman, who terms some of his experiences "ecstatic"—even more so since Swedenborg uses the word himself in his dream diary. Early in the journal (entry 12), he states that he has been in *extasibus vigilibus* almost continuously—in wakeful ecstasy. In entry 14, he refers to his "ecstasies before and after sleep."

From the viewpoint of the psychology of religion, the depth of these trance-like states is of special interest, but the dream diary is not clear on this point, nor are any other of Swedenborg's works. So we are left without particulars, and the argument has to be hypothetical. If the torpor is deep enough, we are dealing with a state of mind where internal vision and dream originate. This dreamy state of mind is born, Arbman writes, at the point where concentration becomes complete and the mind is disconnected from the outer world. The dream then emerges from a complex of conscious and unconscious ideas, forming imagery, thoughts, wishes, intentions, and tendencies toward action.[43]

Besides visions and trance-like states, Swedenborg's "illuminations" should be mentioned, his reports on light phenomena, so-called photisms. Swedenborg experiences these illuminations while awake, and they occur at sudden moments of insight, when he has found a solution or as a sign that he is on the right track. "Flaming light means confirmation," he writes some years after the crisis. He also mentions a very active period of his life as a scientist when "hardly a day passed without this light, which appeared before me as that of an open fire."[44] And he states in *Heaven and Hell* §130:

> *I have often been allowed to perceive that the light that illumines the mind is a true light, quite different from the light that we call natural light. I have also been allowed to see it. I have been gradually elevated into that light inwardly, and as I was raised up, my discernment was enlightened to the extent that I could grasp what I had been unable to grasp before, ultimately things that could in no way be comprehended by thought from natural light.*

BEING IN THE SPIRIT

"Spiritual thoughts," "to remain in spirit," "it appeared to me in spirit"—the dream diary abounds with such expressions denoting a particular inward state, an "internal" or "spiritual" state of mind. The distinguishing quality of this peculiar state is the access to higher knowledge that cannot be reached by reason and sensory impressions. A condition for this mental state is "purity" of mind, liberation from bodily passions and egotistical ambitions. It is a kind of divine intuition. The epilogue of the second part of *Regnum Animale* is on the whole a description of the demands and requisites of this spiritual insight.

Knowledge acquired when "in the spirit" completes the dreams and makes them consistent and comprehensible. This form of revelation is probably the one Swedenborg refers to as "visions." As he explains when writing of his dream of April 19/20, 1744 (entry 156), the vision takes place in a phase that is "neither one of sleep nor wakefulness nor ecstasy." There may be a slight difference: the origin of visions can be either divine or earthly, whereas the nature of "the spiritual" is always incorporeal.

The phenomenon is primarily visual, Swedenborg tells us. When he later attempted to explain the internal sense of the Pentateuch, the channel of wisdom was this faculty of divine sight and hearing. On the title page of the *Arcana Coelestia*, he wrote that the interpretation was the result of what he had "heard and seen."[45]

To reach this spiritual state of mind, Swedenborg used his breathing technique. He was not the only one using this method. On the contrary, he writes in *The Worship and Love of God* §101 that, ever since the Fall, Adam and Eve and their offspring have had to take refuge to this respiratory practice to shield their minds. From the traits of the tree of knowledge, disturbing earthly impulses followed, which have to be screened off to get access to the inner life. The real power of the "internal man" is particularly visible in the prophets of the Old Testament, he says. In *True Christian Religion* §157, a work he composed from 1769 to 1771, he summarizes a good twenty-five years of theosophical experience when he writes:

> As man's spirit means his mind, therefore "being in the spirit" (a phrase sometimes used in the Word) means a state of mind separate from the body; and because in that state the prophets saw such things as exist in the spiritual world it is called "a vision

of God." The prophets were then in a state like that of spirits and angels themselves in that world. In that state man's spirit like his mind in regard to sight, may be transferred from place to place, the body remaining meanwhile in its own place. This is the state in which I have now been for twenty-six years, with the difference, that I am in the spirit and in the body at the same time, and only at times out of the body. That Ezekiel, Zechariah, Daniel, and John when he wrote the Apocalypse, were in that state is evident . . . .

INITIATION AND DESIGNATION

In the Easter vision of April 6/7, 1744, in which Swedenborg meets Jesus, who urges him to act ("Well then, do!"), he seems to have seen an immediate sign of his having been chosen. God has a plan for him; his only question is "What plan?" The day after having this vision, he ponders what to do "if anyone took me for a holy man" and people would begin to revere him. He dismisses that thought at once and prays that he not entice others into such a sin.

The thought nevertheless has occurred to him. Next day he tells of a dream where the apostle Peter—the rock on which the church was built—is carried out of the crypt of St. Peter in Rome. But someone remains, "hiding there." Considering the language of the dream journal, it is not farfetched to see the dreamer himself concealed in the tomb, upholder of a divine legacy and mission.

The meaning of his call gradually becomes clearer, as month by month insight emerges. In a radical way, he must accept the consequences of the religiously tinged epistemology he had laid down in earlier works: all higher knowledge that a person receives is the result of divine influx into his or her soul. Receptivity of this inflow requires that our bodily fires be smothered. In *The Worship and Love of God,* the book that Swedenborg began to write by divine command during the last days of the dream diary, we are given a picture of what he considered divine calling. Adam had been granted the same favor as the author—to sit "in the bosom of love." From Jesus' command recorded in the dream diary—"Well then, do!"—a moral sermon and an apotheosis of love gradually evolve:

> *My ears have told me . . . how eagerly you have striven to know from where the good things come, those that stream into the sphere of your reason. This I will teach you from my heart. My son, there is but one love, the origin of which is the One and only, the first and highest of all, from which all the delights of the senses stem and from which the good comes. . . . Feel in the embrace of love what bliss is, and from where goodness comes. Do not search for the source anymore, since you are dwelling in its innermost! Experience now how the loving feelings you entertain towards me are part of mine! I'll make you perceive this inside yourself and realize that your love is of me. Thus I make you see our father. Through me you are his equal and his image, and since we are both his offspring, you shall not be my son but my brother. Fill now your understanding with the good things which well out of this fountainhead! But beware, little brother, that you do not scoop up anything from the source of the love of self.* (Worship and Love of God §55)

True knowledge is derived from divine love only, and the divine perspective is at the core of all understanding.

At the same time as he approaches this insight, we find in the diary a number of notes regarding acceptance and excommunication, affiliation and independence. The language of the dreams is ambiguous for the most part. When on June 20/21 he writes that the question of his admission is considered by "the society," the Moravian congregation comes to mind. This interpretation cannot be excluded. Yet, the acceptance of a higher society seems to be concerned. He sees his father emerging from that society, uttering kind words on his writings. Three weeks later, on July 7/8, he interprets a dream as foreboding that he will now be accepted by "the society where my father was." He obviously has a presentiment of a heavenly mission here.

By September 29/30, the decision regarding his application has been made. He will become an "immortal member." He observes that he is the first living person to be accepted as a member, adding "which nobody had ever been before, with the exception of one who had been dead and lived." Probably, he is referring to the heavenly society of resurrected souls where Christ, divine and human, had been a member already during his life on earth. There were immortals whom he did want to join, indeed, as we see in entry 219: "I saw a congregation where everyone had a little crown on his head, and two of them stood out front with quite large and magnificent crowns. . . . But who the two were, if one was Huss, I do not know." The Bohemian Johan Huss was a central figure for the Moravians, a martyr to his faith. Is Swedenborg the person standing there at his side?

During the autumn and winter 1744–1745, Swedenborg was working on *The Worship and Love of God*. In April he was granted two new and decisive visions.[46] God appeared to Swedenborg and assigned him his task for the remainder of his life. He was called to explain to humanity the spiritual meaning of Sacred Scripture. God himself would provide the knowledge needed. From that crucial night, *mundus spiritum infernum et coelum*, the world of the spirits, hell, and heaven, were opened to him.

After the experience in April, he began systematically to examine the Old and the New Testament regarding prophesies of the Lord's advent. The result of this investigation—huge lists of references and quotations—has been published as *Concerning the Messiah about to Come*.[47] Under this heading, he first quotes from Isaiah 7:14–16:

> *Therefore the Lord himself shall give you a sign; Behold, a virgin shall conceive, and bear a son, and shall call his name Immanuel. Butter and honey shall he eat, that he may know to refuse the evil, and choose the good. For before the child shall know to refuse the evil, and choose the good, the land that thou abhorrest shall be forsaken of both her kings.*

The name Immanuel, or Emanuel, means "God with us."

CONCENTRATION AND
BREATHING TECHNIQUE

Central in Swedenborg's crisis is a dynamic awareness of the evil sides of his self and his fights against them. To avoid temptations and evil thoughts, he tries to focus on the Divine through prayer, concentration, and contemplation. He is familiar with this mode of screening off the outer world and recognizes the importance of absolute attentiveness. In the *Oeconomia Regni Animalis* (The Economy of the Animal Kingdom), the work outlining the structure and order of the soul's dominion, which preceded *The Animal Kingdom*, he wrote that his thirst for knowledge had led him into domains of consciousness where he felt he was at the center of everything—"not in darkness or in doubt, but in the whitest light and in heaven itself" (*Economy of the Animal Kingdom* I, §10). Now, during the crisis, he tries to focus his thoughts on God and the love of Jesus Christ.

His power of concentration is the effect of a specific breathing control. He minimizes his breath. In the *Spiritual Diary* §3463, he states that he had regulated his breathing in a similar manner ever since the morning and evening prayers of his childhood. The practice of restricted breathing became a habit, and he returned to it whenever he was thinking intensely "because," he explains, "without it, a deep meditation on verity is impossible." In this way one can, as far as possible, liberate oneself from "natural" influences. The soul, which is connected to the Divine, is freed from earthly bounds. During the dream-book period, he uses this practice. In the entry dated April 12/13, he cites the specific theory of breathing he developed, both from a physiological and a psychological point of view, in the contemporaneous *Animal Kingdom*.

It should be pointed out that Swedenborg regarded his breathing control as a talent or gift. According to the *Spiritual Diary* §3463, he later on—at a time "when heaven had been opened to me and I was granted the faculty of talking to spirits"—learned to hold his breath almost for an hour. "Then I had inhaled just the air necessary to keep the process of thought running."

Other mystics, Christian as well as non-Christian, have also used breathing practices to increase the level of concentration and to open up inner vistas. The Greek-Orthodox Hesychasts, in particular, have developed a theory about this, but Roman-Catholic mystics are also familiar with this phenomenon. A comparison with Yoga and Taoist scriptures immediately suggests itself.[48] In these systems of meditation, there are breathing practices that aim at a deeper absorption and at reaching more subtle levels of the soul. By bating the breath, disturbing impulses are eliminated and a state of tranquility and harmony is reached. As matter of fact, Swedenborg seems to have been aware of the importance of breathing practices in Asia. In the *Spiritual Diary* §402, he mentions that, together with spirits from India, he studied "a breathing similar to mine."

Thus, concentration and breathing control are features of Swedenborg's unusually strong will, which comes to play in various aspects of his life. St. Augustine, whom Swedenborg at times studied intensely, writes about "the supersensual eye of the soul" which is opened to those who concentrate on the beyond.[49] Such will, a certain direction of attention, is central in this process, the dream diary bears out (entry 88):

> *Now, while I was in the spirit and yet awake—for I could open my eyes and be awake, and come back into that state— then I saw and realized that the internal and real joy comes from this level, and that only insofar as one can be in it, there is happiness; and as soon as one comes into any other love that does not concentrate thither, then one is far afield right away.*

SWEDENBORG'S HEALTH

Swedenborg's strictly private notes in his dream journal provide us with an unusual opportunity to look into the inner life of an individual. How was the crisis we are witnessing reflected in the dreamer's everyday life?

Shortly after the Easter vision of April 6/7, 1744, Swedenborg observes that he behaved normally, despite the jolting experiences he went through. This entry, number 80, is carefully crossed out and only partly legible:

> *During all this, I remained in the company of all my former associates, and no one could [undecipherable] the least change with me, which was God's grace, but I knew what it [undecipherable] not daring to tell that I realized what high grace had been conferred upon me; for I discerned that this could serve no other purpose than to make people think this or that about me, according to the pros and cons of each, nor perform any use, if privately [undecipherable] from the glorification of God's grace which [undecipherable] for the love of self.*

As we have seen, Swedenborg was already busy with his scientific work a week after Easter. After moving to London at the turn of April-May, he worked with the same diligence as always. Indeed, he seems to have done so during the whole diary period. Anxiety or exaltation was one thing, industriousness, quite another. Did nothing of the former surface?

Only at times are there indications of the inward excitement. On April 15/16, Swedenborg was so upset that he visited the Swedish envoy in The Hague, J. F. Preis, who was an old acquaintance. He did not conceal his worries from his friend. The seventy-seven-year-old envoy sent for pastor Johann Gottlieb Pambo, who arrived in Preis's carriage and gave Swedenborg Holy Communion in a ceremony at the legation.

We also have a witness account from Swedenborg's landlord in London, with whom he lodged from the beginning of May until July 10, 1744. As already alluded to, on his arrival in London, Swedenborg got in touch with the Moravian engraver John Paul Brockmer.[50] Swedenborg took lodgings with him at Salisbury Court, close to the Moravian Church in Fetter Lane. This engraver was later—the year is unknown—called upon by a Swedish clergyman in London, Aron Mathesius, together with the pastor of the local German congregation.[51] To his visitors, Brockmer discussed

Swedenborg's doings and behavior during May, June, and July 1744. In the vast Swedenborg literature, Brockmer's statement, or rather Mathesius' report about it, has repeatedly been called in question. Mathesius was known to be prejudiced against Swedenborg, and for this reason he may have wanted to put Swedenborg in an unfavorable light, critics say.

However, as far as I can see, a number of details in the diary corroborate the testimony, indicating its reliability, at least in these respects.

Mathesius recounts the following:

> Some time in the year 1743 [it should be 1744],[52] a Moravian Brother, by name Seniff, in his return to London from Holland, where he had been visiting his children, became acquainted in a packet-boat with Baron Emanuel de Swedenborg; who desired to be recommended to a family in London, where he could live retired. Mr. Seniff brought him to Mr. Brockmer. This gentleman was very easily prevailed upon to take him under his roof.
>
> The Baron behaved very decently in his house: he went every Sunday to the chapel of the Moravians in Fetter Lane. Though he lived very recluse, he nevertheless would often converse with Mr. Brockmer, and was pleased with hearing the Gospel in London. So he went on for several months, continually approving of what he heard. At last he came to Mr. Brockmer, and told him, that he rejoiced that the Gospel was preached to the poor; but lamented over the learned and the rich, who he said must all go to hell.
>
> Some months after, he told Mr. Brockmer he was writing a pamphlet in the Latin language, which he would send gratis to all learned men in the universities. After that he did not open his chamber-door for two days, neither would permit the maid to come in to make the bed and sweep the room.
>
> One evening Mr. Brockmer was at a coffee-house, and the maid came to fetch him home, informing him, that something extraordinary had happened to Mr. Swedenborg: that she knocked several times at his door, but he had not opened it: upon this Mr. Brockmer came himself and knocked; calling him

by his name, he jumped up from bed. Mr. Brockmer asked, whether he would not let the maid make the bed? He answered, No: and desired to be left alone, for he was about a great and solemn work.

When Mr. Brockmer retired to his room, which was about nine o'clock, he ran after him, looked very frightful: his hair stood upright, and he foamed a little at his mouth. He wanted to talk with Mr. Brockmer, but as he had an impediment in his speech, it was long before he could bring forth a single word. At last he said, he had something very particular to communicate: namely, that he was the Messiah: that he was come to be crucified for the Jews; and that as he had a great impediment in his speech, Mr. Brockmer was chosen to be his mouth, to go with him the next day to the synagogue, and there to preach his words. He continued, "I know you are a good man, but I suspect you will not believe me. Therefore an angel will appear at your bedside early in the morning, then you will believe me." Mr. Brockmer now began to be frightened. He hesitated before he could answer, and at length he said, "Mr. Swedenborg, I am much inclined to think, that a little medicine would be of service to you. There is our dear Dr. Smith, with whom you are intimate; he will give you something, which I am certain will be of immediate use. Now I will make this agreement with you: if the angel appear to me, as you have mentioned, I will be obedient to the angel; but if he does not, then you shall go along with me tomorrow morning to Dr. Smith." He repeated it over and over again, that the angel would appear; upon which they took leave of each other, and went to bed.

Mr. Brockmer lay the whole night restless: however, he got up at five o'clock. As soon as the Baron heard him over-head, he jumped out of bed, threw his night gown over him, and with a night cap half on half off, came running up to Mr. Brockmer in a great hurry, to know if the angel had appeared.

Mr. Brockmer did all he could to divert him before he would give him a direct answer: but he foaming continually cried out, "But how, how, did the angel come?" He answered, "No: and now I expect you will go with me to Dr. Smith." He replied, "I will not go to any doctor." Then he talked a long time to himself, and said, "I am now conversing with spirits, one on the right hand, and the other on the left; the one bids me follow you, because you are a good man, and the other saith, I shall have nothing to do with you; you are good-for-nothing." Quickly he [Swedenborg] went down stairs, as he had no business in his room.

Then the Baron [observing his landlord's fear] sitting down in a chair cried like a child, and said, "Do you think I should hurt you?" Mr. Brockmer likewise began to cry, and the Baron went down stairs.

Mr. Brockmer dressed himself, and when he came down, he found the Baron sitting dressed likewise, in an easy chair, and his door being open, he cried out, "Come in, come in!" Mr. Brockmer ordered a coach, but as he refused going with him, he went himself to Dr. Smith, informing him what had passed, and likewise begged of him to receive the Baron, but the Doctor having no room in his own house, took a lodging for him at a Peruke-maker's [Mr. Michael Caer in Warmer Street] in Cold Bath fields, three or four doors from his own house.

During the time that Mr. Brockmer was gone to Dr. Smith's, the Baron went to the Swedish Ambassador, but on account of that day being post day, the Ambassador could not see him. He then went to a place called the Gully-hole, undressed himself, rolled in very deep mud, and threw the money out of his pockets among the crowd.

Some of the Swedish Ambassador's servants happening to come by, and seeing him in that condition, brought him home to Mr. Brockmer covered over with mud. Mr. Brockmer told him, he had got a lodging for him near Dr. Smith, and asked him if he would go there. He replied, Yes. When he arrived he desired that a tub with water and six towels might be brought to him. Then he went into the back room and locked himself in. Mr. Brockmer being apprehensive that he might hurt himself, had the lock taken off. They found him washing his feet: he had *wetted the six towels, and asked for six more. Mr. Brockmer then left him with two men. Dr. Smith visited him every day, and gave him medicines which did him much good. Mr. Brockmer went to the Swedish Envoy, and told him what had happened, who thanked him much for all his trouble.*

After that Mr. Brockmer continued to visit him: he had often expressed his thanks to him for his great care, but would never give up the point that he was the Messiah; on which Mr. Brockmer always declined to dispute.

One day when Dr. Smith had given him a purging powder, he went out into the field, running as quick as possible. The man who then attended him could not overtake him: the Baron sat down on a stile, and laughed heartily:-when the man came near him, he ran to another stile, and so on. This was in the dog-days, and from that time he grew worse.[53]

Mr. Brockmer had very little conversation with him afterwards, except that he now and then met him in the streets, and found that he still held to his point.

Are these the words of a competent and trustworthy witness? This was discussed along with Swedenborg's mental health in the nineteenth and early-twentieth centuries. The scale of conclusions drawn ranged from declaring Swedenborg to be fit as a fiddle to his being completely insane. Today, the question has lost something of its former importance, since we no longer look upon mental illness as something that, in a definitive way, separates a sick individual from the world of normal people. Nowadays we can understand and accept that Swedenborg may have been ill and confused for awhile: this does not lessen the value of his contributions.

Mathesius' account was printed by the founder of the Methodist movement, John Wesley, in the *Arminian Magazine* in 1781. A decade later, a group of Swedenborgians asked Brockmer if the printed account was correct. In his answer, he made some modifications, but on the whole he affirmed the course of events.

In the following I will focus on five points of coincidence between Brockmer's report and the entries in Swedenborg's diary during the time in question.

First, according to Brockmer, shortly after his arrival in London, Swedenborg pointed out to his landlord that he was delighted that the Gospel was preached to the poor. At the same time, he regretted that the rich and the learned must go to hell. He was working on "a little book in Latin" that was to be handed out to the learned at the university.

The problem of the conflict between faith and knowledge was basic to Swedenborg, before, during, and after this period. Reasoning is one thing, faith another, he wrote in his dream diary entry 49: "I thought that this is the reason that the angels and God showed themselves to shepherds and not to philosophers, who let their understanding enter into these matters."[54] Brockmer observed this central theme in Swedenborg's thought. The purpose of *The Animal Kingdom*, the third part of which Swedenborg was now going to print in London, was exactly, according to the preface, to make the learned believe. Presumably this is the little book in Latin (as Swedenborg modestly calls it) that Brockmer refers to.

Second, did Swedenborg really consider himself a new messiah? As already pointed out, the awareness of a divine mission to humanity is constitutional to his theosophical period. In the dream journal, we time and again meet with this special mission, and it becomes more and more explicit as the months pass. A messianic mission is repeatedly alluded to. I will return to this matter in the final section of this introduction, "The Call." Swedenborg's absolute belief in his calling evidently concerned the pious Moravian Brockmer, who in this sees a sign of his lodger's derangement and his need for medical care.

Third, the landlord states that Swedenborg was foaming at the mouth, a statement that Brockmer denied ten years later. However, in one of his entries of May, number 199, Swedenborg himself writes about a sort of foam or frothing: "I observed that my body is constantly rebelling, which was, moreover, represented to me by scum that must be taken away."

Fourth, Brockmer maintains that Swedenborg went to the Swedish legation, but was not received by the minister since the latter was busy with the mail that day. In the journal entry of July

9/10, Swedenborg recorded that he was "together with the king and spoke to him, who was afterwards in a chamber." We may conclude that the minister shut himself up. In the dream—or in the confusion—he was in the company of the king's princes, probably the clerks or the footmen of the minister. According to the extant documents in the Swedish State Archives, July 10, 1744, was most probably courier day. The Swedish minister, Casper Joachim Ringwicht, dated two official communications July 10, one for the Royal Majesty and the other for the Prime Minister. He thus had good reasons to stay in his office.

The last point regards the washing of feet. It has already been pointed out that pedilavium was an important ritual with the Moravians: thus, Swedenborg was aware of this ritual from his immediate environment, staying as he did with Brockmer.[55] In a journal entry in April 1744, Swedenborg cites the famous episode in John 13 in which Jesus washes his disciples' feet. In the Gospel, the washing was primarily a lesson in humility. To Swedenborg, most likely influenced by the Brethren, the ceremony took on the meaning of purification. The sick man in Brockmer's account, who washes his feet dozens of times, is an image of guilt, of an awareness of sinfulness that has grown into obsession and monomania. A few weeks later, July 22/23, entry 224, Swedenborg records a direct reference to this formal cleaning: "I saw a boy rushing off with my shirt, and I ran after him. *This is supposed to mean that I have not washed my feet*" (the italics are Swedenborg's).

Although the Brockmer–Mathesius report gives us a picture of confusion and of exaltation—or of lunacy, according to one of Swedenborg's fiercest critics—its value is not that of a medical record, but lies in the light it throws on Swedenborg's Moravian connections. It strengthens the framework of his religious seeking in the year of the dream diary and provides a key to obscure passages in the text. A comparison between the Brockmer–Mathesius account and the journal entries brings in immediate focus how the basic structure of a course of events is contained in his dream language, where it is reproduced in a disguise that takes shape from the problems at hand.

SOCIAL CIRCLES

The dream diary introduces us to the social circles to which Swedenborg belonged or in which he moved, and we can follow these connections on three different levels. The first circle is his large family, a group that was both held together and divided by deaths and disputes about inheritances.[56] The next circle comprises Swedenborg's colleagues at the Royal College of Mining, many of them distantly related to him or to his family. The third circle is that of the Hat politician Fredrik Gyllenborg, a relationship probably of a more or less economic nature.

This grouping agrees with the circles we also encounter in the Swedenborg's *Spiritual Experiences*—his private notebooks from the years 1745–1765. To judge from the eternal fates of many of these people, related by Swedenborg in that diary, he did not mourn over their deaths, nor did he miss them.

In the great line of relatives, his father, the bishop of Skara, Jesper Swedberg, stands first in the row. Only once do we hear of his mother, Sara Behm, but her son Emanuel was only eight years when she died. Jesper, on the other hand, turns up very often in the notes. The father's piety, his tremendous vitality, courage, and self-regard must have had an impact, in one way or another, on all eight of his children (one son died at the age of twelve; another at twenty-seven).

The vitality of Swedenborg's father also manifested itself in his marriages. When Swedenborg's mother, the wealthy Sara Behm, died in 1696, Jesper married another rich woman, this one a childless widow by the name of Sara Bergia. When Sara Bergia passed away in 1720, Jesper married another widow, but not a childless one this time. He was then sixty-seven years old. (See the family tree on the facing page.)

Most of Swedenborg's sisters married in accordance with their station, and for extended periods he was in communication with their husbands. In the dream journal, we catch glimpses of one of them in particular, one who was closer to Swedenborg than any of the others—Eric Benzelius, who was married to his sister Anna.

SWEDENBORG'S FAMILY TREE

PARENTS	CHILDREN	GRANDCHILDREN
	1	
Jesper Swedberg	Daniel	
m.	(died as a child)	
Sara Behm		
Sara Bergia	**2**	
Christina Arrhusia	Albrecht	
	(1684[?]–1696)	
	3	
	Anna	Carl Jesper Benzelius
	(1686–1766)	Ulrica m. Petrus Filenius
	m. Eric Benzelius	
	4	
	Emanuel Swedenborg	
	(1688–1772)	
	5	
	Eliezer	
	(1689–1716)	
	m. Elisabeth Brinck	
	6	
	Hedwig	Lars Benzelstierna
	(1690–1728)	five other children
	m. Lars Benzelstierna	
	7	
	Catharina, "Caisa"	nine children
	(1693–1770)	
	m. Jonas Unge	
	8	
	Jesper Swedenborg	Emanuel (1731–1794)
	(1694–1771)	Jesper Gustaf (1736–1821)
	m. Christina Silfverswärd	eight other children
	9	
	Margaretha	
	(1695–1763)	
	m. Anders Lundstedt	

Benzelius was university librarian at Uppsala, a professor, and bishop of Linköping; he was appointed archbishop in 1743 but died before taking up his duties. Benzelius was a brilliant librarian, substantially enriching the university collections. He was also a historian; in his lectures on the history of Sweden, he refuted Olof Rudbeck's view of his country as the original home of civilization. As a member of the priesthood, in the diet of the four estates, he actively participated in the Hat party's policy of revenge, not opposing the war against Russia in 1741. The warm relationship between the brothers-in-law, documented in numerous letters, seems to have cooled in later years. There may be several reasons for the waning friendship: political disagreement, the bishop's deprecation of Swedenborg's religious ideas as they had developed since the 1730s, perhaps even a lawsuit over inheritance. In the *Spiritual Diary* §4749 and §5074, Swedenborg finds Benzelius in hell. One of several reasons for this fate was, we learn, that Benzelius's faith was not from the heart: all was merely memorized by heart and stored in the scholar's excellent memory.

The circle of brothers and sisters, decimated over the years (Swedenborg's brother Eliezer died early, twenty-seven years old), entertained both lively and tense relations, due to the number of large legacies bequeathed to them. The sources of their fortunes were members of the Behm family—both Swedenborg's mother and grandmother—the childless Sara Bergia, and finally, in 1735, the bishop himself.

We also encounter the more-distant relatives. The district medical officer Johan Moraeus, the father-in-law of Carl Linnaeus, was the son of one of Jesper Swedberg's sisters. Johan Hesselius, another physician, was the son of Sara Bergia's sister. Brita Behm, the Rosenadler brothers, Ulrica Adlersten, the Swab family—all were directly or indirectly related to Swedenborg through his father's marriages; and they were all, more or less, heirs-at-law in the division of the estates.

For the most part, these families had their roots in the clergy. Peculiarly enough, many of them seem to have been ennobled at the same time—with exception of the priests—at the coronation in

1719 of Sweden's Queen Ulrika Eleonora. Swedberg was renamed Swedenborg, Benzelius became Benzelstierna, Upmark was transformed into Rosenadler. The family heads—Emanuel was one of them, being the oldest in his line—must regularly have met at the diets in the Age of Liberty.

Bishop Swedberg's ancestors were miners. One of his brothers appears to have studied the science of mining and became, like his nephew, an assessor in the Royal College of Mining. This uncle was ennobled too and changed his name into Schönström. He married Swedenborg's maternal aunt. The father of the two sisters—and sisters-in-law—was the wealthy Albrecht Behm, who had also, in his time, been an assessor in the College of Mining.

Among contemporary colleagues in the college were Assessor Lars Benzelstierna, married to Swedenborg's sister Hedwig, and the Assessors Anders Swab and Johan Bergenstierna, who both, in turn, married Elisabeth Brinck, the widow of Swedenborg's brother Eliezer.

These strange connections are explained, at least partly, by the fact that all the families involved—Behm, Schönström, Swab, and Swedberg/Swedenborg—had their ancestral roots in the Bergslag mining districts and owned shares in mines. The Royal College of Mining was the supervising authority, a civil-service department safeguarding and conducting the most important export industry of the time, iron production, on which the unstable wealth of the country rested. The department was in need of staff with special knowledge in this field, and apparently it was found among people with interests in the trade. Swedenborg's own shares in the mines grew considerably in time. Evidently, it was not considered improper or illegal that the controlling state department, which issued licences and permits, was made up by people with interests in the business.

Among the circle of colleagues, we can also detect a group of young officials, engaged in the religious revival that swept over Stockholm in the 1730s and the 1740s. We do not find their names in Swedenborg's dream diary, but their convictions must have been well known to him. A principal figure among them was

Carl Henrik Grundelstierna (1701–1754), one of the first and most zealous Moravians in the city. He was loosely tied to the college, a trainee in 1722. Grundelstierna traveled to Herrnhut and Marienborn, and corresponded with Zinzendorf.[57] Grundelstierna did not make a career in the College of Mining; he had inherited a rural estate and was economically independent.

Another of these colleagues, Erland Fredrik Hjärne, was closely affiliated to the College of Mining; he was employed as a clerk in 1726 and became an assessor a good thirty years later.[58] Together with his second wife, Hjärne was a central figure of the Moravian revival in the middle of the eighteenth century; earlier, he seems to have taken an interest in other forms of Pietism. The Hjärne couple willed away considerable capital to the Moravian congregation in Stockholm, and for a long time, worship was held in a house once owned by them.

An indirect connection between the circle at the Royal College of Mining and the Moravian Brethren was established in 1741, when Erik Odelstierna entered the college as a trainee. Odelstierna was related to the leading Moravian pastor in Stockholm, Thore Odelius, who in turn was related to the Benzelius/Benzelstierna family, Swedenborg's kinsmen and friends.[59]

The third circle of the dream diary is separate from the other two. These persons seem to be linked together by economic relations, often consolidated by family ties. The central figure is Count Fredrik Gyllenborg, the younger brother of Prime Minister Carl Gyllenborg, the leader of the Hat party.[60] Fredrik had been allied to the court of Fredrik I and held a leading position in the same party. In 1750, he became president of the Royal College of Mining.

On the side of his political activity, Gyllenborg appears to have engaged in somewhat dubious economic interests. His real estate business became notorious. His affairs were on loans where he methodically speculated against the falling Swedish currency, a practice even more problematic since he was the chairman of the National Debt Office, the governmental organ issuing and taking up loans. Gyllenborg's life ended in a bankruptcy of national dimensions in 1759, regarded as the biggest financial catastrophe in

Sweden of the eighteenth century, apart from the national bankruptcy following the death of Charles XII. Liquidation was still going on in 1772, the year Swedenborg died.

Apart from political and economic speculations, Gyllenborg took an interest in science—the science of mining, in particular. Like most other Hats, his general outlook was undoubtedly mercantile and protectionist, a view that was largely in harmony with Swedenborg's. This may partly explain the curious fact that Swedenborg, who otherwise had few friends outside his family, developed a friendship with the count.

Swedenborg's economic dealings with Gyllenborg were extensive and at least partly involved losses. In 1729, he sold his stocks in the Skinnskatteberg works (part of the inheritance from his mother) to Gyllenborg for 45,000 Riksdaler (rkm). Thirteen years later, the count bought the mining shares inherited from Swedenborg's stepmother Sara Bergia for 36,000 rkm. Of the latter sum, Swedenborg entrusted 30,000 into the care of his exalted friend, leaving it as a claim on Gyllenborg. This was a debt against a personal guarantee. The person signing his name as security was a relative, Henning Gyllenborg, who, in the dream journal, symbolizes Swedish *jeunesse dorée* and who was married to a sister of Elisabeth Stierncrona.

I will not detail the many turnabouts in these financial dealings, which for Swedenborg's part proved disastrous—he probably lost about 20,000 rkm in these affairs. For comparison, it should be mentioned that Swedenborg's annual income from the Royal College of Mining was only 3,600 rkm.

His connections to Fredrik Gyllenborg led Swedenborg into the social circles of the house of Gyllenborg, and many of these people appear as minor figures in his dream journal. Carl Broman, who would become county governor, is one of them. He was the brother of Erland Broman, marshal of the court and the entertainment minister of King Fredrik I. Curiously enough, Carl Broman was also married to a Stierncrona, a cousin of the wives of Fredrik and Henning Gyllenborg. Swedenborg appears to have lent Carl Broman a sum of 10,000 rkm. According to F. G. Lindh, who has scrutinized Swedenborg's financial affairs, the loan was probably given in 1742.

The list of connections between Swedenborg and the Gyllenborg–Stierncrona circles can certainly be made much longer. The Countess Hedvig Catharina De la Gardie, who appears in the first entry of Swedenborg's journal, may serve as an example. She seems to have been very close to Erland Broman's circle. If we go to the very last paragraph of the journal, we find the rich banker Petter Hultman, who also belonged to this group in Stockholm. His daughter was married to Fredrik Gyllenborg's son, Gustaf Adolf (1743–1789), heir to Skinnskatteberg, but like all the others ruined by Fredrik's bankruptcy.

THE CALL

The dream diary closes with an awareness of a new task to be fulfilled. In October 1744, Swedenborg realized that all scientific work had to be put aside. Instead, he began writing a *liber divinus de cultu et amore Dei*, a divine book on worship and love of God. In the journal, the meaning of that title is not explained, but an attentive reader will find the answer.

Worship, *cultus*, is a compound concept comprising all that Swedenborg later was to describe as "the outer body and mind" of the believer, as we are told in *The Doctrine of Charity* §173. *Caritas*, a pious life with good works, is half of this concept. In this basic Swedenborgian idea, there is an inkling of Jesper Swedberg's examples and teachings, based on the Old and the New Testaments. Jesus sacrificed his life for humankind, a priest-king as was Melchizedek in Genesis.[61] In a similar manner, each individual must forsake him- or herself, because "a faith without works is not the right kind of faith" (diary entry 166). Christian worship in general, or in the ordinary sense of the word—like prayer, mass, communion—is another side of the same thing. The notes in the dream journal show this.

Worship, in this wider sense, leads nowhere without divine love as the guiding force. Swedenborg dreams of the biblical priests Korah and Dathan, who brought strange fire to the altar and were not able to offer it, but were swallowed up by the earth (Numbers 16). They were not being led by God's spirit: "the spirit of Christ is the only one" that can distinguish between the different levels of spirits (diary entry 247).

Swedenborg probably started on his new book at once, at the same time he finished the third volume of the *Regnum Animale*. On March 11, 1745, he mailed the manuscript of the latter work, together with the already printed first part of *The Worship and Love of God (De Cultu et Amore Dei)*, to his friend J. F. Preis in the Hague.[62] In the enclosed letter, Swedenborg pointed out that the envoy should particularly observe the passage on the first-born's love before the Fall. Swedenborg is then referring to the fifth act of this epic drama, where Adam by celestial interference gets to know the nature of knowledge and becomes aware that truth is part of a divine emanation that the pious human being may receive through the correct worship and love. This is the very insight that the crisis period has given Swedenborg.[63]

The Worship and Love of God deals with the story of creation and the life of Adam and Eve before the Fall. Thus, Swedenborg stops where the difficulties begin, literally speaking. A fragment of a continuation is preserved in a nineteen-page manuscript, which also has been published. Its nature is merely preparatory, however. Already during the winter of 1745, he seems to have realized that the undertaking announced by the title was too extensive. How could he, in a single work, describe how sinful humanity should worship and love the Creator, as this is reflected in the Old Testament, where the coming of the Lord is presaged? From a Christian point of view, the Old Testament heralds the arrival of Christ and should be read with this in mind. Furthermore, according to Swedenborg, all Scripture was divine, written in metaphors that only inspired people can understand. There was a connection between exegesis and the interpretation of dreams. Swedenborg had found that his dreams were made of the same stuff as those of the prophets; "our short life is surrounded with a sleep."

Swedenborg concluded that his assignment presupposed a systematic investigation and analysis of biblical texts. Not before that was done would he be prepared to clarify the true worship and love of God, by means of which the lost wisdom of Adam can be restored.

A month or so after the letter was sent to Preis, in the middle of April 1745, his work was interrupted on divine command, given to him in an inn in London. I quote bank manager Carl Robsahm's famous account of Swedenborg's experience:

> *I was in London and had dinner somewhat late in a restaurant [a spirit-vaults] where I used to eat, and then had a chamber by myself, where I amused myself with thoughts on the mentioned subject [the sciences or Scripture, unclear reference]. I was hungry and ate with good appetite. Towards the end of the meal I noticed something like a dimness before my eyes; it darkened and I saw the floor covered with the most hideous crawling animals, like snakes, frogs, and such creatures. I was startled because I was completely conscious and my comprehension was rational; eventually darkness prevailed, but suddenly it was dispelled and I saw a man sitting in one of the corners of the chamber. Since I was then all alone I was quite amazed when he started talking and said to me, "Don't eat so much." Again it darkened before my eyes, but it cleared up as soon and I found myself alone in the room.*
>
> *Such an unexpected horror hastened my returning home. I did not let the landlord notice anything but considered carefully what had happened, and I could not regard it a random occurrence or as an effect of physical causes.*
>
> *I went home; but in the night the same man appeared before me, and then I was not frightened. He then said that he was the Lord God, the creator and redeemer of the world, and that he had chosen me to explain to humanity the spiritual content of the Scripture, and that he would himself explain to me what I ought to write on the subject. To me was then in the same night*

convincingly opened mundus spirituum infernum et coelum *[the spiritual, infernal, and celestial world] where I recognized several acquaintances of all estates; and from that day I left all worldly scholarly endeavor and worked* in spiritualibus *[in spiritual matters] from what the Lord commissioned me to write. Daily the Lord rather often opened my bodily eyes, so that right in the middle of the day I could look into the other life and in the most joyful alertness talk with angels and spirits.*[64]

He still lived in his rooms at Warmer Street in Cold Bath Fields. We may presume that he started his biblical studies at once; and before he left for Sweden in July 1745, he probably finished one or two of the minor works he produced that year, probably the collection of excerpts called *The Messiah about to Come,* containing quotations from the Bible foreshadowing the birth, life, and works of Christ.

He also started preparing the huge indexes to Old Testament books, which are preserved in folio volumes in the library of the Royal Academy of Sciences in Stockholm. When interpreting his dreams, during the preceding period, keywords and key concepts had been apparent, and likewise he now tried to determine the main components of the prophetic books. He dealt with them as he had done with his dreams, but in a more systematic way. "First," he later wrote to his follower Gabriel Beyer in Gothenburg, "I had to learn the correspondences of which the Bible is made up." It is also likely that he immediately started his studies in Hebrew, which were indispensable in his new pursuit.[65]

Swedenborg went back to Stockholm, following just about the same route as he had taken in 1743. The trip took him a month. On August 22, 1745, he once again took up his duties at the Royal College of Mining.[66]

Thus, we now have an overview of the concerns and tensions that Swedenborg felt as he lived through the remarkable year in which his "spiritual eyes" were opened. The events of this period set the philosophical course for the remaining twenty-seven years of his life. His output after his spiritual crisis, consisting of thirty volumes in his standard edition, testifies to the immensity of his vision and dedication to his call.

Now we turn to the dream journal recorded by Emanuel Swedenborg in 1743–1744 and the crisis that changed the course of his life.

NOTES

1. An illuminating Swedish contribution in this field is Anders Olsson, *Den okända texten: En essä om tolkningsteori från kyrkofäderna till Derrida* (Kristianstad, Sweden: H. Bonniers, 1987).

2. Martin Lamm's *En studie öfver hans utveckling till mystiker och andeskådare* (Stockholm, 1915) has recently been translated into English as *Emanuel Swedenborg: The Development of His Thought*, trans. Tomas Spiers and Anders Hallengren (West Chester, Pa.: The Swedenborg Foundation, 2000). See also Inge Jonsson, *Swedenborgs skapelsedrama De cultu et amore Dei: En studie av motiv och intellektuell miljö* (Stockholm: Natur och Kultur, 1961); Inge Jonsson, *Swedenborgs korrespondenslära* (Stockholm: Almquist & Wiksell International, 1969); and Lars Bergquist, *Swedenborgs hemlighet* (Stockholm: Natur och Kultur, 1999).

3. An interesting psychological interpretation has been made by Dr. Wilson Van Dusen, a clinical psychologist, in his book *Emanuel Swedenborg's Journal of Dreams* (New York: The Swedenborg Foundation, 1986).

4. See Rudolph L. Tafel, *Documents concerning the Life and Character of Emanuel Swedenborg*, vol. 2, document 130 (London: Swedenborg Society, 1875–1877).

5. *Swedenborgs drömmar 1744* (Stockholm, 1859), preface. For more information on Scheringson, see Lars Bergquist, *Biblioteket i lusthuset : tio uppsatser om Swedenborg* (Stockholm: Natur och kultur, 1996).

6. See *Dissertatio sistens observationes nonullas de Philosophia recentiorum Platonicorum, indolem atque originem Fantasmi nostri aevi illustrantes*,

Uppsala University, 1787 (A dissertation containing some observations on Neoplatonic philosophy, illuminating the nature and origin of phantasms of our time).

7. R. L. Tafel, "Swedenborg's Diary for 1743 and 1744," *Morning Light*, no. 112 (1880): 5.

8. Ibid.

9. In addition to Odhner's English translation, there is an earlier translation (1860) done by J. J. G. Wilkinson. This translation was published in *Studia Swedenborgiana* 12, no. 1–4 (1974–1975); a paperback edition of this text was also published (New York: The Swedenborg Foundation, 1977). The Van Dusen commentary, op. cit., uses this translation. There have also been English translations by the Swedenborg Scientific Association (Bryn Athyn, Pa.) and the London-based Swedenborg Society

10. For a better understanding of Swedish domestic policy and international affairs during this era, see Fredrik Lagerroth, *Frihetstidens maktägande ständer 1719–1722* (Stockholm: Sveriges Riksdag, 1934); and Olof Jägerskiöld, *Den svenska utrikespolitikens historia*, vol. II.2, 1721–1792 (Stockholm: Norstedts, 1957).

11. *The Letters and Memorials of Emanuel Swedenborg*, trans. and ed. by Alfred Acton (Bryn Athyn, Pa.: Swedenborg Scientific Association, 1948), vol. 2, p. 497.

12. The topic of possible automatic writing has been debated. In her biography, *Emanuel Swedenborg: Scientist and Mystic*, Signe Toksvig contends that Swedenborg did practice automatic writing (1948; rpt. New York: The Swedenborg Foundation, 1983), 206–207. For a response to Toksvig, see William Ross Woofenden, "Swedenborg's Use of Language," *Studia Swedenborgiana* 5, no. 3 (Jan. 1985): 42–44.

13. As is customary in Swedenborgian studies, the numbers following titles refer to paragraph or section numbers, which are uniform in all editions, rather than to page numbers.

14. See also Tafel, vol. II, part 2, note 164, p. 1093.

15. Cf. Edward F. Allen, "Philosophical Notes," *The New Philosophy* 84, no. 3–4 (July–December 1981): 104ff.

16. *Prodromus philosophiae ratiocinantis de infinito et causa finali creationis; deque mechanismo operationis animae et corporis* (Dresden and Leipzig, 1734).

17. See H. V. Tottie, *Jesper Swedbergs lif och verksamhet*, vol. I (Uppsala University: 1885–1886), 62ff.

18. Ibid., 119.
19. For a discussion of Dippel in Sweden at this time, see Martin Lamm, *Emanuel Swedenborg: The Development of His Thought* (West Chester, Pa.: Swedenborg Foundation, 2000), 57–59.
20. Emanuel Linderholm, *Sven Rosén* (Uppsala: Almquist and Wiksell, 1911), 168ff.
21. Moravian Christology is outlined in Gösta Hök, *Zinzendorfs Begriff der Religion* (Uppsala: Almquist and Wiksell, 1948), 103ff.; in Karin Dovring, *Striden kring Sions Sånger*, 126ff; and in Arne Jarrick, *Den himmelske älskare* (Stockholm:1987).
22. Hök, 22ff.
23. Gösta Hök, *Herrnhutisk teologi i svensk gestalt* (Uppsala: Almquist and Wiksell, 1950), 1ff.
24. See J. Taylor Hamilton, *A History of the Moravian Church* (Bethlehem, Pa.: 1900), 24ff.; and Nils Jacobsson, *Den svenska herrnhutismens uppkomst* (Uppsala: Schultz, 1908) 9ff.
25. Jacobsson, 96ff.
26. N. L. Zinzendorf, "Sendschreiben an Ihro Königl. Majest. von Schweden von Grafen und Herrn Ludewig von Zinzendorf."
27. On Hjärne's conversion about 1750, see Hilding Pleijel, *Karolinsk kyrkofromhet, pietism och herrnhutism 1680–1772*, in *Svenska Kyrhaus historia*, vol. 1 (Stockholm: SKD, 1935), 499ff.
28. Jacobsson, 176.
29. Ibid., 64.
30. Hök, *Zinzendorfs Begriff der Religion*, 40ff., 67ff.
31. Hamilton, 43; Pleijel, 446ff.
32. *Resedagbok* [journal of travel] *af Emanuel Swedenborg under åren 1710–1739*, particularly entries for 1733. See also Tafel, *Documents*, vol. 2, doc. 205, pp. 67–68.
33. Hamilton, 62ff., 94ff.; Wilhelm Lütjeharms, *Het philadelphisch-oecumenisch streven der Herrnhuters in de Nederlanden in de achttiende eeuw* (Zeist, Netherlands: 1935), on Herendyk (Heerendijk), 52; Amsterdam, 54; and Leyden, 58.
34. Jacobson, appendix XV, 5.
35. Hermann Plitt, *Zinzendorfs Theologie*, vol. 2 (Gotha: 1871), 578 ff.; *Vollständige so wohl historisch als theologische Nachricht von der Herrnhutischen Bruderschaft* (1735).
36. See Gerhard Wauer, *Die Anfange der Brüder-Kirche in England* (Leipzig: 1900), on the Fetter Lane society, 91ff.; on Wesley, 103ff.; on the new congregation, 125ff.; on Spangenberg, 119ff.

37. See Plitt, vol. 2, 382ff.
38. Emanuel Swedenborg, *A Philosopher's Note Book: Excerpts from the Sacred Scriptures on a Variety of Philosophical Subjects, together with Some Reflections, and Sundry Notes and Memoranda by Emanuel Swedenborg*, translated and edited by Alfred Acton (Philadelphia: Swedenborg Scientific Society, 1931), 209, 240.
39. Nathan Söderblom, *Svenskars fromhet* (Stockholm: SKD, 1933), 211.
40. Jonsson, *Swedenborgs korrespondenslära*, 260ff.
41. Ibid., 136ff.
42. Emanuel Swedenborg, *The Fibre*, translated and edited by Alfred Acton (1918; rpt. Philadelphia: Swedenborg Scientific Association, 1976), §537.
43. Ernst Arbman, *Vision and Ecstasy*, vol. 1 of *Ecstasy or Religious Trance* (Uppsala: Svenska Bokförlaget, 1963), 348.
44. Cf. Emanuel Swedenborg, *Spiritual Experiences* §6086.
45. *Ex auditis et visis* (from things heard and seen). This announcement appears on several of Swedenborg's religious works.
46. The only full account is found in Carl Robsahm's memoir of Swedenborg (Tafel, *Documents*, vol. 1, doc. 5, pp. 30–51).
47. *Concerning the Messiah about to Come*, trans. and ed. by Alfred Acton (Bryn Athyn, Pa.: Academy of the New Church, 1949), 17.
48. See, for example, Arbman, vol. 1, 273.
49. *Confessions of St. Augustine*, vol. 1, book 7, chapter 10.
50. Brockmer is listed among the original members of the "Moravian Brethren, formerly of the English Communion" registered by English authorities in 1742. The congregation then consisted of seventy-two persons. Regarding this list, see Charles Higham's article in *The New Church Magazine* (London), January 1914. See further Odhner's translation of the dream journal, p. 70. Cf. also Gerhard Wauer, *Die Anfänge der Brüder-Kirche in England*, 126.
51. On the first publication of Brockmer's testimony in John Wesley's journal *Arminian Magazine* in January 1781, and the protests it evoked, see Tafel, vol. 2, doc. 270, 581ff.

    Based on Brockmer's account, the physician Dr. H. Maudsley declared Swedenborg mentally deranged in a paper that attracted much attention, published in the *Journal of Mental Science*, no. 70 (July 1870). In Sweden, the popular historian Anders Fryxell described Swedenborg in similar terms in the forty-eighth volume of his anecdotal Swedish history, *Berättelser ut svenska historien* (1875). A debate followed, in Sweden as well as abroad. In a massive biography of Swedenborg (*Swedenborg: En lefnadsskildring*, 2 vols. [Stockholm: 1917–1920]), Swedish physician E. A. G. Kleen strongly supported this view, as did, for example, the German existentialist Karl Jaspers.

52. As observed by Kleen, vol. 2, 418 ff, who published and discussed this account, which is also published in Tafel, vol. 2, doc. 270, pp. 587–590.

53. According to the English calendar, "the dog days" begin on July 19.

54. Cf. *The Animal Kingdom* II, 356, note c.

55. See also Plitt, vol. 2, 382ff.

56. The most important source regarding economic matters is F. G. Lindh's investigation, "Swedenborg's ekonomi," published in several articles in the journal *Nya Kyrkans Tidning* over the years 1827–1930. Cf. Lars Bergquist, *Swedenborgs hemlighet*, 400–414.

57. Nils Jacobsson, *Den svenska herrnhutismens uppkomst* (Uppsala: 1908), 51 ff.

58. Fredrik Hjärne (1706–1773); on the Hjärne couple, see Karin Dovring, *Striden kring Sions Sånger*, vol. 1, 191 ff.

59. Erik Odelstierna (1723–1805); Thore Odelius (1705–1777). See also the previous section in this introduction on the Brethren of Herrnhut.

60. Fredrik Gyllenborg (1698–1759), a Hat party leader, played an important part in the declaration of war against Russia in 1741. He became a member of the Board of Governors of the Bank of Sweden in 1741 and was appointed president of the Royal College of Mining in 1750. Being a treasurer of the Hat Party, he was responsible for the transactions of French subsidies to politicians who supported an alliance with France. Since his honesty was questioned, the French minister to Sweden transferred the responsibility for these undercover payments to another member of the Hat Party, C. F. Pechlin.

Gyllenborg's wife, Elisabeth Stierncrona, was known for her piety and was the author of a religious work, *Mariae bästa del* (The Best Part of Mary). She was the daughter of the ironmaster Gabriel Stierncrona (1669–1723), who, together with Christopher Polhem, founded Stiernsunds Bruk, where

Swedenborg served as a trainee in his youth. According to an English source, Swedenborg late in his life said that Elisabeth Stierncrona-Gyllenborg was to be his wife in the next life. F. G. Lindh, "Swedenborgs ekonomi," *Nya Kyrkans Tidning* (1928): 115–116.

61. As found in Genesis 14:18. Compare Swedenborg's remarks in *Arcana Coelestia* §1725.

62. Acton, *Letters and Memorials*, 1709–1748, p. 499.

63. See Jonsson, *Swedenborgs skapelsedrama De Cultu et Amore Dei*, 170 ff.

64. This account agrees only in part to the notes Swedenborg himself wrote, which can be found in the *Adversaria*, vol. 2, §1956 f. and the *Spiritual Diary* §397, both dated April 1745, which is probably the time of the experience in London. Robsahm is quoted from Anders Hallengren's annotated critical edition of the memorandum, *Anteckingar om Swedenborg* (Stockholm 1989), §15 (pp. 36 ff).

65. See Tafel, vol. 2, doc. 234, p. 261.

66. See Tafel, vol. 1, doc. 165, p. 462.

PART TWO

The Dream Diary

WITH COMMENTARY BY

LARS BERGQUIST

1

AN ACCOUNT OF A JOURNEY

1743

1

I left Stockholm for Ystad on July 21 and arrived on the 27th after having passed the cities of Tälje, Nyköping, Norrköping, Linköping, Grenna [Gränna], and Jönköping. In Ystad I met with the Countess de la Gardie and her two young daughters and her two young counts; [furthermore] Count Fersen, Major Landtishusen, and Master Klingenberg.—On July 31, General Stenflycht arrived with his son and Captain Schiächta.

The dream diary begins with notes of the same precise and dry character as those of Emanuel Swedenborg's earlier journals of travel. For the most part, these entries account for travel routes, people he has met, and sights he has seen.

The journey from Stockholm to Ystad, a distance of over three hundred miles, took Swedenborg six days. Presumably he went by public coach and stayed overnight at inns in the countryside. At Linköping, as during his earlier journeys, he probably stayed with his brother-in-law, Bishop Eric Benzelius, the husband of Swedenborg's sister Anna. This was the last time they would meet: Benzelius, who had been appointed archbishop, was to die a month later. In June, he appears in a dream, looking "tired and old."

At Ystad, Swedenborg had to wait nine days for fair winds. Since they are part of the picture, we should say a few words about his fellow-travelers.

First, Swedenborg notes the presence of Countess De la Gardie, with her four children. The countess's given name is Hedvig

Catharina, and, for the past two years, she has been the widow of Count Magnus Julius De la Gardie, the late Councilor-of-State and President of the National Board of Trade. In their marriage, she had given birth to twelve children. Now she is on her way to Paris, where she will soon convert to Catholicism and die in 1745.

During the long wait, the countess might have intimated something about the royal court, surrounded by scandal as it was. She may have been the source of some details in a later journal entry (no. 22); with her husband, the countess was close to the influential Gyllenborg–Broman circle.

Since the countess's late husband had been the head of the De la Gardie family in Sweden, Swedenborg must have met him at the House of Nobles during parliament sessions, being himself the head of the Swedenborg family. Like so many others among Swedenborg's Stockholm acquaintances, De la Gardie was later to appear in Swedenborg's spiritual theater. In the so-called *Spiritual Diary*—his later log of spiritual experiences—there is an entry in which he says he has seen Count De la Gardie together with the Russian Empress Elizabeth (Elizaveta Petrovna), whom the count had married after her death in 1762. They had met in the spiritual world and fallen in love; the count's earthly marriage was annulled, since the spouses were found not to share any "mutual affection"— a remarkable piece of information, indeed, when one knows about their twelve children. When the Russian empress marries the Swedish count, their wedding is celebrated with great festivities in heaven, and the two are bodily united. We are told nothing, however, about the fate of the Countess De la Gardie, his earthly widow.

Among those waiting at Ystad to set to sail is "Count Fersen," probably the later well-known Hat politician Fredrik Axel von Fersen, the father of Axel von Fersen, who was to become famous for his affair with Queen Marie Antoinette, whom he tried to rescue from the guillotine. Fredrik was an officer in the French royal army, and—we may assume—was now returning to Paris after being granted leave of absence in connection with Sweden's ill-fated war with Russia. Afterwards, he married one of Count De la

Gardie's daughters, perhaps one of the two girls who are now wait-ing for the boat.

In his dream about the post-mortem marriage of the empress and the count, Swedenborg sees the empress at a party with mem-bers of the Fersen family. "Their spirits were such that although they did not deny God, his Word or the Creed, they thought but little upon it." They are the kind of people St. Paul calls "natural" or unspiritual: a category of spirits that Swedenborg later often tells us about. In his *Spiritual Diary*, the Fersen family's fate corresponds to their indifference in spiritual matters. They are served pastries and delicacies, "but it does them no good." They are anxious and restless—"are fond of eating horseradish," Swedenborg adds. In those days, horseradish was regarded as a cure for the nervous.

Lantingshausen (Landtishusen) was also a Stockholm acquain-tance. His full name was Jakob Albrecht von Lantingshausen; like Fersen, he was a major in the French army. He had returned to Sweden to become ennobled. Lantingshausen was also a member of the Hat party and would afterward become one of its leading figures. At this time, he was on his way back to France, where a year afterward he would be promoted to major-general. He mar-ried one of Fersen's relatives, eventually returned to Sweden, and became governor of Stockholm.

The last name in this little circle of fellow-noblemen, gathering in Ystad on their way south, is Johan Stenflycht, a Swedish colonel and French lieutenant-general. He played a prominent role in the campaign for the election of an heir to the Swedish throne. Repre-senting French interests, and by means of generous dinners, he acted on behalf of a Count Palatine of Zweybrücken, who was sup-posed to be a candidate acceptable to interested parties in Paris.

Captain Skeckta (Schiächta) was also involved in the political storms that swept over Stockholm that spring. He was a Hat Party member and belonged to the circle of Colonel Lagercrantz, who led the Älvsborg Regiment in a successful countermove against the rebellious Dalecarlians. In the flurry of accusations and counter-ac-cusations that ensued as a result of the unsuccessful war, Skeckta had denounced the factory owner and Cap politician Abraham

PART 2: THE DREAM DIARY

Hedman, accusing him of treason. However, the great botanist Carl von Linnaeus—who was related to Swedenborg on his mother's side—regarded the accusation as unfounded. In his work *Nemesis Divina*, the basic idea of which is that we are punished for our sins during our lifetime, Linnaeus observes that, at the diet of 1758, Skeckta was himself accused of "criminal statements"—his wife having secretly supplied information against him—and ended up as a prisoner at the Marstrand fortress.

Magister Carl Klingenberg, finally, seems to have remained outside politics, and his role on this scene is subordinate. He accompanied Countess De la Gardie as the private tutor of her sons, the young counts. In 1747, he became academic secretary at Uppsala University. In contrast to the other people mentioned in Swedenborg's dream journal, he is not a public figure. As a member of the Tankebyggarorden (The Order of Thought Builders), he chose the somewhat defensive device: *Securus sub umbra* (safe in the shadow).

2

Due to headwind, we were not able to sail until 5 August. I was in company with General Stenflycht. On August 6th we arrived at Stralsund, and early on the 7th we went into the city. The same day the Countess and the General left.

3

In Stralsund I once more saw the fortress from the Badenthor up to the Francken, Stripseer and Kniper-thore; and I saw the houses where King Charles XII had lodged; saw the Meierfeld palace; the church of St. Nicholas, the church of St. James, which was laid in ruins during the siege; and the church of St. Mary. I visited Colonel and Commandant Schwerin, the Superintendent Löper, and the Post Director Crivits. In the Church of St. Nicholas, a clock was shown that had been struck by lightning in the years 1670, 1683, and 1688, just as the hand pointed to 6 o'clock. Afterward viewed the new fortifications outside the Kniperthor. I met Carl Jesper Benzelius; saw the water works which supply the city, consisting of two systems of conduits.

4

On August 9, I left Stralsund, and passed through Damm-garten; in the Mecklenburg area through Rimnits to Rostock, where I looked at eight churches, five larger ones and three smaller, and saw a convent of eight women, who nevertheless lived in freedom.

5

From that place, I went on to Wismar, and there were six churches, the finest of them being St. Mary's and St. George's.

Departed on the 11th, and on the way Gadebusk was seen, the seat of war between Swedes and Danes. Then arrived at Ratzeburg, which is surrounded by a swamp, for which reason we passed over a long bridge.

Stralsund was the capital of Swedish Pomerania, a Swedish enclave in northern Germany, which, through the Peace of Nystad in 1721, had been reduced to a third of its former size. It had been the destination of Charles XII's famous fourteen-day ride across Europe after his long sojourn in Turkey. In 1714, when the king and his adjutant were standing at the town gate, on the night between November 10 and 11, Swedenborg was in Greifswald, the provincial capital. The halt in Swedish Pomerania had been the last stopping place during his first, almost five-year-long journey abroad. Soon after the king's arrival at Stralsund, the city was besieged by Danes, Poles, and Russians. In June, Swedenborg was able to take a boat over to Skåne. In December, Stralsund surrendered.

In the capital, Swedenborg saw the sights, made the usual courtesy calls, and met with his nephew Carl Jesper Benzelius, son of the bishop of Linköping and his own sister Anna. He later became bishop of Strängnäs. He admired his famous uncle's research feats and held his teachings in high esteem, and was later to correspond with some of Swedenborg's followers.

By way of Rostock, Swedenborg went on to Wismar, which was also a part of Swedish territory and a remnant of the country's period as a great power, an empire that had finally been dissolved after the Great Nordic war. As he had at Stralsund, he visited the relics of that war at Gadebusch in Mecklenburg, where General Magnus Stenbock and his army had defeated the Danes in 1712. It may be mentioned that Swedenborg's new acquaintance, General Stenflycht, mentioned in the entries 1 and 2 above, greatly distinguished himself in the battle at Gadebusch.

6 _____

On August 12, I arrived at Hamburg, took lodgings at the Kaisershof, where also the Countess de la Gardie was staying. I met with Baron Hamilton, Reuterholm, Trivalt [Triewald], Royal Assessor Awerman, and was introduced to Prince Augustus, the brother of His Royal Highness, who spoke Swedish. Afterwards I was then introduced by Marshal-in-Chief Lesch, to His Royal Highness Adolphus Frederich, to whom I submitted a table of contents outlining what is to be printed, and showed him reviews of the preceding work.

Thus, the successor to the Swedish throne, whom Swedenborg and the parliamentary majority had voted for on Midsummer Eve, was residing in Hamburg. The Council of the State had cherished the hope that the chosen candidate to the crown would go to Stralsund, and there, on Swedish territory, wait for the naval unit which was to bring the king-to-be to his new country. But the prince-bishop obviously stayed where he was. Now, on August 12, when he greeted Swedenborg in Hamburg, the Swedish delegation was only just on its way; it was probably to arrive a week later.

On his visit to the royal personage in Hamburg, Swedenborg presented him with his *contenta*, the plan and contents of *The Animal Kingdom*, together with some reviews of critical praise. Later in his journal, Swedenborg regrets this self-presentation. It had been boasting, he thinks, an act of conceit in line with his corrupt moral state at the time.

As usual in his travel diaries, Swedenborg makes notes on the

Swedes he encounters on his trip. Lack of professional titles indicates that he already knows them, There is no reason to treat in greater detail all these figures, since many of them just pass by. Swedenborg's "little world" has already been presented in outline. Carl Fredrik Hamilton and Esbjörn Christian Reuterholm were both Swedish noblemen. Hamilton and probably Reuterholm were attached to Adolf Fredrik's Swedish court at Hamburg. Johan Fredrik König was a Swedish diplomatic agent in Hamburg, where he was also Swedish postmaster. By "Trivalt," Swedenborg may be referring to Samuel Triewald, member of the Holstein Council of War, author and official, but more likely to his brother, Mårten Triewald, who, along with Christopher Polhem, was the most illustrious engineer of contemporary Sweden and a driving force behind the industrial introduction of steam power.

7

On August 17, I left Hamburg, across the river Elbe to Buxtehude, where, for the space of some ten kilometers, I viewed the most charming landscape I have ever seen in Germany; passing through a continuous orchard of apple, pear, plum, walnut, and chestnut trees, and also linden and elms.

Shortly before this journal of travel comes to a close, the gardens of Buxtehude remind us of Swedenborg's great interest in gardening, horticulture, and dendrology. In particular, he seemed to have had an affection for the disciplined and strictly cultural baroque type of garden, in earlier travel notes speaking enthusiastically of, for instance, the park at Sturefors Castle in Östergötland, Sweden. Swedenborg himself planned such a garden at the island of Södermalm in Stockholm, in the block named Mullvaden (the mole), where, in February 1743, he had bought property.

8

On the 18th, I arrived at Bremen, where there are good ramparts and suburbs, the best being Neustadt. At the bridge leading to it, there are eleven river mills in a row. I saw the town hall in the market square, and the great Roland [statue], which is the sign of a free city: afterward I viewed the Church of St. Nicholas and the cathedrals, and was to the hospital, where there are also some statues.

9

On 20 August, I left Bremen for Leer by way of Oldenburg, which is a county under the Danish crown with fine fortifications and an abundance of waters around. I also passed through Neukants [Neuschanz]. Near Leer there is a fortification called Leerort, belonging to Holland. I journeyed thence to Gröningen, which is a large city under the Prince of Orange. In Leewarden, I saw his palace, moreover the palace of his mother, which is called the Princess' Palace; likewise the town hall, etc. We arrived there by treckscheut [Dutch canal boat drawn by horses].

10

From Gröningen, you have two routes to chose between, one to Harlingen and the other to Lemmer. The former is reached by canal boat, the latter by carriage: but we chose the way to Harlingen through Lewarden [Leeuwarden].

From Harlingen, which is a large town,

Here the travel notes stop. Was there ever a continuation? Page six in the notebook ends with the words "a large town," and then there are empty pages. Four pages seem to have been cut out. Two are left as strips, numbered in large clumsy handwriting.

If there was a continuation of the travel notes, it cannot have been very long. Swedenborg embarked on a boat crossing the sea which was then called Ysselmeer, and probably landed at Amsterdam after a day or so. Here, or later at Leyden, he would visit libraries and look up certain scientific matters, checking for the information he had mentioned in his application for leave of absence. This would have kept him occupied for some time. A note of currency transactions (entry 286) seems to indicate that he was in Amsterdam in September and (through) November. *The Animal Kingdom* was to be printed at The Hague. Perhaps he moved there in January, an assumption that also receives slight support from the note about currency transactions. In any case, it appears unambiguously from his diary that he had settled in The Hague by March 1744, at the latest.

2

GLIMPSES OF THE PAST, KEYWORDS FOR THE FUTURE

————◆◈◆————

Undated Dreams

_____

1. In my younger days, and the Gustavian family.
2. In Venice, concerning the beautiful palace.
3. In Sweden, about the white cloud of the sky.
4. In Leipzig, on one lying in boiling water.
5. About one who stumbled with a chain into the depths.
6. Of the king who showed such generosity in a poor farmer's cottage.
7. Of the farmhand who wanted me to depart.

These seven points seem to constitute dream headlines, keywords that would help the dreamer to remember these strange nocturnal experiences. As I have mentioned in my introduction, a close reading of the dream diary proper reveals that the main components of Swedenborg's dreams and visions are relatively few and recurrent. As is evident from entry 14, which follows below, the laconic captions of the opening page were taken down at The Hague. Even if some months have passed between the seven headings and the notes that follow in the dated sections of the journal, at least some of the summarized experiences should be more or less connected with dreams described in more detail and should touch upon issues in the same sphere of problems.

Assuming that this is the case, we can highlight certain keywords: the dreamer's youth and the Gustavian royal family, the lovely palace, the white cloud of heaven, the fall with chains into an abyss, the farmhand and the journey. Decoding these elements in the same fashion as Swedenborg himself was about to do, we arrive at the following reading with reasonable accuracy. His dreams are about his father, the bishop, and about God. Furthermore, they concern his grand effort to demonstrate scientifically central Christian doctrines. It seems to Swedenborg that he is being granted the opportunity to behold heavenly truths, the knowledge that God's light also reaches the unworthy. The dreamer realizes he has been fundamentally mistaken and has sinned, but has been saved from the depths. As a servant of truth, the time has come to make a new start, abandon his old lines of thought and the work he is engaged in.

The last two points on the list are particularly noteworthy. After Swedenborg's great Easter vision in April, he will ask himself what Christ's exhortation could mean: "Well then, do!" Does this refer to the royal visit to the farmer's house? Had he been promised a departure from his old ways of thinking?

We will continue to encounter these themes, in elaborated and varied forms, in the rest of the journal, and now we leave the strange poetry of the dream catalogue.

12 _____

8. **On my nightly amusements.**
—Wondered at myself that there was nothing left to do for my own glory, which I began to feel very strongly.
—that I was not inclined toward sexual relations, which I had been all my days.
9. **how I have been in wakeful ecstasy almost continuously.**

From point eight and onward, he begins describing physical and psychological phenomena that he has observed in himself. The conflict between love of self and the love of God is one of the diary's leitmotifs. Another is the sexual theme. Swedenborg observes that he has lost his erotic desire. As we read on, we shall find that this serene state of mind was only temporary. The ninth point, about continuous rapture, indicates that the dream diary period was preceded by days and weeks of exaltation, an excitement where he is "beyond himself." Even after the period covered by the dream diary, he describes a similar state of ecstasy as "visions as in clearest midday-light while awake, but with eyes closed."

13

---

10. How I opposed the spirit
—and how I then liked it, but afterwards found it to have been foolish things, devoid of life and coherence.
—and that, consequently, parts of what I have written must be of such nature, whereas I had not altogether resisted the power of the spirit, for which reason the faults are all mine, but the verities are not my own.
—yes, I sometimes fell into impatience and defiance. I wished to do things my own way when progress was slow, since I did not labor for my own sake. Less did I see my unworthiness and give thanks for the grace.

As already mentioned, the epistemological problems connected with the relationship between secular and divine knowledge were not new to Swedenborg. The implicit contradiction— the question of how to combine analysis and intuitive synthesis—was already addressed in his work *On the Infinite and the Final Cause of Creation* (1734), was treated in *The Economy of the Animal Kingdom* six or seven years later, and is further discussed in *The Animal Kingdom* series. His introductory self-reproach for having "opposed the spirit"—and the elaboration of this theme in the diary—thus has a frame that has been constructed for a long time. He enters into a house that he has built for himself.

When Swedenborg turns to pure intellectual analysis alone, the only result is "hideous specters," complex and horrible illusions of truths, he later observes (entry 15). Therefore, we must allow ourselves to be led by spiritual power, our only way of achieving enlightenment. The earlier, undated notes seem to indicate that he is now, even before the actual dream diary, entering into the process of purification described later. To go on writing for the sake of his own fame and honor seems meaningless. This is a change of attitude compared with the one mentioned in his application for leave of absence from the Board of Mines, which he had submitted only a year earlier. Then he had given his journey's motive as a desire to produce a work that would satisfy his grand capacity and intentions, one that would also, secondarily, be an honor to his native country.

14

> **11. How, after arriving at The Hague, I found that the impulse and ambition for my work had passed away, at which I wondered.**
> **—how the inclination toward women, which had been my chief passion, so suddenly ceased.**
> **—how the whole time I have enjoyed the best sleep at night, which has been more than pleasant.**
> **—my ecstasies before and after sleep.**
> **—my clear thoughts about things.**

15

> **How I had resisted the power of the Holy Spirit, and what then happened; how I saw hideous specters, without life, in horrible shrouds within which they moved. With a beast that attacked me but not the child.**

Entries 14 and 15 are largely reflections of those immediately preceding them. Note, however, his astonishment at his lengthy and beneficial sleep. Later on, we frequently find him amazed at this—he declares that he has slept soundly for more than twelve hours at a stretch and that he continues to do so.

When we read the records of Swedenborg's contemporaries, people who followed his life closely, we find that they often mention his regular habits and long hours in bed. The Amsterdam banker John Christian Cuno, for example, reports that Swedenborg went to bed as early as at seven o'clock and got up at eight in the morning. Cuno noted this when Swedenborg was eighty-one years old, but we have earlier reports to a similar effect. Perhaps it was during his long nights that the "clear thoughts about things" came to him. However, and more important, we know from the dream diary that the crucial visions appear during the hypnagogic states of evenings and mornings. His regular and early habits may have been established because of the experiences during this period.

16

I seemed to be reclining on a rocky mountain, beneath which there was a chasm. Lying there among the knobby cliffs, I tried to get on my feet by holding onto a rock, without a foothold; an abyss beneath. This signifies that I wished to rescue myself from the precipice all by myself, and that was not possible.

17

How a woman lay down by my side, just as if I had been wide awake; I wanted to know who she was. She spoke to me softly, but said that she was pure, but I stank badly. She was, I believe, my guardian angel, for the temptation then began.

The bottomless pit of evil often returns in Swedenborg's texts. Fundamental to his thinking is the idea that since human beings possess free will, we can very well help ourselves out of these depths—but not without aid. We must pray for God's help and adapt our way of life to the divine commandments. The "rocks" he is clinging to, of whatever kind, do not suffice.

A woman lies beside him on the mountain side. She talks to him gently and gets him to realize his own sinfulness. Can she be his guardian angel? This concept, certainly not one of Lutheran orthodoxy, had been common in his father's teachings.

This moment on the rocky hillside is crucial because temptation starts here. Swedenborg often returns to this opening day in his thoughts. On one occasion (in entry 186), he counts the days from that event.

Temptations on high mountains are, of course, a biblical paradigm. As we shall see, Swedenborg will emerge from his crisis convinced of his calling—a calling that, in due course, became increasingly messianic.

Temptation, as such, is synonymous with everything that prevents a person from being ruled by his or her divinely inspired soul: selfishness and egotism of all kinds, refusal to see one's own doings and sayings within a greater context. It is at the intersection between the incurable fires of the body on the one hand and an awareness that inner truths lie within his reach on the other that Swedenborg's torment begins, an agony of a unique and genuine stamp, producing a marked melancholy and pain.

3

MARCH 1744

———◆•✕•●———

Here the dated dreams begin. As is usually the case with Swedenborg's diary, they appear to have been written down shortly after the moment of awakening. As we will see, Swedenborg from time to time also summarized his experiences.

1744 March 24–25

18

> **1. I was standing by a machine which was moved by a wheel; its spokes entangled me more and more and carried me up so that I could not escape. I awoke. [It signifies] either that I need to be kept in further difficulty, or else that it concerned the lungs in the womb, on which subject I then wrote immediately afterwards; both.**

Here we are immediately faced by one of the characteristic traits of the diary, namely, the intimate connection between its entries and Swedenborg's current scientific work. The visions guide him forward, not only ethically and religiously but also practically. For Swedenborg, it is only a question of different aspects, of different sides of the same thing.

We are plunged straight into the question of the lungs' development and function in the womb, as described and discussed in the prologue to *The Animal Kingdom*. It is one of the cornerstones of his thought and is a portend of the future. The basic idea is that the fetus is isolated from the outer world and that it has only one immediate concern: to develop according to the laws of its own being. The exclusion of all exterior human influence is the most significant characteristic of this developmental phase. The embryo grows in accordance with its own nature.

According to Swedenborg, the influences bearing upon an infant in the womb through its mother are wholly beneficial, and its development is guided by "God's love and wisdom." Its birth into the world alters this situation completely. The infant begins to breathe, and with each breath, "nature" flows into this new human being. From now on, the infant is prey to worldly influence, opposed to goodness and the love that pervades the world. In his short work *The Interaction between the Soul and the Body* (1741), Swedenborg had already described the paths taken by this outside influence, which he calls an "influx." He also pursued this theory in two other works, *The Fibre* and *Rational Psychology*, written at approximately the same time as the dream diary. It is this line of thought he continues in *The Animal Kingdom*.

The problems are epistemological. Throughout the crisis, the relationship between knowledge and faith, or science and religion, is the topic at issue. One question emerges: if all illumination, all clarity and insight stem from God, what is the scientist supposed to do? What is the correct scientific attitude under such conditions? Swedenborg undoubtedly accepted the Christian faith and the idea of divine providence, but he also made allowances for his worldly aims. He wanted to become famous, to be the one to discover the location of the soul and reveal its true function. However, this ambition is also a source of hubris, and Swedenborg became increasingly aware of this.

It is his own personal machine, with its spokes and wheels, that squeezes him.

19

2. **I was in an herb garden containing many fine beds, one of which I desired to own. I looked around to see if there was any other path; I saw one and thought of another. There was someone who was picking away a heap of invisible creeping things and killed them; he said they were bugs that someone**

had carried thither and thrown in, infesting the entire place. I did not see them, but saw some other crawling creature, which I dropped on a white linen cloth beside a woman; it was the impurity which ought to be rooted out of me.

We have already come across Swedenborg's interest in horticulture. In the emblematics of the dream diary, the word *garden* signifies paradise. Now he dreams of being in Elysian fields, but at the same time he is trying to get out. The reason is that he is littering paradise with rubbish, bringing in lice. (The impersonal pronoun "one" or "someone" often refers to himself.) Another reason is that he simply is reluctant to be here.

Indeed, he is not suited for this garden. In his later writings, Swedenborg will allow a taste of paradise to those spirits who in their earthly lives have been victims of their egotism. However, they do not feel at home in paradise and long to return to their natural atmosphere. The same is true of our world.

Swedenborg the dreamer is blind to the creeping things, with the exception of one that he leaves with a woman, one of many females in the diary. In his vocabulary, all these women (*fruntimmer*) whom he dreams of month after month, and whom he either loves or rejects, represent theoretical subjects or fields of research. Thus, this dream appears to tell him that there is something dirty in the work he has in hand at the time. He can see the flaws in his conceited ambitions and in his vanity—a constant theme of his self-accusations.

These traits are fatal character flaws. From the 1740s onward, he believed that truth discloses itself only to someone who has liberated himself from earthly bonds.

To be soiled in this fashion is dangerous indeed:

20 _____

3. I boldly descended a huge stairway, which after a while turned into a ladder; below it, there was a hole that went down to quite a great depth; it was difficult to get to the other side without falling into the hole. On the other side, there were persons to whom I reached out my hand to help them

cross over. I woke up. This is the danger in which I am: of falling into the abyss unless I receive help.

This is the second time Swedenborg is threatened from the depths. Chasms, ladders, or stairs, usually associated with rescue from danger, with progress, or with initiation, are rather common elements in our dreams; and they appear frequently in Swedenborg's diary. For the assessor of the Royal Board of Mining, an expert on mineralogy inspecting drifts and pits in the country, this imagery was certainly not farfetched.

21

4. I spoke long and familiarly with our successor in Sweden, who had changed into a woman; then I spoke with Carl Broman, saying that he ought to be in favor of him, and he said something in reply—and then with Erland Broman, saying that I had returned here. I do not know what this means unless it has something to do with what follows.

The "successor" was the successor to the Swedish throne, Adolf Fredrik, whom Swedenborg had met in Hamburg, about six months before. The prince-bishop had been fetched from Rügen by a naval ship and was now installed in Stockholm Castle, which he shared with the old monarch, Fredrik I. Baron Erland Broman, the court marshal, played an important but morally dubious role here. We shall see him again in the diary. This minister of pleasure and entertainment had to delight the sixty-nine-year-old king with various spectacles, and the diversions the monarch demanded were invariably of the more frivolous variety—any other kind of amusement was simply alien to his nature. In his memoirs, Admiral Carl Tersmeden, a man whose personal preferences were not far removed from the king's, gives the following portrait of the monarch:

> *The king is of such humor that he cannot tolerate any words against any of his favorites, and he lacks all discrimination regarding those who are dear to him and those who are good*

advisors, since his passion for sex is so indescribable, and nothing so amuses him as speaking in private about such voluptuousness.

Erland Broman appears to have been addicted to much the same pleasures as his master. In this regard, he showed an ingenuity of sorts. This talent, together with his gift for raising money in no time (Broman's estate left the beneficiaries bankrupt) made him the king's favorite.

In Swedenborg's dream diary, Erland Broman symbolizes sensuality, superficiality, and impiety and constitutes a threat to the dreamer's integrity and peace of mind. In his *Spiritual Diary,* Swedenborg notes that he has studied Broman's posthumous destiny. The court marshal ended up in a "hell of excrement," associated with fornication and rape and appropriate to someone given to sexual depravation of the special types to which Broman had been so committed. "The angels were horror-stricken," Swedenborg wrote.

Carl Broman, on the other hand, is a secondary figure in this context. Although his family relationship to Marshal Broman had earned him the governorship of the little Swedish county of Älvsborg in southwest Sweden, he moved for the most part in President Fredrik Gyllenborg's social circles; like the president, he had financial dealings with Swedenborg. Again, this may have been inspired by family relationships. Carl Broman was married to a cousin of Fredrik Gyllenborg's wife, Elisabeth Stierncrona. Presumably, Broman was involved in the agreement regarding the inheritance of Sara Bergia. Swedenborg, writing in 1765, says that he had lent Carl Broman a sum of 10,000 riksdaler.

Now, however, Swedenborg seems to think that Carl Broman should be affiliated with the court of Adolf Fredrik.

This dream of the two Bromans, which Swedenborg says he is unable to interpret, is followed by another dream sequence, also related to the royal court in Stockholm. Besides Adolf Fredrik, who is mentioned merely in passing, this dream features Fredrik I, a widower, and his mistress Hedvig Taube, as well as his former wife, the late queen Ulrika Eleonora, who had died in 1741.

22

5. I came into a magnificent chamber and spoke with a woman who was governess of the court. She wished to relate something to me; then came the queen and passed through to another chamber; it seemed to be the same one who represented our Successor. I went out, for I was rather meanly dressed, as I had just returned from a journey, wearing a long, old surtout, and being without hat and wig. I wondered that she deigned to come after me. She told me that a certain person had given all the jewels to his mistress, but that he had got them back in this manner: she was told that he had not given her the finest, whereupon she had thrown away the jewels.

23

She asked me to come in again, but I excused myself on the score that I was so unworthily dressed and had no wig, and must go home first. She said it did not matter. This refers to what I was then about to write and to begin with, the epilogue of the second part, to which I wanted to add a preface, but which was not needed. I acted accordingly. What she told me about the jewels referred to the truths which one has discovered, but which have been taken away again, because she was offended that she had not received all. I afterwards saw the jewels in hand and saw a great ruby in the middle.

On the surface, this dream seems to tell about Swedenborg's meeting with Queen Ulrika Eleonora and her gracious manner toward him, even though he was improperly dressed. The queen mentions her husband's affair with Madame Taube, relating how she had refused the second-rate jewelry he had tried to give her. Go back to the first entry in the diary: the royal romances might have been brought up by Countess De la Gardie.

The king's romantic liaison was known, both to the queen and the court, as well as in leading circles. In time, it was even in some measure "legitimized" when Hedvig Taube gave birth to two sons, who were given the title Count of Hessenstein; their mother was then raised to the same rank, becoming the Countess of Hessenstein. The king often brought presents to his mistress. Now Swedenborg informs us that she could return them if they did not strike her fancy.

However, as is evident from Swedenborg's own interpretation of the dream, the scenery takes another shape in his interpretation. Suddenly, it is transformed into the preface to the epilogue of *The Animal Kingdom*. The question was whether it was necessary to write such a foreword. When we look at the text again, we let the key-words take on a secondary meaning, a meaning that they also have in the diary.

The dreamer finds himself in "a magnificent chamber." With Swedenborg, these words mean that the dreamer is successfully drawing the outline of a doctrine, a true teaching. The queen is an image of wisdom. She comes to him, although he is not yet quite prepared for this important encounter. She tells him of a man whose mistress has refused his gifts, since they were not of superior quality. This is a recurrent image: love, which is knowledge, expects its adepts to do their utmost, whereas the inferior is rejected. The queen—wisdom—asks him to follow her, but he excuses himself: he has no wig nor is he properly dressed. The excuse is overruled.

This pattern, or its constituent concerns, is constantly repeated and pervades the whole vellum-bound notebook. For his analysis, Swedenborg on this particular occasion, on March 25, chooses a topic that requires immediate attention: whether or not to write a foreword. The queen urges him to come, without delay. Thus, the question is settled. The epilogue is standing there by itself, without support of any introduction.

This hermeneutics applies elsewhere and works even outside the parchment cover of the dream diary. When Swedenborg later deciphers the hidden meaning of the Pentateuch, and thus reveals the heavenly secrets, he operates for the most part in a similar fashion.

[March] 25–26

24

It seemed as if I took a key and went in. The doorkeeper exam- ined the keys I had; I showed them all, in the case I should have two, but it seemed that Hesselius had another. I was arrested and put under guard. Many went to see me. I thought that I had done nothing wrong, but I realized that I might be put in an unfavor- able light if it turned out that I had taken the key. I awoke. There may be various interpretations, such as that I have taken the key to anatomy, while the other one that Hesselius had was the key to medicine; or that the key to the lungs is the pulmonary artery, and thus all the motions of the body; or, spiritually.

To sum up the subjects, we have one or two keys, Hesselius, im- prisonment, many visitors, anatomy/medicine, the relation be- tween the lungs and the pulmonary artery, and bodily and spiritual motion.

A possible reading is as follows: Swedenborg had already con- sidered the area of anatomy in *The Economy of the Animal Kingdom,* the work on the structural order and congruence of the animal king- dom. Now he is concerned with his new work, simply titled *The Animal Kingdom.* We should note that the Latin *Regnum Animale* also may have the meaning "kingdom of the soul." The question he puts to himself is whether he is now forced to investigate yet another field—medicine. The physician mentioned is Johan Hesselius, a relative who in his youth had stayed in Swedenborg's parental home in Skara. Hesselius had become an assessor of the National Board of Health and Medicine. What would happen if Sweden- borg, as a layman, trespassed into Hesselius' territory in his search for the keys of the soul? Was this really permitted? Or would he be prosecuted? This was a venturesome pursuit, although he would at- tract many readers. Perhaps, he ponders, he had better refrain from this digression.

Another angle of approach is that Swedenborg had clarified the importance of the lungs and the pulmonary artery to *motum corporis,* the bodily movements. He considers them crucial to spiritual life.

Is it permissible for him, a scientist, to use a theological key? The latter question is, as we already have seen, the cutting edge of his deliberations.

25

> I asked for a cure against my illness, and I was offered a heap of rags to buy. I took half of them and selected from the other half, but finally I gave back all the rags. He said that he would himself buy me something that would lead to a cure. The rags were my corporeal thoughts by which I wished to cure myself, but they were good for nothing.

The dream now takes a different turn. What is the illness for which he seeks a cure, and what is the doctor prescribing? Dr. Hesselius certainly cannot help him. The illness is the imprisonment in bodily thoughts—the "illness to death" of St. John. This explains the impurity and the indecision on the edge of the precipice.

This was one of the fundamental problems occupying his mind at this time, and he had already expounded it extensively, for instance, in his works *The Fibre* and *De Anima*, his treatise on psychology. A human being is mentally sick when ruled by the senses alone and when the soul has no control. In such a case, the sense of being part of a larger context is lost, as is the connection with the Divine. From this loss follows melancholy, which, in its turn, is derived from pangs of conscience when temptations are getting the better of us.

Swedenborg is offered a heap of rags. In the following paragraph in this night's entry, he finds his own thought—referred to as *ratio naturalis*, natural reason—to be fragmentary and incoherent since it is devoid of the higher meaning.

In his dream, Swedenborg abandons the tools he has so far been using. "He said that he would himself buy me something that would lead to a cure." To the reader, the pronoun *he* appears to refer to the physician, his relative Hesselius. To the writer himself, *he* was certainly God, Jesus Christ. Only Christ can buy the truth

that cures; it is not for sale to human beings. This insight Swedenborg expounds in the last, undated, entry in the diary.

26 _____

**Afterwards I went out and saw many black images; one was
thrown to me. I saw that it had no use of its foot. This meant, I
think, that natural reason could not accommodate to spiritual
reason.**

We may assume that the black images are caricatures of Swedenborg himself. We find such distorted self-portraits in the first part
of the *Opera philosophica et mineralia* (Philosophical and Mineralogical
Works) published ten years earlier. Which self-portrait shall he
choose for his new book?

There is no portrait of the author. But when he sees himself in
his dream, he limps along on one lame foot. Natural reason and
spiritual reason do not go together. This piece of information is
very useful, since it supplies us with a key to a disability found in
this dream world time and again: he hobbles around or has one
foot bandaged.

As will shortly become evident, Swedenborg's dreams have a
strong erotic tinge. Especially after the great crisis experienced
during Easter time 1744, he is confronted night after night with
women, approaching him one after another, as it were, attractive as
well as repulsive, always partners in a sexual relation. He invariably
interprets these female characters as topics he has chosen appropriately or inappropriately for his research or as different ways of scientific approach.

That physical love is given a scientific role in this manner is certainly due to an identification between love and the enthusiasm of
discovery. This aspect takes on a new dimension when, in the
1740s, Swedenborg associates scientific clear-sightedness with the
intercourse between the soul and a higher reality. In this perspicacious state of mind, a feeling of happiness emerges, and this sense of
joy is often described in the dream notes as a bliss with erotic over-
tones to which numerous mystics have sung their praise. The soul

provides us with a special power of discrimination, Swedenborg tells us in the epilogue to the second part of *The Animal Kingdom*:

> *and it can finally be determined whether the ideological forms are in unison with the order of soul, or stand out in contrast. In the former case she will receive it in a mood similar to that of love, in the latter case she will experience hatred.*

[March] 30–31

27 _____

Saw a number of women, one of whom was writing a letter. I took it, but do not know where it went. She was sitting, and a yellow man struck her on the back. He thought that she should get more of a beating, but it was enough. It concerns, so I believe, what I am writing and have written; our philosophy.

Swedenborg interprets this dream in a way that is most logical to him. His divine insight—the woman—has given him a missive that is now gone. The woman is maltreated by the worldly: to Swedenborg, yellow is the color of the earthly, the mundane.

28 _____

I saw an absolutely gorgeous woman by a window where a child was placing roses. She took me by the hand and led me. I believe this signifies what I am writing and my suffering, which should guide me.

The beautiful woman, the roses, and the child belong to the recurrent imagery of Swedenborg's dream play, constellations in an ethereal solitaire. Only tender innocence may serve as guidance on the narrow track toward truth and knowledge. At the end of the goal he dreams of attaining, the torment will wither away, and the temptation and the darkness will be gone. His present affliction is the same one as that earlier described in entry 25.

29

Saw a magnificent procession of men, so adorned that I never saw anything finer, but it soon disappeared. It was, as I believe, experience, which now is in its heyday.

The vogue for empiricism forms a kind of procession. Here Swedenborg may be referring to the number of scientists of the seventeenth and the eighteenth centuries, who, on the basis of observation, had made epoch-making discoveries. On the other hand, he may also be referring to his own grand plans for the Animal Kingdom series. *Experience* is the keyword to an understanding of his scientific pursuit, and it is of central importance in the dream diary.

In *The Economy of the Animal Kingdom*, completed in December 1739, the foundation of Swedenborg's intellectual structure is laid. From a limited number of facts, he intuits analogies, syntheses, and outlines connections and ends. He terms the basis of this method "intuition," and in the introduction, he points out that this way of thinking is vouchsafed primarily to poets, musicians, and artists alone. This is a way to truths otherwise inaccessible to us.

During the period between finishing *The Economy of the Animal Kingdom* and the beginning of *The Animal Kingdom* (1741–1742), Swedenborg decided to try a new method. To convince the skeptics in religious matters and perhaps also to obtain a more firm ground for his reasoning, he intended to tackle his main problem—the nature and function of the soul—in a more empirical and scientific way, making more use of observation.

Indeed, empirical science was in its bloom. Books written by the leading English thinkers behind the advancement of learning in the era, John Locke and Francis Bacon, were in his library, urging empirical knowledge. But even more important to Swedenborg were contemporary scientists like Hermann Boerhaave and Jan Swammerdam, to mention two other authors in Swedenborg's library.

He needed more facts. In *The Animal Kingdom*, he writes that "we must master all sciences . . . and from those already known we shall deduct and explore new ones." The dream diary was written when this scientific work was in progress. The religious crisis led him from a reconsidered Christian stand into an existential experience of the doctrines. He turns from passive abstraction to active engagement. As a consequence of this change, the blossoming experiences never were to form that magnificent procession of which he had dreamed.

4

APRIL 1744

———◆▸◉◂◆———

April 1–2

30
_____

I rode in the air on a horse; went into all the rooms, the kitchen, and other places, searching for one whom I did not find. The rooms were badly kept; finally I was carried through the air into a dining hall where I received two splendid loaves of bread, and then I got him back. Quite a number of people were there, and the hall was tidy. Signifies the Lord's Supper.

As we have already observed, the basic elements of his dream language tend to be fixed. Dreams 30–32 are illustrative examples.

The "horse" represents the dreamer himself; it is a metaphor of his work and, in a figural sense, serves as its vehicle. Horses gallop through the diary, by themselves, harnessed side by side, or in procession. The particular significance of horses is found in all of Swedenborg's later works. In his _Spiritual Diary_ §688, he remarks:

> _I have frequently seen horses, and also chariots drawn by horses, and often they are of different colors and of various sizes. . . . Today I realized that they are images of human knowledge, and in a good sense signify intellect, and in a bad sense that condition which inverts true intelligence._

In a similar fashion, Swedenborg associates the concepts "room," "hall," and "chamber" (cf. dream entry 22) with an outlook on life or a doctrine, and, in some instances, a particular state of mind. Accordingly, doctrine and the psychological or spiritual state, in general, lie close to one another within Swedenborg's works. "In ancient times," he writes in *Arcana Coelestia* §7353, "human states of mind were often compared to houses. The mind's contents were compared to chambers, rooms. And indeed the human mind is of that nature, because the things inside it are separated from one another in much the same way as a house is divided into rooms." Certain recurrent epithets are given to the rooms: "tidy" or "untidy" signify pure or impure states of mind.

Thus, through his work, Swedenborg is searching for the right doctrine, the true relationship to God. His exploration takes place "in the air," in heaven. Finally, he arrives at the hall he has been looking for. In this grand dining room, different from the "untidy rooms," he is presented with the most magnificent and appetizing loaves. And he notes that this "signifies the Lord's Supper."

The pieces of bread are associated with the bread used in the Communion. At the same time, the two loaves probably refer to the two parts of *The Animal Kingdom*, which, at the time of his dream, were at the printers. While this entry is made in early April, less than a month later, Swedenborg will repeatedly dream of the inadequacy and deficiency of these works. Swedenborg was always oriented toward the future—probably he is thinking of other volumes still to come.

After he has received the loaves, we read, "I got him back." This presumably signifies that he sees the God he thought he has lost; or perhaps his own self, seen in a divine context.

According to the last lines, the hall is kept in good order. Furthermore, other people are present. In 1914, a ledger was found among some documents from the old German Lutheran congregation in the otherwise Reformist Hague, in which the names of communicants were recorded. On Maundy Thursday, April 2, 1744—the same day this entry was written—we find Swedenborg's name inscribed.

One of the congregation's clergy was Johann Gottlieb Pambo, mentioned later by Swedenborg in his diary (entry135), where he then calls him "Pombo." It is most likely that this clergyman was a Moravian believer. As early as 1725, Pambo had become a member of "The Lutheran Congregation of Brethren"; nine years later, he published a book, the very title of which clearly announces his adhesion to Zinzendorf's teachings: *True Christians as the Loving Wetnurses of Foundlings.*

The point is worth noting as evidence that, while at The Hague, Swedenborg was already in contact with the Bohemian Brethren. As earlier mentioned, Zinzendorf had influential friends in Holland. A Moravian conference had been held in Amsterdam in 1742, and the movement had at that time established itself to some extent and bought a property, Herrendyk, in Ysselstein, for its activities. This German clergyman in The Hague thus was probably one of the count's many connections in the Dutch republic.

31

King Charles was sitting in a dark room and said something, but somewhat indistinctly; afterwards asked one at the table if he had not received the information he had asked for, and he replied "Yes." Then he shut the windows, and I helped him with the curtains. Afterwards, I mounted a horse, but did not take the road I had intended but went across hills and mountains, riding rapidly. I had a full cartload in tow that I could not get rid of, and eventually the horse got exhausted by the burden and I wanted to get him into some stage; he came in, and he became like a slaughtered, blood-red beast, fallen down. This means that I have received all that I have thought of for my instruction and that I am perhaps on the wrong track; the load was my remaining work, which followed me, who that way became so tired and lifeless.

32

I stepped out of a carriage that was driven into a lake. While driving into it, the coachman cried to the other carriage to watch out, as there was danger when he drove in. I looked at the other carriage; behind it, there seemed to be a screen unfolded like a hood. Together with the man who sat behind, I took down the screen, went in, and folded it together. This meant that the beginning of my work was difficult: the other

carriage was warned to look out, and that I ought to tally my sails and not make the notes so long.

In entry 31, for the second time, we meet with King Charles XII. As will become evident, that king, along with Swedenborg's father, will be one of the figures to appear most often in the diary. Swedenborg's fascination with the taciturn "Lion of the North" was probably mixed with fear. The king's absolute power and strong personality had made him very special. Regarded as king by the grace of God, he demanded that everyone about him play the subordinate roles they had been allotted in his political drama, which finally turned out to be a tragedy.

Some time after the king's flight from Stralsund in 1714, the two men came together at the royal headquarters in Lund. King Charles, who took a deep interest in mathematics, discussed one of his favorite ideas with the gifted young man: how the decimal system could be replaced by another mathematical system, based on the numeral 8. Indeed, like Christopher Polhem, the great mechanic, Swedenborg had been entrusted with a number of authoritative missions by the king, which lie outside the framework of this book.

On the whole, Swedenborg's relationships with the king seem to have been good. Yet Swedenborg realized that the king's singular character combined with his dictatorial powers were threatening to throw Sweden into a catastrophe of apocalyptic dimensions. In his letters of that time to his brother-in-law Erik Benzelius, and also in a poem called *Festivus Applausus*, which saluted the king upon his return from Turkey, we can glimpse his worries on that score and his criticism of the king.

Shortly before the king's death, Swedenborg seems to have fallen out of his favor. One hypothesis is that, despite Charles's insistence, he had declined an officer's commission in the army. There is, in fact, a hint of such a commission in the diary (entry 255), albeit in a completely different context.

In the diary, the earthly autocrat appears in another shape: he is God himself. Once again the dream language draws on the dreamer's mental reality, where the enigmatic king, twenty-six years after his death in the trenches at Fredrikshald, is still very much alive.

Knowledge of the diary as a whole enables us to see the clear implications of what is going on at the windows in this dream of the king. God asks "someone"—namely, the dreamer—whether he has not been given a clear answer. He replies "Yes": he knows what he needs to know, after which the king and the assessor help each other to draw curtains across the false and confusing world of "experience." Knowledge is to come from above.

The wagons in entry 32 may refer to the same entity as do the horses—his intellectual work. A carriage is being driven into a lake, but Swedenborg has managed to get out in time. There is an accompanying carriage. In the rear, a screen has been stretched out to its fullest extent. Curtains and screens serve the same purposes: to shield, to isolate, or, more precisely, to prevent outside impressions from penetrating into the room or the carriage where all knowledge is already to be found.

But the dreamer finds he is unfolding too much of the screen, or producing too extensive digressions. This implies that he is not giving divine insight, or intuition, the role it ought to play or should play. On the contrary, he is persisting in the empirical-analytic path, encumbering his statements with lengthy footnotes.

To sum up, entries 30–32 indicate that Swedenborg feels he is now on his way to formulating a doctrine that accords with truth and that, in doing so, he is, or will be, in contact with the Divine. God tells him he must not rely on his empirical knowledge, but instead on knowledge of a higher nature. Despite this insight, he is still following the paths he is used to traveling and therefore risking a fall. His work is foundering. But a new one is rising, where he is safe. In this new work, he will rely on God, renounce and screen off his former knowledge.

This theme will reappear a number of times. Both in content and in his choice of symbols, these are typical entries. There is also another factor to consider. As elsewhere in the diary, we see how successive dreams of the same night in different forms express the same basic notions. The dream events change, only to clarify the idea symbolized.

[April] 2–3

33 _____

Two persons came and entered a house which, although built, was not yet in order. They went about it, but did not seem favorably impressed. We saw that our power was gone and feared them. One of them came up to me and said that they intended to inflict a punishment on me the following Maundy Thursday, unless I took flight. I did not know how to get out, but he told me he would show me the way. Woke up. Meant that I had invited the highest to visit me in an unprepared and untidy hut and that they had found it untidy and that I ought to be punished, but I was most graciously shown the way by which to escape their wrath.

These notes refer to Easter Week: April 3 was Good Friday. There is talk of a punishment that will befall the dreamer on Maundy Thursday of the following year if he does not make his escape. In other words, he is granted a year's grace. As mentioned in the introduction, Swedenborg dated his definitive calling, which came to him at the London inn, to April 1745: next Easter, that is.

Again, his dream about being visited by two eminent persons certainly concerns *The Animal Kingdom*. He has just handed the printer his work, a house that, although built, was not yet fully furnished. It is too late to change its contents. The two visitors express their disapproval and threaten to punish him. The dreamer realizes his presumptuousness. He has invited supreme love and supreme wisdom to enter a disorderly, untidy cottage. But real insight and higher knowledge are only possible if his mind is purified from earthly slag. As yet, all talk about following "the power of the spirit"—see, for example, dream entry 15—is presumptuous. Although the visitors first threaten to have him punished, in the end they let mercy go before justice. God, love, will show him the way.

34 _____

There was a beggar who cried that he wanted pork. They wished to give him something else, but he insistently called for pork. I woke up. It has the same significance, I believe.

Here, the dreamer sees himself as a beggar obsessively craving only one thing, pork. "They"—supposedly the same eminent visitors as in the preceding dream—want to give him something else: something, we may suppose, less down-to-earth. Conclusion: he is heading in the wrong direction, asking for the wrong favor (compare a later dream, entry 239).

In these two dreams, Swedenborg seems to be questioning himself and his own intellectual capacity. Perhaps the tone is more personal than before. In light of what is to follow, one gets a presentiment that he is intuiting a change of course, both radical and imminent, which he both fears and hopes for.

35

> I saw two soldieries, blue, marching in two corps past my windows, which stood ajar. I wanted to look out and watch the marching of the first corps, which seemed to me magnificent. I woke up, awakened by a gracious guard that I may not perish.

Soldiers, a window open, ajar, a watchman guarding him. The most obvious interpretation, of course, is Swedenborg's own, "a gracious guard that I may not perish." In the visual vocabulary of his dreams, "window" signifies communication with the sensory world. The empirical scientist obtains his information through that window: it is remarkable how often this image will recur in the following. Reading his dream in this way, the guard is there to protect him against onslaughts of empirical methods, here presented in the shape of an alluring parade of magnificent Carolinian soldiers marching towards the end, faithful as steel to the Lion of the North.

Up to April 4, 1743, Easter Eve, the dreams have essentially revolved around two questions: first, has he been approaching his task—the exploration of the role and function of the soul—in the right way? And, second, if he has failed and gone astray, is this not due to shortcomings in his spiritual and moral state? Behind both questions lurks a doubt, a sense of being on the wrong path, which grows stronger with each passing day.

April 3–4 NB—the day before Easter

36 _____

Found nothing during the whole night, although I often woke up. I thought everything was gone and settled and that I was left behind or driven away. Towards the morning, it seemed to me that I was riding, and the direction was shown to me; but when I looked, it was dark, and then I found that I had lost my way in the darkness. Then it lightened up, and I saw that I was lost. I saw the road and the forests and groves to which I should go, and behind them the sky. I awoke. There came then a thought, spontaneous as it were, about the first life [*prima vita*], and thereafter, about the other life [*altera vita*], and it seemed to me that everything was full of grace. I fell to crying because I had not been loving but rather had offended Him who has led me and shown me the way even unto the kingdom of grace, and that I, unworthy one, have been restored to favor.

Thus, the night had passed without any dreams—*"Found nothing during the whole night, although I often woke up. I thought everything was gone and settled."* Swedenborg analyzes his disappointment. He has already become accustomed to the nocturnal experiences and welcomes these signs or messages. But in the early hours, probably in that "hypnagogic" state of light sleep bordering on waking, where we usually dream our clearest dreams, he sees how he has gone astray in the dark. Furthermore, his dream shows to him his future path, which will be the right one: *"I saw the road and the forests and groves to which I should go."* Then he wakes up. A thought immediately presents itself. It concerns the first and second life—earthly life as a first existence, followed by another new reality. *"It seemed to me that everything was full of grace."*

The dream diary accounts for a continual process of spiritual development. There are no definitive changes of direction, no abrupt conversion. Yet this flow of experiences comprises changes, modifications of attitude, of which this is one. He weeps over his own lack of love and realizes he has rewarded good with evil. His despair is so much more striking in that it comes from, and is formulated by, a man who in the ordinary way of things is a taciturn and reserved researcher and humble civil servant.

We can see his feeling of having rejected all that he has been offered, as well as his strong exaltation, as part of an ongoing searching of the heart. Easter is certainly important in this context. His longing for purity and divinely inspired knowledge is being accompanied, day by day, by the story of Christ's passion, death, and resurrection, and the lesson of how bliss is attained through faith. This message, which had set its stamp on his childhood in the episcopate, is now being revived by regular churchgoing (see entries 30 and 38). Moreover, he sees presumptuousness, self-love, ambition, and a lukewarm love of God as the great obstacles to union with the Divine. The Easter mystery is a reminder: there is an answer, a way. He is crushed but forgiven. During the night leading into Good Friday, he had seen himself as protected by an army guard. Now, on eve of Easter, he is sure he is forgiven.

Before these entries, Swedenborg wrote a *nota bene*. He is perfectly aware of the importance of his experiences, the vision of *prima vita*, heaven and paradise. Perhaps this is the very experience he was referring to in the cryptic words his dream catalog, *"In Sweden, about the white cloud of the sky."*

[April] 4–5

37

I went to God's table.

It was told that a courier had just arrived: I said that this should mean that [the rest of the sentence is crossed out].

Sang the melody, and a line I remember, of the hymn *Jesus is My Best of Friends.*

It seemed to me that buds were put forth, green.

During this night between Good Saturday and Easter Sunday, Swedenborg seems to hear the tune of the hymn *Jesus is My Best of Friends* and remembers a part of the lyrics. We may presume that it is the same line as later recurs in the diary:

> *neither . . .*
> *darkest abyss [n]or the deepest need,*
> *whether coming or nigh,*
> *make me leave God's love*
> *Which is with Jesus on high.*

This hymn, which we come across several times in his diary entries, was written by Jacob Arrhenius, a professor of history at Uppsala, more than ten years' Jesper Swedberg's senior and his colleague at the university. It had been included in the 1695 hymnbook. The tune, by Gustaf Düben, remains unchanged today. Here are the first three verses, which Swedenborg has in mind:

> *Jesus is my best of friends,*
> *His equal you will nowhere meet.*
> *To leave him now would that be fair,*
> *abandoning him as people here?*
> *Naught shall ever make me retreat*
> *from the one to whom I'm dear;*
> *The will of one be the will of both,*
> *ever here and ever there.*
>
> *For my sake he suffered, made up for the past:*
> *a new life began that forever will last.*
> *He prayed to his father with innermost care*
> *of eternal blessing for me as for others.*
> *Who can then freely forsake someone*
> *by whom you've been chosen and spared?*
> *Who really wants to depart from the one*
> *who is so cheerful and lovingly bothers?*
>
> *My trust is complete and such is my creed:*
> *that neither will life and nor will death*

ever estrange him from my lead,
nor any baseness or angels above,
darkest abyss or the deepest need,
whether coming or nigh,
make me leave God's love
Which is with Jesus on high.

In view of Swedenborg's later religious development, the primary theme of this hymn is noteworthy. Arrhenius paraphrases St. Paul's words in the eighth chapter of his Epistle to the Romans, where the apostle declares that God "spared not his own son but delivered him up for us all," making amends for the sins of humankind by his *satisfactio vicaria.* According to Reformation theologians, the fact that Christ has died for all people makes salvation possible. No person can justify him- or herself by good deeds, but human weakness and innate sinfulness are cured by Christ's sufferings on the cross for all our sakes. This is a notion that Swedenborg, both in the period covered by the dream journal and in his later writings, will energetically revolt against. Each human being has free will: he decides how he shall live his life and presides over his own destiny. By sincerely turning to God both in faith and with good deeds, he can be sure of salvation. To Swedenborg, the notion of a vicarious suffering gradually loses its importance.

But now, as the crisis begins, theological dogma is assumably of less importance. Crucial is Swedenborg's increasingly strong hope of being taken up in God's love, that no abyss shall separate him from Jesus, "my best of friends."

His experiences between Good Friday and Good Saturday (entry 36) implied a first surrender or submission, a deep insight into his inability to implement his own demands and into his reliance upon God. Easter Day, Easter night, and the whole of Whit Monday can be seen as an intensified prolongation of these experiences.

His observations are presented dialectically. First comes anxiety, then dread, and, finally, in all its force, temptation. Afterwards follows purification, a catharsis that points forward toward the first acme of the diary, the vision of Christ in the third night, Easter Monday night.

First, the temptation. In his later writings he often returns to these afflictions—*tentationes*—expounding their nature and functions extensively. As already pointed out, it is not merely a question of being enticed or tempted to thoughts and actions that conflict with the Ten Commandments. The temptations also include moods of skepticism and doubt, even denial, regarding God's presence and grace. Yet, he writes, these trials are necessary elements in the process of regeneration. The greater one's love of God, the greater temptations.

[April] 5–6

38

Easter day was on 5 April; and then I went to God's table. The temptation was persistent, mostly in the afternoon up to six o'-clock. There was nothing definite, but an anxiety as if one were damned and in hell; and yet all the time remained the hope which the Holy Ghost inspired, and very strongly so, according to Paul's Epistle to the Romans, V:5. The evil one had power given him to produce inquietude in my innermost by various thoughts.

39

On Easter day, after communion, I was inwardly content, but still outwardly distressed. The temptation came in the afternoon, in an entirely different manner, but strongly; for I was assured that my sins were forgiven, but yet I could not govern my wayward thoughts to restrain some expressions opposed to my better knowledge. It was from the evil one, by permission. Prayer gave some relief, and also the Word of God; faith was there entirely, but confidence and love seemed to be absent.

After receiving communion in one of the churches in The Hague—maybe it was in the German church with Rev. Pambo, mentioned in entries 30 and 135—he feels satisfied, yet sad. He uses different expressions for this dual state of mind. At one and the same time, he feels anxiety, as if doomed and in hell, yet has hope and cites Paul, "And hope maketh not ashamed; because the love of God is shed abroad in our hearts by the Holy Ghost which is given unto us."

40

Went to bed at nine; the temptation and the trembling continued until 10:30. Then I fell into a sleep, where all my temptation was represented to me, how Erland Broman in various ways tried to get me on his side, to become a member of that party of voluptuousness, wealth, vanity; but he did not manage to get me there. I became even more obstinate because he instilled contempt.

41

Afterwards I was together with a crawling, dark-gray snake, which was Broman's lapdog. I repeatedly tried to strike it with a club but all attempts to hit its head were in vain. It wanted to bite me but couldn't. I seized it by the throat, and it could not bite me, nor was I able to do it much harm. Finally, I got hold of it by the jaws and squeezed hard, and also by the nose, which I squeezed so that something like venom burst forth. And I said that, even though the dog was not mine, I had to chastise it since it wanted to bite me. Thereupon, it seemed as if he had not got me to say one word to him, and then I quarreled with him. When I woke up, the words I said were: Shut up!

42

Without further interpretation, the nature of my temptation can be seen from this. But, on the other hand, also how great has been the grace of God, through the merit of Christ and the workings of the Holy Spirit, to whom be glory from eternity to

eternity! The thought at once occurred to me, how great is the grace of the Lord who accounts to us that we have really resisted in temptation and which [resistance] is imputed to us, when it is nevertheless nothing but the grace and operation of God, being his and not our own; and he overlooks the weakness that we have shown in it, which have been manifold; and also how great a glory our Lord bestows to us after a little time of tribulation.

Trembling in anxiety, torn between abominations and longing for God, Swedenborg eventually falls into a sleep "where all my temptation was represented to me." The expression may refer to the experience that marks the beginning of the dated entries, to which he will return later on, "for the temptation then began" (entry 17). The previously mentioned Erland Broman is evil's representative, the royal favorite and court marshal, but also a part of Swedenborg's own "sinister nature." Broman's character has earlier been described.

Probably one had to look for a very long time in contemporary Stockholm to find more striking opposites than these two gentlemen. A conscientious person, hard-working and frugal, Swedenborg was nevertheless "drawn to the sexual" too, and he likewise had financial interests and, as we will see, a mundane pride that offered him stubborn resistance. Broman, the base courtier, becomes increasingly aggressive. He changes shape, turns into a snake, then a dog. Yet temptation is overcome, and steadfastness gets its reward.

43

Then I fell asleep, and it seemed the whole night that, in various ways, I was first united to others by what was sinful, and then that I was enveloped by strange and indescribable circumvolutions, so that during the whole night I was inaugurated in a curious manner. And then it was asked, "Is there any Jacobite superior in honesty?" Then, in conclusion, I was received with an embrace, and it was said that "he ought not to be called this or that, or thus named." But how, I do not remember: if it was not Jacobite, this I cannot describe; it was a mystical series.

44
_____

Subsequently, I woke up and fell asleep a number of times; and everything was in response to my thoughts, yet in such a manner that there was a life and a glory in the whole of it that I cannot in the least describe, for it was all heavenly. At the time, it was clear to me, but now, afterwards, I cannot express anything. In short, I was in heaven, and I heard a speech that no human tongue can utter, nor can anyone describe the glory and bliss of that life.

Apart from this, I was wakeful, in heavenly ecstasy, which is ineffable too.

45
_____

At nine o'clock, I went to bed and arose between nine and ten, having been in bed from twelve to thirteen hours. To the Highest be praise, honor and glory! Hallowed be His name! Holy, Holy, Lord God Zebaoth!

After temptation its opposite follows: a feeling of lucidity, of being led toward and introduced into an ever broader context, where he glimpses heavenly secrets. During that night, he sleeps for brief periods, awakens, drops off to sleep again. A recurring theme is his circuitous path toward lucidity. In his dreams, he sees how earlier, in a sinful fashion, he has been allied with "others."

Is he a Jacobite? A man who wrestles like Jacob with God, thereafter to build the church of the elect? Or, is he referring to James, the author of the New Testament epistle of which Luther disapproved, the St. James who also emphatically stipulated, as Swedenborg does, that salvation does not come by faith alone, that Christianity is also practical, and that good deeds are also needed? We are not told. Gradually, all becomes a series of *mystica*, arcane things. His experience beggars description, he tells us in entry 44, an impression he shares with many mystics—Christian as well as non-Christian—who have experienced similar states. An example can be drawn from the pseudo-Aristotelian tract *On the Secret Parts of the Divine Wisdom, According to the Egyptians*, which Swedenborg excerpted, and quoted in *The Animal Kingdom* §12:

Plato used frequently to say . . . that when his soul was engaged in contemplation, he seemed to enjoy supreme good and incredible delight: that he was in a manner fixed in astonishment acknowledging himself as a part of a higher world and as feeling his own immortality with the greatest assurance and light: at length, that his understanding, wearied with this contemplation, relapsed into fantasy, and that he became sorrowful as the light decreased. That again leaving the body and returning to the former state, he found the soul abounding with light and this light now flowing into the body. . . . The soul, freed as it were from the body, ascends and is enlightened; descending again, it is obscured, but it is afterwards purified and reascends.

Here we meet the same elements as in Swedenborg's ecstatic elevations and illuminations: indescribable, jubilant bliss, a feeling of being part and parcel of the ineffable, of the light.

In one respect, his dreams are explicit:

46 _____

How I learned by trying what it means not to love angels more than God, which had nearly made the whole work turn over. In comparison with our Lord, no account should be taken of them, except in respect to their assistance where love is concerned, being much inferior.

This note portends a long series of remarks about angels during the years to come: on their position, their nature, their origin, and their language. The angels of later years are part of his "doctrine of spirits." They are from earth, good people who, after death, have come so close to the light that Swedenborg calls them angels, although they do not call themselves as such. Evidently, Swedenborg already at this point realizes that worshiping them would be absurd. From the dreamer's angle of vision, their position is under the light they are reflecting.

47 _____

I found within me, as it were, a radiance: that the greatest happiness would be to become a martyr, because the indescribable

grace connected with love of God makes one desire to stand that suffering, which is nothing compared to the eternal torment, and the least thing would be to sacrifice one's life.

48 _____

Had also in my mind and my body a kind of sensation of indescribable delight, so intense that, had it been increased, the body would have been, as it were, dissolved from delight alone.
  This took place in the night between the first and second day after Easter, and during the whole of Whit Monday.

The torment, martyrdom, is related to the temptations and tribulations that now begin to appear in almost every entry. An experience often repeated in Swedenborg's writings is the calm and intense joy that follows after these temptations have been happily overcome, what he calls a "sensation of indescribable joy." At the memory of this joy, as described in, for example, his later work *Heaven and Hell* §289, his usually dry and pedantic style suddenly changes note:

> *That peace is like the morning time or dawn in spring, when, once the night has passed, all things of earth begin to take new life from the rising of the sun; the dew that falls from heaven spreads a leafy fragrance far and wide, and springtime's gentle warmth makes meadows fertile and instills its charm in human minds as well. This is because morning or dawn in springtime corresponds to the state of peace of angels in heaven.*

The experiences between Easter Monday and Tuesday were to be fundamental to Swedenborg's subsequent development. He would often refer to them as one of his life's turning points. In his diary, he marks the entry three times with "N.B." (*nota bene*).

Regarding its content, the following record falls into five parts: first, his temptations and mood (entries 49–50); next, his vision of Christ (entries 51–54); then, thoughts about the character and implications of his experience (entries 55–57); dreams of his father's approval (entries 58–59); and, in conclusion, his own analysis of the night's events (entries 60–61).

April 6–7 NB NB NB

49

In the evening, I came into another sort of temptation, namely, between eight and nine in the evening, while I read about God's miracles performed through Moses. I observed that something of my own understanding interfered and made it impossible for me really to believe this as I should; I both believed and not believed at the same time. I thought that this is the reason that the angels and God showed themselves to shepherds and not to philosophers, who let their understanding enter into these matters: then you can always ask why God made use of the wind to call together the locusts, why he hardened the Pharaoh, why he did not set to work at once, and other such things, at which I smiled at to myself, but which nevertheless made me incredulous.

50

I looked at the fire and said to myself: thus, I should not believe that the fire exists, because the external senses are more fallacious than the words of God, which are truth itself and which I should believe more than in myself. With such musings, I spent some hour and a half and inwardly smiled at the tempter. It is noteworthy that, the same day, I walked to Delft, and all day was granted the deepest spiritual thoughts, deeper and more beauteous than ever, and all that day I was influenced by the Spirit, which I found within me.

On Whit Monday, Swedenborg went to Delft, some five kilometers south of The Hague, all day obviously being absorbed in the most wonderful thoughts. We know nothing about his reason for visiting Delft. Perhaps this Easter excursion had something to do with the Moravians—the entries for the night before Easter

Tuesday are of so special a character that they may well justify such an assumption.

He probably returned to The Hague the same day. Thus, it was in the evening he was reading the *Exodus*, concerning the children of Israel and their troubles in Egypt and of God who "hardened the heart of Pharaoh." Time and again, the Pharaoh had been given warnings, the implications of which were clear: the children of Israel should be given permission to leave his country. But none of God's warnings—darkness over the country, grasshoppers, pestilence—affected him. When Swedenborg, in the light of his fire, asks himself why God did not immediately allow the Jews to depart, we hear an echo perhaps of his father's pondering on this same problem thirty years before. In a sermon, which was afterward printed, the bishop had expounded the danger of so superficially "rational" an explanation of the biblical events. Seen in a broader context, they could be fitted into a higher logic. Even so, the bishop had thought, this apparently needless prolongation of the Jews' captivity was "rather hard to accept."

Up to this diary entry, Swedenborg's inner struggle has essentially been over conflicts between a Christian life and Christian ideas on the one hand and "voluptuousness, wealth, vanity" on the other. But now he is confronted with another temptation: his skepticism, which we have caught glimpses of earlier, in entries 3 and 16, his doubts whether the Word of God is indeed the "wellspring of truth." He forgets his own inferiority; and, in doing so, he has lost that innocent vision and uncorrupted relation to the Divinity that once had made it possible for the shepherds to see God and his angels.

He is sitting beside the fire, comparing the flames and his own senses, probably thinking that the real is always there, regardless of his ideas and of the speculation of philosophers through the ages.

51

At ten o'clock, I went to bed and felt a little better. After half an hour, I heard some din under my head, and then I thought that the tempter left. Immediately a shiver came over me, starting from the head and spreading throughout the body, with some rumbling, coming in waves, and I realized that something holy had befallen me.

52

Whereupon I went to sleep, and about twelve o'clock, or perhaps it was at one or two in the morning, such a strong shivering seized me, from my head to my feet, as a thunder produced by several clouds colliding, shaking me beyond description and prostrating me. And when I was prostrated in this way, I was clearly awake and saw how I was overthrown.

53

I wondered what this was supposed to mean, and I spoke as if awake but found that the words were put into my mouth. I said, "Oh, thou almighty Jesus Christ, who of thy great mercy designest to come to so great a sinner, make me worthy of this grace!" and I clasped my hands and prayed. Then a hand emerged, which pressed my hands firmly.

54

In a little while, I continued my prayer, saying, "Thou hast promised to receive in grace all sinners; thou canst not otherwise than keep thy words!" In the same moment, I was sitting in his bosom and beheld him face to face, a countenance of a holy mien. All was such that I cannot describe. He was smiling at me, and I was convinced that he looked like this when he was alive. He spoke to me and asked if I have a health certificate; and to this I replied, "Lord, thou knowest better than I." He said, "Well then, do!"—that is, as I inwardly grasped this, "Do love me" or "Do as promised." God give me grace thereto! I found it beyond my powers and woke up, shuddering.

Thus, it all starts with noise and shivering. Swedenborg's biblically tuned dread, fear, and trembling are recurrent phenomena. His shudderings are holy, he tells us in dream entry 228; they seem to augur the approach of the numinous.

Later on, in the *Arcana Coelestia*, he will make his point even
more clearly: "Those who are in the good tremble in the presence
of the Divine, a sacred shuddering which precedes acceptance."

After a few hours of sleep, he has a shivering fit, hears a noise
like thunder, and finds himself lying with his face to the ground.
He has tactile sensations: his hands are folded, words are placed in
his mouth, and he begs forgiveness for his sins.

Then the dreamer finds himself sitting in Christ's lap, sees him,
as in the famous passage in Paul, Cor. 1, "face to face." Christ asks
him whether he has a *sundhetspass*, a proof that he is sane. This unusual Swedish word has been discussed by Swedenborg scholars.
Some of them see in it an echo of what had happened on the occasion of his first visit to England. Having left his ship without any
appropriate "bill of health," he had been apprehended and threatened with severe punishments for defying the strict quarantine
rules of the harbors.

Although the word might be explained in this way, from a bio-
graphical fact, the point is surely that, in the context of the diary,
questions of sickness, torment, and health refer to moral states.
Thus, the question may be whether he has sufficiently liberated
himself from temptation and the bondage of the senses to be able
to relate to the Godhead. From Swedenborg's point of view, a certificate of sanity surely meant mastery of temptation and implied a
mobilization of his own will to turn toward God completely and
submit fully.

His reply to the Lord—"Thou knowest better than I"—is followed by a brief exhortation: "Well then, do [so]" or act! To the
practical-minded Swedenborg, who thinks in concrete terms,
Christ's answer seems deeply significant. Pious thoughts, refraining
from evil, are only one aspect of virtue. Action is also needed. We
should bear in mind his father's incessant reminders of the importance of acting in accordance with Christian morals. It is a demand
that Bishop Swedberg repeatedly dwells on in his *Autobiography*, a
copy of which he had left to each of his children. In the following
paragraph, the bishop paraphrases the Sermon on the Mount to his
children's edification:

By no means will anyone who shouts "Lord! Lord"' enter the kingdom of heaven, but only those who do my heavenly Father's will. The day will come when many will appeal to me, "Lord, Lord, have we not prophesied in your name, and in your name cast out devils, and in your name done many great deeds?" I will then condemn them and say: "No! Get away, you evildoers!" Anyone, however, who hears the words and acts accordingly can be compared to a wise man who built his house on a rock. And the rain fell, and the flood came, and the wind blew and struck that house, and yet it did not fall down; for it was founded on the rock. But the one who hears these words and still does not act in unison with them, he is like a vain man who built his house on sand. And the rain fell, and the flood came, and the wind blew and struck that house which then collapsed, and tremendous was that fall.

Immediately after his revelation, Swedenborg seems to have asked himself what the words can have implied. It is likely, he writes, they mean "Do love me" or "Do as promised." Here is evidently an allusion to some earlier promise. Do these lines about a promise refer to the royal visit to the humble cottage referred to in entry 11?

The vision of Christ may, of course, also be seen as a timeless religious experience, the result of distress and longing. Neither is it in any way unique that a believer in a strong state of exaltation should see Christ appear to his inward eye. Still, considering what we know about the Bohemians and the wave of emotional religiosity that had swept over Stockholm during the year before he had left and bearing in mind the clear signs of Moravian influence to be found in diary entries to come, it is reasonable to relate Swedenborg's thoughts and his remarkable experiences to Count Zinzendorf's ideas.

Easter, according to Moravian beliefs, was by far the most holy day of the year. As in the Greek Orthodox Church, Christ's suffering and death on the cross were presented as the very foundation of Christian doctrine. Only because of it could a human being be sure of his or her salvation. Thanks to this self-sacrifice, humankind has conclusively been forgiven, a necessary act of grace inasmuch as our evil is innate and otherwise indelible.

The emphasis Zinzendorf laid upon the divine suffering as crucial to salvation lent his theology a peculiar emotional character. Devotees had to use all their strength to identify themselves mentally with all that the Divinity had gone through in the drama of passion—the pain, the wounds, the blood. Zinzendorf believed that, by thus sacrificing themselves, those who meditated or prayed could at least momentarily thrust aside personal sinfulness. But to do so, worshippers had to activate all their senses: feeling, smell, sight, hearing, and, above all, sight. Christians ought to try to reach such a degree of compassionate insight and identification that they actually saw the Man of Suffering. In such a moment, writes Zinzendorf, "all theology is summed up."

Therefore, all members of the Moravian congregation prepared themselves to celebrate Easter in a manner that was regulated in detail, the purpose of which was to make the Passion come alive for and within them. Here Zinzendorf's Easter hymns, with their blood mysticism, were one instrument out of many. The ceremony, by which the congregation actively joined in the divine services, was generally more intense than in the ordinary Protestant churches of those days. The count had written a special "Litany of Wounds" for Easter. On Easter morning, imaginative and emotional participation was stimulated by celebrating divine service in the open air, beside an open and empty grave: Christ is arisen! For the Moravians, the crux of the matter was to experience Christ. As it happens, it is precisely this total experience we find outlined in dream entries 51–55 of Swedenborg's diary, both in the preludes to his vision of Christ and in its central passage on submission. Prostration formed part of the Moravian ritual. The devotees flung themselves to the floor as an outward sign of their strong awareness of sinfulness. There may be a connection between this strange element—so alien to sober Swedish Protestantism, which often, in a negative sense, referred to such Moravian rites as "enthusiasm"— and the fact that Swedenborg is prostrated in a very similar manner. However, the question of the importance of good deeds to justification would soon enough become a point of disagreement between Swedenborg and the Brethren and make him reject them.

55

> Once more I came into such a state that, in my thoughts, I was neither asleep nor awake. I thought: What can this really be? Have I seen Christ the son of God? But it is a pity that I doubt this. However, as we are commanded to try the spirits, I carefully thought all this over; and from what had occurred during the night, I concluded that the Holy Spirit had been purifying me all night and that it had encompassed and preserved me, preparing me for this. And from the facts that I fell on my face; that the words I spoke and the prayer did not come from myself, but that the words were put into my mouth, although it was I who spoke; and that everything was holy, I saw that it was the son of God himself who descended with such a resounding noise that I was spontaneously prostrated, offered up the prayer, and said it was Jesus in person.

56

> I prayed for my long-term doubts to be forgiven and that in my thoughts I had demanded miracles, which I now saw was not reasonable. Thereupon, I fell in prayer, and I prayed only for grace. That was all I could express, but afterwards I added that I pray for love, which is the work of Jesus Christ and not mine. When I said this, tremors repeatedly passed over me.

57

> Later, at dawn, I fell asleep again when having all this in mind, considering how Christ binds himself to people, and then sacred thoughts emerged that I cannot get down in writing, nor what then passed: I only know I had such ideas.

In the morning, still half asleep, Swedenborg contemplates his experiences. As on later occasions, he calls to mind the biblical demand for an examination of spiritual experiences. Here the important thing is his own passivity. The grace that has befallen him, his entire experience, has come from outside himself. He has been thrown down on his face, as by itself. "The words were put into my mouth." He has been seized by God's power, has become, as he writes in entry 55, "purified," "preserved." He also observes how Jesus joins or "binds himself" (in the Swedish original: *binder sig*) to humankind.

Indeed, the way in which Swedenborg accounts for his experiences is very close to Moravian thinking. Christ really catches hold of a person, who becomes a tool in this type of religious experience, Zinzendorf says. Furthermore, to be bound and drawn are important concepts in Moravian terminology, the main source of which is John 6:44: "No man can come to me, except the Father which hath sent me draw him." The Holy Writ and the Gospel are not—as for Luther—primarily a promise, but a mystical experience in which Christ binds himself to the human being.

> *Please now call me, tempt me, draw me*
> *Seek and find me, take me home!*
> *Bend my heart, O dear Jesus*
> *That it also seeks for Thee!*

To use a word that constantly recurs in their hymns, the believer in his turn clings to Christ's bosom.

What this "binding" to Jesus implies more exactly we do not know. These are, as he says, "holy ideas," beyond comprehension. Yet we may surmise that they are not altogether remote from the experiences described in his book *The Worship and Love of God*, his work on the creation story on which he—in obedience, as he believed, to a divine command—would begin working in October this same year and in which he has Adam experience a vision where he sees himself sitting in the bosom of love, as Swedenborg himself had done. After this experience, the first human being, like the diarist, asks himself what it really is he has experienced. I quote a few lines from the lengthy reply, found in §56:

> *You are still sitting in his bosom. For he is in our innermost sphere as in the highest, he and his heaven. All the inward is*

filled with rays of his light, and where his rays are, there is also his sight, from the highest or from his throne. . . . But he is also in the outermost. However, if our reason does not turn inwards, like a door is opened inwards, he will not be seen . . . but heaven, which is also called the Kingdom of God, is also to be found deep within ourselves.

Here, as we shall see in later diary entries, we have the most important aspect of being joined to Christ. Swedenborg has been passively thrown into a state of prostration, vision, and insight. As he writes later (entry 149), he must refrain from mixing his reason with matters of faith. Then he will have paradise within.

Swedenborg, the systematic scientist, also systematized his dreams and later on his revelations as well. In February 1746, he was to distinguish between four forms of visions: first, "dreams," which he has been having "for some years"; second, "revelations," clear as daylight, in which he is awake but with eyes closed and which occur "very often"; third, revelations in a state that resembles waking, so that one fancies one is awake, "and yet is not awake." These have occurred "several times." The fourth and last form is probably of the same crucial type as his Easter vision. "The inner senses seem to have left the outward," he wrote in *The Word Explained* §1893.

In the next dream entry, we are for the first time directly confronted with his father Jesper Swedberg—the figure who, together with Charles XII, will appear most frequently in the diary. As mentioned in my introduction, even though there must inevitably have been clashes between them, the relationship between father and son may be assumed on the whole to have been harmonic. While Emanuel had to be aware of his father's monumental egocentricity and self-complacency, he must also have seen his courage, his faith, his remarkable vitality, and his constant concern for his family. Conflicts, we may suppose, arose in connection with Emanuel's first trip to London in 1710. The bishop was dubious, even critical, regarding his son's almost manic activity as inventor, engineer, mathematician, astronomer, physicist, etc. But when Emanuel by and by "settled down" and became an official, specializing in mineralogy and mining science, and, by inheritance, a mine-owner, his father cannot have been dissatisfied. The more so as his other son was "rather wild" in his youth and so little disposed to accept advice and guidance that Swedberg at long last had found it advisable to pack him off to the Swedish colony of Delaware.

When the Episcopal mansion in Skara was ravaged by fire in 1712, one of the objects saved from the ashes was a copper engraving of Jesper Swedberg. To his temporarily homeless father, Emanuel—probably then on his English journey—wrote some admiring verses. They provide a closing scene of this father-son relationship:

> Porträttet, mitt i den brinnande askan
> låg oskatt när hemmet förtärdes.
> Så, min far, skall ditt namn och ett kärleksfullt minne
> trotsa eldens och gravens makt!

> [When our home was consumed by the fire,
> your picture passed through in the burning pyre
> Likewise your name we so dearly admire
> will brave the grave and ordeals by fire.]

Swedenborg's first dream about his dear dad—not surprising in view of his shaking experiences of only a few hours before—is about a task and a calling. His notes are complicated for us by the special ambiguities characteristic of his dream world, such as will recur on several occasions:

58

I then saw my father dressed in another costume, almost reddish. He asked me to come, and he took me by the arms, which were in half-sleeves but with detachable cuffs in front. He took both the cuffs and tied them with my bands. That I was wearing cuffs meant that I did not belong to the clergy but am, and should be, a civil servant. Then he asked for my opinion about a certain question, that a king has permitted some thirty ordained clergy to marry, thus changing their state. I replied that I

have written something about such matters, but it has no bearing on this.

In the introductory scene, we see the late bishop—dead since 1735—busy attaching lace cuffs to his son's sleeves, carefully fastening them at Emanuel's wrists. Starched cuffs were worn by members of the aristocracy and middle class, whereas the clergy, as a sign of a more ascetic way of life, usually only wore the so-called "half-sleeves." Naturally, the bishop's action has something to do with his son's vision and Christ's *vademecum*. Does his action mean that his son shall not change his estate and take holy orders? Or, on the contrary, remain what he always has been? The father's performance constitutes a clear statement regarding what his son should do or not.

The problem of Swedenborg's estate—the word *stånd* in the original Swedish refers to both "[unmarried] state" and "[the four] estates"—was a matter of principle here. Could he, or should he, as nobleman and head of his family, now become a clergyman? Northern Europe already offered one example of such a change of estate: to the indignation of his fellow aristocrats, Count Zinzendorf had taken holy orders and even had himself installed as a bishop.

Thus, "estate," in this context, is an ambiguous concept, as is the whole question of which estate anyone belonged to. On the one hand, the term can refer to the estates of the realm; on the other, to whether one was married or not. This ambiguity, together with the possible reference to Zinzendorf, leads on to his second thought in entry 58.

Having ostensibly given his blessing to his son's future religious calling, without a change of his estate, the bishop asks Emanuel what he thinks of the king's having given thirty clergymen permission to marry. Here Swedenborg is certainly alluding to the well-known mass weddings within the original Bohemian congregation. Zinzendorf himself—the congregation's "king"—had arranged simultaneous weddings of a great many people in his congregation. The couples were joined by lot, and often immediately sent out to the movement's congregations overseas, in Pennsylvania or elsewhere. The dreamer, we read, had thought or written something about this. Yet it is irrelevant, has no "bearing," or, as the original reads, *rapport*, on the matter.

59

Shortly, I collected my wits and answered according to my conscience, that one should not be allowed to change one's estate like that, of whatever kind it may be; and he said he was of the same opinion, whereas I added that it will certainly be as the king has decided. He said that he would submit his vote in writing, and, if they were fifty in number, it would be accordingly. I observed, and this I found to be very strange, that I never called him my father, but only my brother. I thought the matter over for a while: it seemed to me that my father was dead, and that this one, who is my father, thus must be my brother.

Swedenborg returns to his initial idea: no nobleman has the right to enter holy orders. The bishop agrees: but what the king—God or Zinzendorf—decides, must stand.

He calls his father "my brother," which he finds remarkable. Swedenborg means that his dream has given rise to a confusion of ideas. His father having been dead for nine years, the figure he is speaking to might as well be his brother Jesper. The word *brother* is pregnant with meaning here, however. It is not too far-fetched to suppose that Emanuel, a member of the laity, now feels he has come closer to his father, the bishop, his "brother in Christ."

But the change from father to brother may also have a more specific application to the Moravians, calling themselves the Brethren. Zinzendorf and his followers laid special store by their readings of Paul's Epistle to the Hebrews, especially to 2:11, which treats of brotherhood or fraternity, but on a higher plane. "For the one who sanctifies and those who are sanctified all have one Father. For this reason, Jesus is not ashamed to call them brothers and sisters." We come across this emphasis on brotherhood, of which Swedenborg was certainly aware, in the Brethren confession of faith and in their hymns. What applied to the relationship between

God and humanity should reasonably be supposed also to apply to father and son.

The subject of brotherhood in and with Christ recurs later in Swedenborg's epic drama *The Worship and Love of God*. In §55, it is love, the Godhead, who is speaking to Adam: "Since we are thus both of one and the same, you shall not be my son, but my brother."

60

Not to forget, it also occurred to me that the Holy Ghost wanted to guide me to Jesus and introduce me to him, a work he had this way brought about, and that I should not ascribe anything to myself, but everything is his, although he imputes to us the same.

Then I sang the hymn I had chosen for the occasion; Jesus is my best of friends, No. 245.

61

This I have now learned of the spiritual: that the only thing is to humble oneself to the grace of Christ, in all humility to ask for no more than that. I had added something of my own—to receive love—but that was presumptuous. Because when one delivers oneself to the grace of God, one is at the mercy of Christ and acts according to his wishes. One is happiest when in God's grace. In the humblest prayer, I had to ask forgiveness before I got ease of conscience, because I was in temptation when all this happened. I was taught by the Holy Ghost; but in my sententiousness, I fell away from complete submission, which is the basis of everything.

In the last sentences of this entry, Swedenborg sums up his impressions in two main thoughts. First , he is a "work" that, thanks to the care and efforts of the Holy Spirit, is already fully prepared. In all this, the dreamer has been passive, a figure borne up by powers outside himself. Second, a relationship to God must be based on the insight that faith is more important than knowledge or reason. Here the key word is *humility* or, to quote the Moravian clergyman

Arvid Gradin's book *The Secret of the Gospel* (*Evangelii hemlighet*), "the living insight into your own corruption and wretchedness, which on our Savior's lips means poverty of spirit." This is an aspect of the childlike mind Swedenborg later on is to praise in his diary.

We are now entering upon the longest entry of the dream diary. Swedenborg thinks he is now being instructed on his future religious stand and on his mission—which means that he has now begun to intuit that he is approaching a turning point in his life, the nature of which is not clear to him. The emotional crescendo of Easter time slightly calms down. He is still exalted, fighting various whims and thoughts and crying with joy when he finds himself embraced by God's grace.

[April] 7–8

62

> All night my dreams were about how I went far down, on ladders and through other rooms, but got back safe and sound, so the depths were of no danger to me; and in my dream also that verse came to my mind, *neither depths nor anything else, whether coming or nigh.* . . .

In this way, Swedenborg summarizes the night's experiences. He has been penetrating into hitherto inaccessible depths and mine shafts. Just as he formerly had to descend ladders and pass along subterranean galleries while carrying out his duties for the College of Mines, he is now descending other ladders, going into the depths of his own self. His former official visits to the bowels of the earth, however, are different from his new venture. The new descents are not dangerous. With God's help and at his bidding ("Well then, do!"), he must now undertake such expeditions. And once again Arrhenius' hymn *Jesus is My Best of Friends* comes to his mind:

My trust is complete and such is my creed:
that neither will life and nor will death
ever estrange him from my lead,
nor any baseness or angels above,
darkest abyss or the deepest need,
whether coming or nigh,
make me leave God's love
Which is with Jesus on high.

63

Thereafter it seemed to me that I was at a clergyman's dinner table together with many others. I paid about a louis-d'or for the meal, much more than I should. But, when I left the house, I brought two silver chalices that I had taken from the table. This troubled me, and I tried to return them. It seemed to me I had a plan for this, which means, so do I believe, that in the temptation I had paid my due (by the grace of God), with interest (God's grace), but that, at the same time, I had learned much in spiritual things, signified by the silver chalices I wanted to return to the clergyman, that is, for the honor of God to give something back to the established church in some manner, which, as it seemed to me, will also be done.

The key concepts of this dream seem to be the clergyman, the meal, the payment (a French gold coin being the actual currency), the chalice or vessel of silver, and remission. His interpretations, here as elsewhere when taken out of the full context of the diary, are partly difficult to follow. That wider angle of vision, however, may open up the following analysis and purport of the entry.

In his works—in his dream, he is in company with "many"— Swedenborg the scientist, mining expert, and philosopher has been making use of Christian doctrine at his pleasure (ate a meal in a clergyman's house) or in a way that suited him personally. To use an expression frequent in his later writings, he has relied on *proprium*, "his own." This he has done too often ("much more than I should"). His dues, caused by hubris, he has accounted for in his works ("in the temptation I had paid my due"), even with gold.

Now he has brought with him two silver articles from the clergy-man's table, a figure for his debts to church doctrine ("had learned much in spiritual things"). There is not any remission, however. When it is returned "in some way," it will be an "honor of God." This implies a special Christian mission. What he has learned about divine reality shall benefit the public or general church, be it the State church or the universal church, "to give something back to the established church in some manner, which, as it seemed to me, will also be done," his wording [*allmenna kyrckian* in the original] being both ambiguous and por-tentous, implying an estrangement: the position of an outsider or a nonconformist connection.

64

Afterwards I went with quite a large company to the house of another clergyman, where it seemed to me I had been before. When we alighted, it occurred to me that we were so many that we would overwhelm the clergyman and trouble him, which bothered me. This meant that I had so many unmanageable thoughts, which should not be such and which were like roving Poles and hussars, but it seemed to me they went away.

To stick to goodness—the new clergyman—presupposes concen-tration and a wholehearted effort, which proves to be hard won. The great number of attendants, or the escort, is his unruly ideas, like the bands of drifting hussars and any rabble of soldiery. They return in yet another shape in the following note, where they ap-pear as afflictions or visitations.

65

I was also in such a temptation that my fancies went out of con-trol, yes, with such a force that I could think only of keeping a close check on them, to counter the spiritual power, which is heading in another direction; yes, with such a force that had not God's grace been even stronger, I'd have fallen or been driven crazy. At times, I was not able to focus on Christ at all, whom I

had seen, but for a little while. The power and agitation of the spirit fell upon me so strongly that I would rather become insane. This referred to the second clergyman.

In a way, the content of this paragraph is partly the same as that of the foregoing or a continuation and accentuation of the theme. Temptations hinder him from contemplating Christ, a kind of experience that, when achieved, in the Christian tradition has an intrinsic value, connected with feelings of peace, harmony, happiness, and energy. To Swedenborg, another element is even more important in this endeavor: contemplation is a form of knowledge, and happiness, to him, equals wisdom. In *The Animal Kingdom* II, §463, he writes:

> *If we thus want to receive real truths—natural, moral, or spiritual . . . in our understanding, we must extinguish the impure bodily fires and thus our false beacons, and . . . allow our reason to be enlightened by the rays of spiritual power, undisturbed by bodily influences. Then truths flow in for the the first time—because this power is their special source. When they reach us, they identify themselves by a number of signs: the plentiful joy, that is, which accompanies insight . . . since as soon as a truth emerges, reason is jubilant.*

Now, when a sense of call is constantly on his mind, the question of focus assumes a double significance.

66

I compare this to the two scales of a balance. In one of them is our own will and our evil nature; in the other, the power of God. In temptation, our Lord so arranges these that at times they come into an equilibrium, but as soon as one of them weighs down, he helps it up again. This is what I have found to be the case, expressing it in a worldly manner, from which follows: that this is very little by our own power, which draws everything downwards and is opposed rather than cooperating with the power of the Spirit, and consequently it is the work of our Lord alone, which he thus disposes.

At last, then, as transpires from the concluding sentences of entry 65, the temptations were over; the powerful movement and strength of the Spirit have come over him, a Spirit he would not forsake for anything. To explain what has happened, he employs an image to which he will often return in his works: the simile of a balance or a steelyard. This thought is clarified by some lines in *True Christian Religion* §504, written in 1770, and published the year before he died:

> God allows human beings to feel life within themselves as if it were their own. And God wants them to feel that way, so that they, as if by themselves, shall live according to the order, the rules of which are as many as the Commandments. . . . Nevertheless, God never ceases to keep his finger on the needle on top of the steelyard, moderating softly, without ever interfering with the freedom of will and thought.

Evidently, the basic idea, one of profound consequence, is that God maintains a balance that is the very condition of free choice.

67

Then I perceived that things were brought forth in my thoughts, which had been put into them long before, so that I thereby found the truth of the Word of God: that there is not the least word or thought that is not known to God and that, if we do not receive the grace of God, we are responsible for this.

68

Thus I have learned, and beyond that I know nothing, that the only thing in this state is this: in humility to thank God for his grace and to pray for it, and that we consider our own unworthiness and God's infinite grace.

The last four points do not directly concern his dreams. They are reflections on his present mental condition and God's concern with it. Here old thoughts reappear. Swedenborg is thinking about the pair of scales, an image earlier used in his *Rational Psychology*. This is still another example of something that is obviously true as we proceed, namely, the recurrence of themes and basic structures: Swedenborg's experiences have a notable tinge of déjà vu and recollection.

This singular character of his series of experiences appears to him as a confirmation of God's universal presence, and, likewise, they reflect his own development. As with so many other mystics, Swedenborg's call will be his screen. "When I look back on my past life" he writes several years later in the *Spiritual Diary* §3177, "I realize that all has been guided by God."

69

It was strange that I was able to have two thoughts at one and the same time and quite distinct from one another: the one for myself, which arrested all thoughts of others; and at the side of this, the thoughts of the temptation, and this occurred in such a manner that nothing was powerful enough to drive them away. They held me captive so that I did not know where to flee, for I carried them with me.

Here, for the first time, Swedenborg describes how he seems to entertain mutually contradictory ideas. Of these, one seems to dominate—the pious insight he has already developed in the foregoing paragraph. Yet, at the same time, he is still exposed to temptations that nothing is strong enough to counter. Later we shall see how this theme of diffidence and "being in two minds" will develop in various directions. Soon he will be using his special breathing technique to overcome such mental distractions. Yet this duality, this mental struggle between a conviction of salvation and a despair of his own sinfulness, a dialectic between evil and bad impulses, agony and bliss, will run all through his later writings.

70

Later on, because various things occurred to me that I had thought and fixed in my mind long ago, it was as if it had been said to me that I found reasons for excusing myself, which was also a great temptation, or to attribute to myself the good I have done or, more correctly speaking, what has been done through me. The Spirit of God removed this also and inspired me to regard it otherwise.

71
_____

This last [temptation] was more severe than the former, insofar as it reached to the innermost; but over and against this, I received a still stronger evidence of the Spirit, for at times I broke into a perspiration and what then came to my mind was no longer anything that could condemn me. For I had the strong confidence that I was forgiven for this, but that I should excuse myself and set myself free. Every now and then, I burst into tears, not of sorrow but of inmost joy that our Lord has been willing to show such great grace to so unworthy a sinner. The sum and substance of all I found to be that the one and only thing is to cast oneself in humility upon the grace of our Lord, to perceive one's own unworthiness, and to thank God in humility for his grace; for if there is anything great that does oneself credit, be it a glorification of the grace of God or anything else, then it is impure.

Both entries touch upon the classical problem of how far the merit of a person's good deeds, if any, shall be ascribed to God. Zinzendorf had an emotional and most positive answer to this question— nothing can be ascribed to our own power! In Herrnhut, the awareness of absolute sinfulness and complete incompetence was considered the only passable way to salvation. Everything depends on God's grace. Swedenborg is tempted to take the credit and take the opportunity of gaining honor for his achievements, or, the other way around, to excuse himself for his shortcomings. This view, no doubt, is quite different from the radical relation to God he is now approaching and is also opposed to the epistemological conviction touched upon in my remarks to dream entry 65. Good (the Divine) and desire (Evil) are in the balance. If good takes command, human credit goes to only that volition which lets the higher influence pass. If that passage is open, the question of excuses seems to lose all relevancy.

Very upset, Swedenborg is summarizing this insight in entry 71. For the scientist Swedenborg, who has recently gone to press with a new book, this has vast and serious consequences. What was the value of scientific work?

72

These thoughts often occurred to me, and I wondered what would happen if anyone took me for a holy man, and therefore esteemed me, yes, as with some simpleminded people, not merely to venerate but also to adore a putative holiness or saint: I then perceived that, in the excitement in which I then was, I would be willing to inflict upon him every evil, even unto the extreme, rather than any such sin cleave to him. And that I must entreat our Lord with earnest prayers that I may not have any share in so damnable a sin, which should be inherent in me.

73

For Christ, in whom dwelleth the fullness of the Godhead, is alone to be adored in prayer, for he takes the greatest sinner to his grace and does not regard our unworthiness; wherefore, we must not in the prayer address ourselves to any one but him. He is almighty and is the only mediator. What he does for the sake of others who have become saints is his concern and not ours, that we should . . . [The rest of the sentence is crossed out].

This bizarre notion, that simple people might worship him as a saint, is one indication out of many of the strength with which Swedenborg is absorbed by the idea of a divine calling. His emotional life is still dominated by the vision of the previous night. His immediate acceptance of a new state and a new mission indicates his readiness for changing his life in a radical way.

He realizes that this idea, too, is presumptuous. In entry 74, he formulates a confession, correct from the orthodox Swedish point of view, of Christ as intercessor and bearer of our sins. It is Arrhenius' hymn again, now sung in a Moravian mood.

74

> I perceived that I was unworthy above others and the greatest sinner of all. Yet our Lord has granted me [permission] to penetrate more deeply with my thoughts in certain matters than many others have done. This is the very fountain of the sin, that in this manner my sins come from a deeper source than in the case of many other persons. From this, I saw my unworthiness and my sin to be greater than those of others; for it is not enough to call oneself unworthy, since this may be done while yet the heart is far away from it and it may be a pretense; but to perceive that one is such, this is of the grace of the Spirit.

In fact, Swedenborg is more burdened with sin than others. As in the first lines of his entry for April 6–7, he emphasizes that his thinking and his research have carried him further than others from the Divine. His specific sin, due to the natural self-absorption inherent in scientific work, is thus firmly established. To realize that one is unworthy—that is the grace of the Spirit. In the concluding words of the entry, Swedenborg's moral and epistemological credo is repeated: to be superior is to be rescued from impure fires, and this way become enlightened by higher truth.

75

> Now, while I was in the spirit and in [such] thoughts, I sought by means of my thoughts to gain a knowledge of how to avoid all that is impure; but I noticed that, every time something from the love of self intruded and was turned about in the thought—as, for instance, when someone did not show the proper regard for me according to my own imagination—I always thought, "If you only knew what grace I am enjoying, you would act otherwise," which at once was something impure, having its source in the love of self. After a while, I perceived this and prayed God to forgive it; and I then desired that others might enjoy the same grace, and perhaps they possess it or will obtain it. Thus,

I observed clearly that there was still with me that dreadful apple which has not yet been converted, which is the root of Adam and original sin; yes, and in addition to that, the roots of my sin are infinite in number.

Swedenborg says he is "in the spirit" (*uti andan*), an expression he will often use henceforth. Here, he seems to refer to a state of mind where he has succeeded in extinguishing the "bodily fires" and to a kind of lucidity or calm in which he can be directed and enlightened "from above." It is in this contemplative state, or in something resembling it, that he will later find he is being granted participation in a higher knowledge.

In this state of purity or incorporeality, Swedenborg tries to analyze "all that is impure" in order to avoid it in the future. But in this self-examination, he stumbles, not surprisingly, upon the Lutheran outlook on human nature, according to which the power of inherited sin is stronger than our will. Everywhere, in every thought, he is faced by his own conceit. He wishes others to experience the same grace, the grace that has now been granted to him or is in the process of fulfilment. As soon as he expresses his wish, he notices, by introspection, that conceit is hiding in this too, that dreadful apple of original sin. As Luther writes in his remarks to the Credo: "I believe that I do not have in myself the understanding and the power to believe or to come to my Lord Jesus Christ."

The topic "original sin" (*arfsynd*, hereditary sin, is Swedenborg's term) will turn up again—the next time in entries 109 and 110 of April 11–12.

76

I heard a person at the table asking his neighbor the question whether anyone who had an abundance of money could be melancholic. I smiled in my mind and would have replied—if it had been proper for me to do so in that company or if the question had been addressed to me—that a person who possesses everything in abundance is not only subject to melancholy, but to something higher, that of the mind and the soul, or of the

spirit, which operates therein; and I wondered that he had put such a question.

77

> I can testify to this so much the more because, by the grace of God, there has been bestowed upon me in abundance everything that I require of temporal things. I am able to live richly on my income alone and can carry out what I have in mind and still have a surplus of the revenue; thus, I can testify that the sorrow or melancholy that comes from the want of the necessities of life is of a lesser degree and merely of the body and is not equal to the other kind. The power of the Spirit prevails in the latter, but I do not know whether it is so also in the first kind, for it seems that it may be severe on bodily grounds; still, I will not enter further into this matter.

Can a rich man really be melancholic? Someone has asked such a question in his company or at an adjoining table, and Swedenborg jots down his ideas on the subject. It is the same question of agony or "sickness" we have met with before, but the problem here is of a radically different nature: anxiety from money worries and its effects are even worse. Later, in his *Spiritual Diary*, coloring his examination with theological reflections, he will explore the psychology of melancholy. In this dark mood, he writes, a struggle is going on in the depths of a the person's soul between his or her innermost "real" love and temptations that are trying to distract that person from it. He also points out that these temptations have their source in the spiritual world. This line of thinking, however, belongs to a later stage of Swedenborg's development.

78

> I saw a book shop, and immediately the thought struck me that my work would have greater effect than the works of others; but I checked myself at once by the thought that one person serves another and that our Lord has many thousand ways of preparing every one, so that every book must be left to its own

merits, as a close or remote medium, according to the state of the understanding of each. Nevertheless, pride immediately pushed itself forward. May God control it, for the power is in his hands.

Once again, self-importance raises its head and swells with pride, this time in the shape of the notion of his own works being more valuable than those of other authors. But he instantly realizes that one writer complements another; everything collaborates to endow existence with a higher meaning. Each book, seen in such a perspective, has a relative value. And this, in turn, implies that his own oeuvre is only important to those whom God has prepared to receive his message.

Having now put down this reflection in writing, he is stricken, probably in the very instant, by another insight: even in this acknowledgment of his own books' relative value is an element of self-love. The "dreadful apple" turns up again. He is aware of his inconsistency, and he carefully watches the oscillation between joyful faith and tormenting temptation in his mind.

79 _____

Had so much of the Lord's grace, that, when I was determined to keep my thoughts in purity, I perceived an interior gladness; but, still, there was a pain in my body for it was not able to bear the heavenly joy of the soul. I therefore submitted myself most humbly to the grace of God, that he might do with me what he wants. May God grant me humility, now when I see my frailty, my impurity and unworthiness.

We now turn to page 29 of the manuscript diary. The twenty lines found on this page are extremely difficult reading, since the text is hardly legible. Swedenborg has tried to cover the text with thick layers of ink, concealing them. By careful examination and conjecture, the learned librarians and philologists of the Royal Library in Stockholm, G. E. Klemming and F. A. Dahlgren, extracted the following paragraphs:

80 _____

> During all this, I remained in the company of all my former associates, and no one could [undecipherable] the least change with me, which was God's grace, but I knew what it [undecipherable] not daring to tell that I realized what high grace had been conferred upon me; for I discerned that this could serve no other purpose than to make people think this or that about me, according to the pros and cons of each, nor perform any use, if privately [undecipherable] from the glorification of God's grace which [undecipherable] for the love of self.

81 _____

> The best comparison I could make of myself was with a peasant who had been given the power of a prince or king, so that he would possess everything his heart could wish for, but still there was something within him that made him desire to learn what he did not himself know; but from the comparison one finds that [undecipherable] thy gracious hand which causes the great joy. Still I was distressed because I feared that he cannot maintain that grace with me.

At the time of all these trembling and upsetting occurrences, Swedenborg is seeing the same people as usual, and he notes that no one observes any changes with him. He is careful not to reveal anything to anyone, and, in this matter, he is successful too. It is important to see that he does not look upon himself as a person in crisis but as one who is particularly favored and chosen.

A few weeks earlier, Swedenborg wrote that he "enjoys being in the world." We do not know much about the company he was keeping at that time or under what conditions. He was in the habit of retiring and rising early, but there is also occasional dissipation, at least when in London. At The Hague, one is certain to find Swedenborg from time to time in the house of the Swedish envoy Joakim Fredrik Preis; they had known each other for a long time. Preis had been a Swedish envoy since 1714; at this time, he was seventy-seven years old. There is an indication in another entry, that of April 15–16, that Swedenborg may have opened his heart and spoke of his crisis to the old diplomat.

The notes of April 7–8, the longest in the diary, conclude with an image showing how he regards himself these days. His is aware that he has the most undeserved and exalted position and that he can afford to meet any material wish. His craving for knowledge, however, never leaves him in peace. From the eradicated sentences, we may surmise that he sees God's grace as the fountain of knowledge and wisdom and fears he cannot get full access to this source, since he knows that unconditional humility and wholehearted submission were, as yet, not fully within his reach.

The emotional summit of the dream diary is passed; the remainder of the time covered by the journal offers no further experiences of the same crucial and groundbreaking character. Instead, the entries reveal ambivalence between feelings of divine presence and absence, happiness and despair. At the same time, the author will gain ever deeper insights into the nature of his mission. In these veering turns of mind, Swedenborg does not differ essentially from other Christian mystics. Most of them experienced a feeling of being "called" or of being granted divine insight, followed by the demand for "purity," clashing with the natural desire to cling to habits, customs, and old ways of thinking.

[April] 8–9

82 _____

I seemed to have a dog on my lap, and I was astonished that it could speak. I wonder if Swab, his former master, knew this. It was swarthy, and it kissed me. I woke up and prayed for the mercy of Christ, because I cherish much pride, flattering myself.

Afterwards, it seemed to me that, on my day of prayers, which was yesterday, many things were packed up for the army.

The dreamer is kissed by a black dog, lying in his lap. It also speaks to him. As he himself has sat in the lap of the Savior, so now evil—his own self-righteousness—is sitting on his knee. It may be worthy of note that the owner of the dog probably was his relative and colleague Anders Swab. Possibly it was he who stood for what Swedenborg several times calls "my temptation," a fundamental experience immediately preceding the diary's dated entries and mentioned again later (entries 17 and 40). I shall return to this point in connection with entry 126 of April 14–15.

The previous day, he writes, was "my day of prayers." Special days of prayers, stipulated by the Moravian Brethren in Saxony, had perhaps been adopted elsewhere by other Moravians. His intercession days may thus be another instance of Moravian influence, which would set the tone of his stay in London.

The crucial point seems to be that on this day "many things were packed up for the army." We are, he was to write later in his diary, "soldiers at war with Satan." He certainly means that, during the course of the day, his resources for this struggle have been strongly reinforced. The rest of the long entry of April 7–8 supports this reading.

83

> Then a young woman dressed in black entered and said that I ought to go to . . . Then she got behind me and grasped my back and my hands so firmly that I could not move at all. I asked for help from a person nearby, and he helped me get her away, but I was not able to move the arm myself. This referred to the temptation during the day and means that I am not capable of doing anything good by myself. I then heard as if someone were whistling, but he went away, and I shivered.

The young woman in black exhorts him to go to a particular place, but which place the note does not tell. A temptation? The dreamer feels trapped. The woman embraces his back, clutches him. He is helpless, unable even to move his arm. He asks for help, appeals to "one" who is standing nearby and is partly released. The moral of this dream: by himself, he can do nothing without God's help.

The woman/temptress's way of attacking him is typical of Swedenborg's world of imagination. We shall later see him again bound from behind (entry 232), possessed. Someone withers away with a whistle. Is it the woman, passing through a metamorphosis of gender, or is it the helper?

84

> Then I saw someone in St. Peter's church going into the vault underneath, where Peter lies. He was carried out, but it was said that yet another is hiding there. It seemed that I was free to go in and out. May God lead me.

This reference to St. Peter's in Rome is of special interest. According to Christian tradition, Peter the Apostle—the rock on which the Lord's congregation would be built—is buried in the crypt. Now the dreamer sees him carried out of the grave, whereas someone else is said to be hiding down there.

No doubt we may interpret this as still another sign of the importance Swedenborg is attributing to his call. The apostle disappears, but Emanuel Swedenborg remains there to found a new congregation, an idea that he will later explicitly claim to be a matter of fact. God is leading him, he writes. Isn't that the Hebrew meaning of his Christian name, "God with us"? He feels free to move in and out, and it is precisely this freedom he will later adduce as evidence of the special grace he has been granted, by virtue of which he can pass freely to and fro between this world and the world of spirits.

85

> After that I saw all that was impure, and I acknowledged that I was impure, head to foot. I cried for the mercy of Jesus Christ.
>   Then it seemed that the words "I, poor sinful creature" occurred to me. I also read them the following day.

Swedenborg realizes that his dream about his place of honor in St. Peter's is presumptuous. Praying for forgiveness, he uses the opening words of the "confession of sin" in the Swedish liturgy of 1697. The words seem to echo a Lutheran conviction of absolute human incapacity to exorcize original sin:

> *I, poor sinful creature, who was begotten and born in sin, and who likewise in all my days have lived a sinful life, acknowledge from my whole heart before Thee, Almighty and Eternal God, my dear Heavenly Father, that I have not loved Thee above all things, and that I have not loved my neighbor as myself. Like my fathers, I have time and again sinned against Thy Commandments, both in thoughts and in deeds. And I know that, on this account, I would be worthy of hell and eternal damnation, Thou to judge me according to the demands of Thy stern justice, and as my sins deserve. . . . But I ask Thee according to Thy promise to show leniency and forgive me my trespasses. . . . Thy Holy Name be Praised!*

The confession of sin thus concludes in a hope of redemption.

[April] 9–10

86

All day, on the ninth, I was in prayers, songs of praise, reading the Word of God, fasting, except in the morning, when I did some other things, until the same temptation came over me, that obsession with thoughts I did not want to think.

The week after Easter was drawing to a close. April 9 was a Thursday. In those days, not only Easter Monday but also Easter Tuesday and Wednesday were holy days. Swedenborg is still living under the spell of his vision: praying, reading the Bible, and fasting. His temptation of the previous day returns. Had it taken the shape of a woman in black?

From experience, he will later emphasize that praying does not suffice against this class of temptations. Only in active combat can one stand up to these torments, he observes in *Arcana Coelestia* §8179:

> *For they who are in temptations are wont to fold their hands and pray with fervor, not knowing that prayers do not work on them, but a combat must be waged against the falsity and evil then infused by the hells. The only weapon is the truths of faith, which are victorious, since they counter falsity and evil with truth and goodness.*

87

During the present night, I slept very tranquilly until three or four in the morning, when I woke up and lay awake, as in a vision. I could open my eyes and be awake when I wished, so I was not otherwise than awake, but as to the spirit there was an inward joy that could be felt all over the body.

Everything seemed in a consummate way to be fulfilled, flew upwards as it were, concealing itself in something infinite, as a center, where love itself was, and it seemed as if it issued thence round about and then down again, thus moving around in incomprehensible circles from a center that is love, and back.

This is apparently not a dream. At about three o'clock in the morning, Swedenborg wakes up from a good night's sleep and lies there in his bed, noting with closed eyes "as in a vision." I want to stress the terms he is using in describing this experience: "an inward joy that could be felt all over the body"; "Everything seemed in a consummate way to be fulfilled [*abouterade*]"; "flew upwards"; "concealing itself in something infinite, as a center, where love itself [*amor ipse*] was"; "issued thence round about and then down again, thus moving around in incomprehensible circles from a center which is love, and back."

The main features of this ecstatic experience are to be found elsewhere in his work, both before and after his crisis. In his prologue to *The Economy of the Animal Kingdom*, which he would write eight years later, he described how, "while intensely seeking for knowledge," he at times felt he was at the innermost center of all being. At such moments, he was "not on earth, but on high . . . in the whitest light and in heaven." The vision also reminds us of the "paradise play" of *The Worship and Love of God*. There this takes the form of a dance, by which the celestial intelligences celebrate the birth of humanity, a dance they resort to when they want to "revoke the state of virginity and childishness." They move in circles toward the center, where they are united into one, from which they extend outwards again, forming new rings, "in an ever more world-embracing swing," return to the center, and so forth.

These experiences of concentricity and whirling illumination are reserved for those who, freeing themselves from sensory limits, place themselves under the "heavenly light." This is an element of the transcendent state of mind, which in the *Spiritual Diary* is referred to as "being in the spirit" or "inspirited." A few lines from *Arcana Coelestia* §5128 provide us with a more systematic account:

> When sensory matters are placed before [higher] reason . . . they are enlightened by . . . the light of the Lord through heaven. When sensual things are put in this light, they do not pose hindrance [to the truths]. . . . Those [truths], that are in unison, then appear as a center . . . and are lifted up towards heaven, as it were. . . . This takes place when man is regenerated.

That is to say that at the center of the universe is divine love, and anyone in this perspicacious state of consciousness will find him- or herself enfolded in these swirls of circumvolution.

88

This love, which then filled me, in a mortal body is like that delight a chaste man enjoys when he really is in love and makes love to his spouse. Such an extreme joy was suffused over my whole body, and this for a long while. I have experienced this before, particularly just before falling asleep and after the sleep, for half an hour or even a full hour. Now, while I was in the spirit and yet awake—for I could open my eyes and be awake, and come back into that state—then I saw and realized that the

> **internal and real joy comes from this level, and that only insofar as one can be in it, there is happiness; and as soon as one comes into any other love that does not concentrate thither, then one is far afield right away.**

Swedenborg's tangibly erotic manner of describing his feelings can be related to similar accounts taken down by numerous mystics of various confessions during centuries past. It is noteworthy that he feels free voluntarily to enter and to exit this state of bliss. His joy, intimately connected with the direction taken by his love and his mental focus, also depends on control of his will. At every worldly distraction, joy departs.

This beatitude, conditioned by a turn of the mind, is also described in the contemporaneous epilogue to *The Animal Kingdom*, mentioned earlier in this book. The account of the conflicting sources of light, rays of the "light of spiritual power" and of the "impure fires of the body," may have its origin in this experience of April 1744.

89

> **When there was some love of self or love that did not concentrate itself in that direction, then one was out of this. A chill crept over me, a kind of shiver and some anguish, from which I understood the source of repeated pains, since the soul is grieving and finally may end up in eternal suffering and take to hell, as when one unworthily receives Christ in Communion and the sense of disgracefulness then is the torment of spirit.**

A relapse to conceit is, per se, torturous. The superior pain is much worse than the sense of being dwelling in the "bodily" sphere, however. The real agony comes from the conflict between higher will and the desires of self. In remembrance of purity, this agony is born at the core of the ego. The paradigm is, he explains by means of illustration, going to the Lord's table and unworthily partaking of the Holy Sacrament.

Swedenborg returns to this point on several occasions, both in the diary and later. To appreciate his notions correctly, as well as his simile, we must set them in a historical context. We should then bear in mind the stress laid on "right preparation" for taking the sacraments. Only after confession shall the communicant, then in a state of purity or vacancy, approach the great mystery of Holy Communion. The matter had been carefully stipulated in the Swedish canon of 1686, where the clergy had been ordered to warn their listeners of the *själavånda*, i.e., spiritual torment, entailed in misuse of the sacraments and to exhort them to prepare themselves properly for receiving them. Church Law also stipulated the forms under which this should be done: in towns, by going to confession on Saturday.

In Moravian circles, special emphasis was put on these preparations. In my introduction, I have explained Zinzendorf's view of these matters. In practice, these preparations were meant to sharpen and enhance the congregation's insights into the various elements in the divine service. Members were urged to confess privately to the congregation's elder, who advised anyone not in the right state of mind, to refrain from taking communion.

Swedes influenced by Moravian thinking likewise stressed the importance of right preparation. In their hymnbook, *Sions Sånger*, we find reminders of this:

> *Beforetime I consoled myself*
> *and felt no fear at all.*
> *Trespassed to my heart's content,*
> *thought myself as blissful,*
> *as any other soul.*
> *Since my conscience has awakened*
> *naught can me console.*
>
> *To pray and sing was then my haven,*
> *the sole refuge in my perdition;*
> *Went to confession time and again*
> *devoid of any pangs of pain.*
> *Went to Supper as a swine,*
> *which provided no remission;*
> *Dead was then the soul of mine.*

90

> In the state I was in, I came still further into the spirit; although I was awake, I could not control myself, but there came as it were an overwhelming impulse to throw myself on my face and to fold my hands and to pray, as before.
>
> About my unworthiness and to ask for grace with the deepest humility and reverence, that as the greatest of sinners I may receive forgiveness of sins. I then noticed that I was in the same state as during the night before last, but more I could not see, because I was now awake.

He is thus penetrating still deeper into the state he calls "being in the spirit," becoming even more aware of his own imperfections. He is turning his attention inwards and focuses on inner reality. Again, as in his great Easter vision, he feels guided by some power outside himself. It obliges him to clasp his hands and prostrate in prayer. He does not glimpse Christ, because now he is waking up.

The contents of his prayers are worth noting. They concern his own great burden of sin, and, despite his unworthiness, they implore Christ's grace. To Zinzendorf and his followers, awareness of sin was conditional and crucial. For them, "to be a sinner" and even "to wish to become a sinner" was synonymous with "desiring salvation" and "to see the light."

91

> I wondered at this, and then it was shown to me spiritually that a human being in this state is like a person who has his head down and his feet up; and it occurred to me why Moses had to remove his shoes when he was to go into the presence of the Holy One; and why Christ washed the feet of the apostles and answered Peter that all is sufficient when the feet are washed. When in the spirit, I then perceived that which proceeds from the center itself, which is love, is the Holy Spirit which is represented by the water, for there was mentioned water or wave [aqua eller unda].

Still "in the spirit," Swedenborg sees how, in his impure state, he resembles a man who is upside down, with head down and his feet in the air. He has uplifted the lowest parts of the body, those closest to the ground, using them to think with, meanwhile perpendicularly averting his head. His thoughts run on: he who would approach God must try to rectify himself by achieving purity and humility. Was this not why Moses had been told to take off his shoes when approaching the holy place of God?

In line with this thought, Swedenborg next interprets the washing of feet, in its Christian sense, as described in chapter 13 of the Gospel of John. Since the episode is important to our understanding of Swedenborg's attitude and spiritual state during the dream crisis, we should here recall the main features of this biblical passage.

Immediately before Passover, Jesus had his last meal with his disciples. Supper being over, Jesus, as an "ultimate proof of his love," took a basin and the towel wherewith he was girded, washed their feet, and dried them. Upon Peter's objecting, Jesus summarized the action's meaning in these words: "He that is washed needeth not save to wash *his* feet, but is clean every whit: and ye are clean, but not all." To his own question to his disciples, whether they understood what he had done or not, Jesus provided the answer. Henceforth, they were under an obligation to behave toward one another as he had acted toward them. "For I have given you an example, that ye should do as I have done to you." In the Roman Catholic Church, the episode is celebrated in the papal ceremony of washing the feet of the poor as a reminder of Christian humility.

This *pedilavium* of Christ—to use the common Latin term—had evidently made a deep impression on Swedenborg. In entry 91, Swedenborg primarily interprets it as a purification procedure: the numinous may only be approached in a state of spiritual purity. Its other aspect—humility—he seems not to stress in this context. Later, in entry 233, he will write about how "in the night" he has observed the soles of his feet to be white, which he interprets, in line with his dream of the washing of feet, as a symbol of redemption and remission.

Later, in July, as we have seen when considering Swedenborg's state of health these months and as emerges from Brockmer's narrative, this *pedilavium* idea at some point appears to have become an *idée fixe*. This is also faintly echoed in entry 224 of the diary.

The importance Swedenborg ascribes to the passage in the Gospel of John, and to his own special interpretation of it, is another indication of the power exerted on his mind at this time by Zinzendorf's teachings and Moravian practices. To Zinzendorf, the washing of feet was a ceremony of purification and, like marriage, "a Sacrament in the broader sense." In Moravian congregations, *pedilavium* was used at feasts and on ceremonious occasions, preparation for Communion being one.

Arvid Gradin, as mentioned, was a Swede who was active as a clergyman at Herrnhut. In 1743, he published a book for the bookseller James Hutton, in London, entitled *A Short History of the Bohemian-Moravian Protestant Church.* Hutton was in charge of the congregation of Brethren in London. In his book, which Swedenborg had in his library, Gradin describes the ceremony of the washing of feet thus:

> Once a month, we all partake of the Lord's Supper publickly [sic] together. . . . Just before the Administration of this venerable Sacrament, and after the Lovefeasts are ended, our Elders are us'd to wash the Brethren's Feet, as likewise the Female Elders the Feet of the Sisters.

This ceremony, writes Gradin, was observed at so-called love feasts (*agape*). These were held a day or night before the service. In his later doctrines, Swedenborg retained the purificatory element of Communion, regarding it as a continuation and perfection of Old Testament purification ceremonies.

92

In sum, when a person is in such a state as not to possess a love that centers upon self but upon the common good, which on earth or in the moral world represents love in the spiritual world, and all this not for the sake of self or of society but for the sake of Christ, who is love itself and the center, then one is

in the right state. Christ is the ultimate end, all other ends being intermediate ends, leading on directly to him.

Swedenborg summarizes the experiences recorded in entries 90 and 91. Only by liberating oneself from self-love—according to Arvid Gradin "the bitterest enemy of the cross and Christ's merits"—can anyone take the right track and his soul get to know God. In a characteristically analogous piece of reasoning about various levels of love, Swedenborg declares that love of the general good has its counterpart in spiritual love of Christ, which is the center and end of all. One's earthly love must accord with that higher love.

This reasoning concludes the spiritual experiences we have just been reading about in the preceding entries, thus forming an explanatory subsection of the interpretation of dreams.

93

Afterwards I fell asleep, and I beheld one of my acquaintances sitting at a table. He greeted me, which I did not notice at once; and before I returned his greeting, he became angry and spoke to me harshly. I wanted to excuse myself and finally thought of saying that I am often in deep thoughts and do not observe when anyone greets me, that at times I can pass my friends in the street without seeing them, and I asked an acquaintance there to testify to this, and he said Yes, and I said (and God grant this be true) that nobody wants to be more polite and humble than I do. Because of the preceding night, when I had been in other thoughts than I should, our Lord wanted to forgive me in this way. My friend did not reply, however, but seemed to be convinced, as I believe.

"During all this I was in the same company as before, and no one could notice the least change in me," he had written after his Easter vision. Yet he is distracted, or, at least in his dream he sees himself as being so. Contemporary eyewitnesses confirm his own assurance that he wanted nothing better than to be "polite and humble." "Pleasant and far from stubborn," according to his contemporary,

Count Carl Gustaf Tessin. "Not touchy or self-sufficient, but kind, polite, open-hearted; has a good judgment of times and people, makes the best construal of everything, and appears to be a philanthropist," the count further observed.

Experiences and reflections encircle a central set of opposites: God's grace and his own unworthiness, the joy from knowing that his sins are forgiven, and agony caused by remaining self-righteousness. He prays for a stronger faith, wishing "not to resist the spirit."

[April] 10–11

94

> I entered a lowly place, where there were many people, but I had eyes only for a friendly woman dressed in black, She walked far into a chamber, but I did not wish to follow her, although with her hand she beckoned me towards the door. Then I went out, and I found myself attacked many times by a clinging specter, which stuck to my back; finally, it disappeared.

Many aspects of this dream resemble his experiences of April 8–9, entry 83. A woman in black is tempting him, enticing him in vain. He immediately finds himself several times clutched from behind by a hideous ghost. This tribulation continues:

95

> I came out, and a sordid specter approached me, acting likewise, and there was a nasty old man; at long last, I got rid of them. These were my thoughts on the previous day: while indeed I regarded myself as completely unworthy and felt that I would not be able to endure like this for the rest of my life, still I trusted that God is mighty in everything and that his power will accomplish it. Nevertheless, there was still something within

me that prevented me from submitting to the grace of God as I should, letting him operate with me according to his wish.

The attractive woman in black goes into a bedroom—going "far into a chamber," he adds—and turning to Swedenborg, again wants him to come (compare entry 83), but he refrains from doing so. According to the encoded language of the dream diary, this means that a "love," an aim and direction of life, presents itself.

His hesitance and refusal are punished, and his lot is to dwell in the world of agony and affliction outside, which he knows he will not endure for long. Later in the diary, Swedenborg explains his reluctance by his longstanding selfishness: he simply could not let himself go and give himself up to the Divine. He knows that naive innocence is the sole condition, but he cannot restrain his wilfulness.

96

When I came out, I saw many people sitting in a gallery, and, lo!, a mighty torrent of water was pouring in through the roof, and it was so strong that it thrust itself through everything in its way. There were some who tried to close the opening so the water would not come in, others who tried to get away so it should not reach them, others again who tried to dissipate it into drops, and one who tried to divert it so it would pass outside the gallery. This, I believe, refers to the power of the Holy Spirit that flowed into the body and the thoughts, which in part I shut out and diverted and in part avoided, since the people signify my own thoughts and my own will.

As we saw in the notes from the preceding night, water symbolizes the Holy Spirit, and so it will continue in his theosophical writings. The dream of the crowded gallery or stand and the water pelting in from above illustrates his situation as a whole. The gallery is his outlook, the exalted seat in the stand from which he views the subjects in the middle below, as would a student in the anatomy classrooms of that time, at Uppsala University and elsewhere. Many people are there, surrounding him as in the chamber where he saw the woman in black.

Above the packed gallery, water is flooding in. The people present, which he interprets as his thoughts and his will, protect themselves in various ways, fighting or fleeing. The waters are, to quote
Bishop Swedberg, "the rain of Grace," the compelling divine love.
His son, however, tries to escape it. As in the dream of the beck-
oning woman, he declines.

97

**Finally, I got out of there; and in my thoughts, I began as it
were to measure and divide into parts that which proceeds from
the center to the circumference. It seemed to be heaven, for afterward there was a heavenly shining light. I may indeed consider this, but I dare not yet regard it as certain, for it refers to
something that is to take place.**

Swedenborg's dream continues. He leaves the anatomy lesson,
giving way to a wider scope and a heavenly perspective. The
image of the inflowing power lingering in his mind, he relates it
to his future task. He perceives, as yet intellectually, that divine
love emanates from the center of all things; and as a sign, he experiences a strange illumination. Perhaps he has been given the
task of studying this instead, to describe and analyze the anatomy
of this universal love, examine distances and susceptibility. However, he dismisses this big question, since he thinks it is too soon
to consider it.

98

**While I was in the first assault of evil temptations, I cried to
Jesus for help, and it went away; I also kept my hands folded
under my head, and then it did not return a second time. I was,
nevertheless, in tremors when I awoke, and now and then I
heard a dull sound, but I do not know where it came from.**

99

**Afterwards, when I was awake, I began to consider if this might
not be sheer fantasy. Then I realized that my faith was faltering,**

and I prayed with clasped hands that I might be strengthened in my faith, which also happened at once. I also fell into thoughts about my being more worthy than others; but I prayed in a similar manner, and then these ideas vanished at once. So, when our Lord withdraws his hand, even in the least manner, from somebody, that person is out of the right path and out of the faith itself, as has been the case with me, who so manifestly has experienced this.

The moment Swedenborg prays for help, the ghastly vision evaporates, the moods of conceit are quelled, and doubts vanish. Again, during his Easter vision, he is overtaken by shivering and fancies, and he hears a dull sound of thunder.

Finally awake, his thoughts come down to earth. His faith falters, and he is tempted by moods of transcendency and self-sufficiency. Once again he realizes—underscoring this as he has many times before—that all must be submitted to the Divine, an insight which, from theory to practice, has a long way to go.

100

This night I slept about eleven hours; and during the whole of the morning, I was in my usual state of internal joy, and yet there was a certain pang along with it, which I supposed came from the power of the Spirit and from my own unworthiness. After a while, and by the assistance of God, I came into thoughts such as these: that a person ought to be content in all that the Lord pleases to do, because it is of the Lord, and that he should not resist the Spirit when he receives from God the assurance that it is the Grace of God, which leads everything for our best. For since we are his, we must be content in what he pleases to do with that which is his own. Still, one should pray for this to our Lord, for it is not in the least in our own power.

We have already seen an entry (45) where Swedenborg tells us that he has spent some twelve or thirteen hours in bed. Here he says that he has slept for eleven hours. There will be more entries of that sort.

Perhaps the explanation of his unusual need for sleep is the exhausting intensity of his emotional life, his violent oscillations between joy and despair. It is hardly surprising, he records in entry 102, that he is faint with exhaustion (in Swedish *matt* or *utmattad*) in body and mind, sometimes ready to drop in fatigue. On the other hand, he is also perhaps consciously trying to prolong the hypnagogic states that precede and follow ordinary deep sleep—the state in which mystics of all times mainly seem to have had their visions. As we have already observed in entry 52, Swedenborg emphasizes the frequency of his revelations (*uppenbarelser*) in this state. His prolonged sleep, or anyway his lying in bed, seems to have become a habit that continued after his crisis was passed. According to contemporary witness reports, he always seems to have been concerned to get home early in the evenings. Considering that one's need for sleep normally decreases with increasing age, this peculiar trait may partly be due to his readiness for and susceptibility to visions and revelations, which taxed his powers and certainly also presupposed an abundance of time for REM-sleep.

His usual state of mind, as he will assure us later in his diary too, is one of inward joy, *jucunditas interna*. At the same time, Swedenborg also suffers from agony. As in entry 89, his torment stems from the conflict between grace and his own sinfulness. At the moment of writing this down, he thinks that his transgression is his reluctance to accede to a love, the existence and universal power of which he is convinced of. To use his later term, he cannot give up "his own," his *amour propre*, or love of self. In his later works, this Latin concept, *proprium*, will become a key word and be seen as the major obstacle to divine influence in each individual, where it is opposed to all higher wisdom.

In *The Apocalypse Explained* §318, Swedenborg put it this way:

> For what constitutes one's own man (proprium) is nothing but evil and falsity: self-will (proprium ejus voluntarium) is sinister, and comprehension from self-interest (proprium ejus intellectuale) is fraudulent. . . . Unless an individual is elevated from his ipseity (a sua propria) by the Lord . . . it is utterly difficult for him to be wise and sensible.

For the one who has become conscious of God, as has the author of the dream diary, "our evil nature," *vår arga natur*, is the source of agony. Let alone being aware of this state of affairs, he cannot do anything about it but give himself up and trust the Lord. The weak human can only pray for this confidence.

101

He then gave me his grace to this end. I then began turning it over a bit and wanted to understand why this happens, which was a trespass. The thoughts should not go in that direction, but I must pray to our Lord for power to control them. It is enough that it is as he pleases. Throughout we ought to call upon him, pray to him, give thanks to him, and in humility acknowledge our unworthiness.

102

I am still weak in body and thoughts, for there is nothing that I know except that I am a wretched creature, good for nothing, which torments me; and from this, I really see how unworthy I am of the grace I have received.

In this state of dejection, Swedenborg finds it a transgression even to try to understand the heavenly meaning of such agony. Weary in body and thoughts, he simply resigns himself to his fate. Swedenborg's universal scientific knowledge has at this moment been reduced to a vague insight into divine grace and into his own complete worthlessness and earth-bound nature, which disgusts him. St. Paul's famous words about "sighs" are not distant.

103

I also observed that the down-pouring current pierced the garments of a person who had been sitting there, just at the moment he was getting out of the way. Perhaps there had fallen upon me a drop, which is penetrating so hard. What, then, would have happened if the whole stream had fallen upon me? I therefore took this for my

SYMBOLUM:
God's will be done, I am Thine and not mine. [crossed out]
This is all by the grace of God, it is not mine.

This entry, too, shows some sign of exhaustion. Clearly, the allusion is to the passage about the gallery where water from heaven had been pouring in. Perhaps a few iridescent drops have fallen on his clothes and passed through the cloth. What would have happened if he had been hit by the waterfall? Many years before, he had pondered upon a similar question in his *Rational Psychology*:

> *If the loves of the Animus [mind] had wholly submitted themselves to the loves of the Anima [soul], there would have been no combat, and the human being would live supremely blessed; blessed namely, as he once had been in his first age, the Golden Age, his infancy. In that case, however, there would not have been any intellect that must be formed and instructed by the senses and the affections of the Animus, and which, in order to be free, must know what Good is, and what Evil is, which it would not know if all things proceeded in their due order. The several passions, therefore, are so many heats and inciters of the corporeal life, and they are all allowed us, if only they are of service and are called into use with moderation.*

Swedenborg certainly perceives the errors necessarily inherent in his thought. His *symbolum*, his motto, is a wording of surrender. Still, apparently finding his first line—"God's will be done, I am Thine and not mine"—rather presumptuous, he immediately crosses it out. To decide whether he is prepared to subordinate himself to the Divine and to let divine will be done does not lie within his own power. In his next sentence, he is even more self-abnegating: there is nothing but the great mercy.

104

I found that one can be in anguish spiritually, even though one is assured of absolution by the Spirit and harbors the hope and

confidence of being in the grace of God. This appears to . . .
[The last two words are crossed out]

Here he is describing a lasting predicament: a dichotomy of mind.
One moment, he feels secure in the "the spiritual" or in his "internal
man" (entry 133). While dwelling there appeased, he can smile at
his afflictions, and he can even afford to greet or shoo away his old
thoughts at his pleasure. At other moments, he is sunk into the acid
test of agony, yet always safely clinging to a higher grace.

The following entry consists of five numbered dreams, supplemented by two explanatory notes. The dreams are about the omnipotence of sin: how hard it is to hold one's own against sin and
how difficult it is to distinguish between good and evil.

[April] 11–12

105

Was all night in a dream: I can recollect only a little, it was as if
I was being instructed the whole night on various subjects, of
which I cannot recall anything. I was asleep for nearly eleven
hours. As far as I remember, something was mentioned of (1)
substantial or essential things, which one should seriously search
for; and of (2) thymus and glandula renalis, from which I conclude: just as thymus sorts out the impure serum of the blood
and glandula renalis remit into the blood that which has been purified, something similar might go on within us spiritually.

When writing down these experiences in the morning, Swedenborg first notes that he thinks he has heard the word *substantialia* or
essentialia uttered, that is, the innermost or matters relating to being
itself; and this is what he should now turn his attention to and diligently study. From his earlier diary jottings, we can figure the substantial as that great center from which divine love winds out in

spiral form. In entry 97, he had asked if his task might not be to explore the nature of that power and, in a profound sense, divide and define what that transcendent center emits.

His thoughts under the second head are allied to one of the diary's central problems: how can we, in our thoughts and actions, rightly distinguish between good and evil? Later, in his October entries, the question will recur in the form of "distinguishing between the spirits," then concerning the worship of God.

The entire mode of reasoning is typical. Swedenborg hears the words "thymus and glandula renalis" (Latin in the Swedish original), i.e., the thyroid and renal glands. In his contemporaneous work *The Animal Kingdom*, he wrote about these organs and their purificatory functions. Now the soul mirrors the body. Spiritual purification occurs when reason, turning to God, permits the soul's lucidity to govern the intellect. *The Animal Kingdom* §293 treats of this "correspondence:"

> As the blood is continually making its circle of life; that is to say, is in a constant revolution of birth and death; as it dies in its old age and is regenerated or born anew; and as the veins solicitously gather together the whole of its corporeal part, and the lymphatics of its spiritual part; and successively bring it back, reflect it with new chyle, and restore it to the pure and youthful blood; and as the kidneys constantly purge it of impurities, and restore its pure parts to the blood; — so likewise Man, who lives at once in body and spirit while he lives in the blood, must undergo the same fortunes generally, and in the progress of his regeneration must daily do the like. Such a perpetual symbolical representation is there of spiritual life in corporeal life; as likewise a perpetual typical representation of the soul in the body. In this consists THE SEARCHING OF THE HEART AND REINS, which is a thing purely divine.

106
_____

(3) My sister Caisa was seen; let herself get hurt and lay down and shouted; but when our mother showed up, she put on

another face and talk: the interpretation of this will be given in the following.

107

(4) There was a minister, who preached to a large congregation, and, at the end, he spoke against another. If that person was mentioned by name, I do not know; but somebody arose and rebuked the preacher, saying that such a thing may not be. I was afterwards with them in private company; and on inquiring, it was then told that the punishment for libeling anyone is three Swedish marks. He did not seem to know that this was that criminal; but it was said that the fine begins with one mark, then two marks, etc., which signifies that it is wrong to preach against anyone, or to talk or write likewise, this being a punishable offense since it is defamatory and calumnious.

These dream sequences, of his sister and the clergyman, are about dissemblance and spite. The first concerns a childhood memory. His sister Caisa pretends to be hurt, screams, but quickly changes her attitude when her mother enters the room. The little girl is putting on a show. Thus, the sin of dissimulation or mendacity is observable even in small children. The priest is celebrating divine service in church and preaching against someone, whom we do not know. This priest says he is ignorant of the fact that, in doing so, he is breaking a law. But the implication is that, even when one believes one is acting in a manner pleasing to God and preaching Christianity, evil enters the scene, in this case in the shape of libel.

108

(5) Afterwards, my knees moved by themselves, which might indicate that I have been somewhat humbled, which, by the grace of God, is actually the case, and I thank him very sincerely for this.

Being the prey of evil, we can only pray in a humble spirit for grace. Not before a purified state of mind is attained can we get in touch with the essential, Being itself.

109

Subsequently, I found within myself, and perhaps also from the third point in the dream, that in every thought, yes, even in those we believe to be pure, there is concealed an endless quantity of sin and impurity, as also in every desire that comes from the body into the thoughts, which spring from quite deep roots. Although the thoughts may appear pure, underneath there is nevertheless the fact that a person thinks thus from fear or hypocrisy, and many other causes, so that, on reflection, it is found that nobody can make himself so free from sin that there is not mixed into every thought much that is unclean or impure. It is therefore best to acknowledge every hour and moment that one deserves the punishment of hell and to trust that the grace and mercy of God, which are in Jesus Christ, overlook it.

We are born into sin because of Adam's desire for the horrible apple, Swedenborg observed the day after his epiphany. The Fall was to follow Swedenborg all his life, as sense of immanent wickedness he had almost imbibed with his mother's milk. His father, the bishop, preached about it; and on all Sundays, from his earliest years, the harsh confession of sin was mumbled by the congregation at church:

> *Like my fathers I have time and again sinned against Thy Commandments, both in thoughts and in deeds.*

The revivalism of the 1730s and 1740s, with its strong emphasis on personal unworthiness, can only have heightened this awareness. The Pietists in general were calling for a conversion in faith and deeds, preferably after a penitential struggle. For Zinzendorf, on the other hand, insight into one's own sinfulness sufficed: all depended on attaining the true and sincere "poor-sinful-creature" awareness. To the Moravians, sin is inveterate and ineradicable. We can only pray for mercy. More closely examined, mind and heart are wicked, pure thought is impure, and good intentions are mere hypocrisy.

110

Yes, I have also observed that our whole will, which we have inherited and which is ruled by the body and introduces thoughts into the mind, is opposed to the spirit. For this reason, there is a continual strife, and there is no way for us to unite ourselves with the spirit, which by grace is with us. And hence it is that we are, as it were, dead to all that is good, but to the evil we are ourselves. A person should, therefore, at all times account himself guilty of innumerable sins, for the Lord God knows everything, and we know only a little about those entering into our thoughts and are only aware of those that are implemented in action, and then we are persuaded.

It is also worth noting . . . [crossed out]

Thus, body and soul are in constant combat. Even worse, we are even unable to perceive our own sinfulness. Only when wicked ideas and impulses materialize in actual deeds and they are accomplished facts does their sinfulness stand out and grate on us. We had better plead guilty beforehand and conclusively avow and admit whatever trespasses we may commit, consciously or not.

Swedenborg had described this endless struggle with less heat in his *Rational Psychology* §369, treating the matter more distantly:

> *[I]t is the desires of the body that take on command. The love of the soul can vaguely be grasped but by simile, by comparing it to intelligible things. The soul cannot teach us, because it lacks words.*

In that account of the struggle between body and soul, Swedenborg allotted human reason, aided by lucidity from above, to stand as judge, to achieve a balance between our physical and spiritual selves, and to let the Divine flow into us. In his *Rational Psychology,* he had used the same simile of a balance as he used in entry 66 of the diary. But now, in his despondency, he seems for a moment to overlook this divinely inspired, yet free will.

In the epilogue to the second part of *The Animal Kingdom*, Sweden-borg summed up his theory of the importance of breathing to emotion and will. He means that inhalation is followed by sensory impressions that are transformed into thoughts and wishes and that, when we exhale, these impressions leave the body. Our lungs serve as a bellows, and our way of inhaling is crucial not only to our oxygen supply but also to our apparatus, both physical and psychological.

The sensual impress, which follows the stream of air, may be pleasant or unpleasant. Already before writing about this in *The Animal Kingdom*, he had outlined the importance of these sensations to the intellect in his *Rational Psychology*. When we find an impression attractive, we long for more; we entertain specific *amores*, loves, appertaining to our perceptions. We encountered this thought in dream entry 110, where it is stated that our will is ruled by the body, and there are other similar observations to the same effect.

It is these basic ideas, developed in his scientific works, that we find again in dream entry 111. He feels he is inspirited, undisturbed by sensory desires, which is confirmed by a shining spiritual text. Apparently, the illumination here referred to does not affect the actual state of affairs, however, only the conclusion that suddenly strikes him.

[April] 12–13

111

I noticed it to be a fact—as, indeed, I had been inspired to think during the day and as was also wonderfully represented to me by a kind of luminous writing—that the will has the greatest influence on the understanding. When we inhale, the thoughts fly into the body, and when we exhale, the thoughts are in a peculiar way expelled and rectified; so the very thoughts possess their alternations of activity like the respiration of the lungs. For the inspiration belongs to the will and the expiration to nature, so that the thoughts have their alternations in every turn of respiration because, when wicked thoughts entered, I only had to draw the breath, whereupon they ceased.

A point of consequence here is Swedenborg's observation on how he can free himself from distracting thoughts and improve his power of concentration by controlling his breath. He provides himself with a summary and conclusion in the next entry.

112

Hence, from this may also be seen the reason that, when in deep thought, the lungs are kept in a state of equilibrium and at rest, more according to nature, and that the inhalations are then faster than the expirations, when at other times the reverse is the case; and, furthermore, that a person in ecstasy holds the breath, the thoughts then being as it were absent. Likewise in sleep, when both the inhalation and the expiration are governed by nature, when that is represented which inflows from above. The same may also be deduced from the brain, that by the inhalation all the internal organs together with the brain itself are expanded, and that the thoughts thence have their origin and flux.

The experiences he describes here have in fact been familiar to him for long. According to the *Spiritual Diary*, he had already in his childhood learnt consciously to minimize his breathing at moments of profound contemplation. His theory of the influence of lung movements on mental activity he seems, as far I can see, to have first developed in *The Economy of the Animal Kingdom* II, §10, where it forms a part of the organic structure outlined:

> For as often as the brain has intent, and is thinking deeply, or is occupied by anxious cares of some kind, the lungs draw their breath tacitly and slowly, and the breast either rises to a fixed level, and fears by any deep breath to disturb the quiet of the brain, or else compresses itself, and admits only a small amount of air to pass. When the brain is exhilarated and joyous, the lungs expand and unfold. When the brain draws back with fear,

the lungs do the same. When the brain is disturbed by anger, breathing is likewise disturbed. And similarly is the case with all other affections, where analogous states are observed to be super-induced upon both, and sometimes without any perceptible change in the rhythm of the heart and in the arteries of the body.

There is a simple explanation as to why Swedenborg is so eager to describe his earlier observations. One of the diary's recurrent elements is his struggle with "ungovernable thoughts," his inability to concentrate and thus to remain "in the spirit." In his persistent awareness of the importance of breathing control, he can presumably find a much desired remedy. He makes comparisons with his experiences of ecstasy and hypnagogic states. There too, where concentration is a fact, inhalation is either reduced or even ceases completely.

Many others besides Swedenborg have drawn the practical conclusions that follow from these observations. Numerous mystics, Christian as well as non-Christian, have sought to approach the transcendental, the numinous, to the Godhead, by breathing control and a conscious screening of physical sensations. Then another kind of awareness is established, and normally hindered perceptions surface from the inward. Sometimes these perceptions conform with discursive human reasoning; sometimes they appear as irrational as real.

This particular concentration from now on becomes Swedenborg's method and theme. In his persistent and consequent attempt to get a clear view of the spiritual—which in reality has been going on for decades—we can perceive a strong-willed and purposeful mind searching for another consciousness and accordingly another kind of knowledge, which he is now about to explore.

113

Next I came to a place where there were wonderfully large and tall windmills going at a terrible speed. I then came into a darkness, so that I crept on the ground, being afraid that one of the sails would catch me, which would have been the end of me. I did come beneath a wing which then stopped, and brought

myself well within it, so that the wing helped me further. This meant that during the day I had been in conflict with my thoughts, which are signified by the wings of the mill, and that sometimes I did not know where I was going. Yet by the grace of God they were calmed, and I was helped onward safe and sound; wherefore glory and praise be to God, who overlooks my weakness.

Swedenborg's fight with the windmills reflects earlier unrest caused by roving free companies of Poles, hussars (see entry 64), and whatever stalkers or charmed marksmen moving about in the terrain he is now exploring. The brain worker, striving hard for acumen and lucidity, is at war with his unruly musings and associations. However, as mostly with Swedenborg, there is a happy end to the story. God interferes, the battle is settled, and the alarm is quieted in a reassuring way.

114

Afterwards it was as if I were in company with some people who appeared desirous to make gold, but they saw that they would have to climb upwards, which they were not able to do, and that otherwise it would be impossible to make gold. This continued for some time, until, after a while, I was together with two persons who insistently attempted the ascent; but our Lord was not with them. I said that this will not do and went up before them with a rope. I pulled but noticed that there was something beneath that pulled strongly against me. Finally, I saw that it was a man, but I was stronger and pulled him up; then I was glad and said that it was as I had said.

115

I think this refers to the gold that is the good, *aurum quod bonum est*, and well pleasing to God, which you can only gain by ascendance, and that this is impossible to do on one's own. When we administer all our strength in an attempt to achieve this, we become aware of an opposing force, but finally the attempt succeeds by the grace of God.

116

> Afterwards I remained for a long time in the same thought, which became increasingly luminously rosy; this light signifies that the grace of God is written within it and that the whole thing amounts to the importance of doing good, which we may faithfully achieve by the grace of God and which God may grant us to perform. This is to make gold, for then we receive from our Lord everything that is needed and useful. This was very powerfully illustrated, that what is good ought to be put into effect and that the gold consisted in this.

This time Swedenborg adopts some terms from the gold-makers, the alchemists, a reminder of the currency of their ideas. Naturally, the alchemy in question is transcendent and figurative, representing elevation, persistence, good deeds, and trust in God's help; and the outcome—gold—is that which is well pleasing to the Most High. In the diary, there are, in fact, several instances where Swedenborg, in his accounts of his own process of moral and spiritual purification, appears to draw his parallels from the alchemist's slow combustion and purification of matter in the Great Cauldron (see, for example, entry 136).

117

> When I eventually got up, I was in a great fear of our Lord, as in a cold that made me shiver at the least hint or thought of that which I was afraid of. It was the grace of God showing me that I must seek salvation in fear and trembling. And as I have my motto, THY WILL BE DONE, I AM THINE AND NOT MY OWN, and have given away myself to the Lord, may he accordingly do what he wants with me. In my body, there seemed to be some discontent; but, in the spirit, there was joy, for it is the grace of God that brings this about. God give me strength.

118

> I was continually in dissension with double thoughts, opposed to one another. I pray thee, O Almighty God, to grant me the grace to be thine and not my own! Forgive me if I have said that

I am thine and not mine; this is not for me to determine but falls to God. I pray for THE GRACE OF BEING PERMITTED TO BE THINE AND THAT I MAY NOT BE LEFT TO MYSELF.

The first lines of entry 117 appear to paraphrase Psalm 55:

> *My heart is in anguish within me:*
> *the terrors of death have fallen upon me.*
> *Fear and trembling come upon me,*
> *and horror overwhelms me.*

Swedenborg calls to mind his motto: "I am Thine and not mine." As in entry 105, he finds his promise presumptuous. Whom he belongs to does not depend on his own will.

Swedenborg is still tormented by the duality, too, although the wholesome breathing control and this inner divided loyalty will upset him for a very long time, well beyond the limits of dream diary. A few years later, he described this split state of mind in *Arcana Coelestia* §3696:

> *[A]t first [a human being in the process of regeneration] is in a state of tranquillity, but as he passes into a new life he also comes into a state of distress. For the evils and falsehood he has earlier acquired keep arising and intrude in his consciousness, and by and by they begin to trouble it in such a way that he is tempted by the devil's hosts, which incessantly try to upset the order of his new life. Nonetheless, his innermost being remains in a state of peace, and unless this stillness were within him, he would stop fighting.*

[April] 13–14

119
_____

It seemed that the grace of the spirit was operating with me all night. I saw my sister Hedvig, with whom I did not want to have anything to do. This signifies that I should not touch the

Economy of the Animal Kingdom but leave it. Afterwards, when time dragged, it seemed that she first said to her children, "Go out and read," and later on that they could play backgammon or cards, whereupon they sat down to do this as a pastime and then to have a meal too. I think this is meant to say that there is nothing wrong in this, when done in a proper way.

This is Swedenborg's first reference since his Easter vision to his scientific work. At the height of his crisis, it seems to have been so far from his thoughts that he apparently even refers to it, a bit absentmindedly, as the *Oeconomia Regni Animalis—The Economy of the Animal Kingdom—*a work already completed four years ago, instead of as *Regnum Animale, The Animal Kingdom.*

As we see, his formal reason for doing this is the dream he has had about his sister Hedvig, wife of Lars Benzelstierna, his colleague in the Board of Mines, a person by whom he, as we have seen, set little store. Wishing to have nothing to do with her either, he projects his rejection of Hedvig onto his science. He first interprets the dream as indicating that the current work should be abandoned. But then, impressed by the dream's continuation, he reconsiders the question. He sees his nephew and nieces playing cards and backgammon and, after a while, also having a meal at the table. His interpretation of the scene with the playing children is that, even if our occupations are deprived of deep meaning, they will be allowed. The implication is that he can go on with his scientific work at least for the time being.

120 _____

I lay with one who was not beautiful, but whom I liked. She had what others have, and there I touched her; but, in front, there seemed to be some set of teeth; it appeared to be Archenholtz [Arckenholtz] in a woman's shape. What this means I don't know, perhaps that I should not touch any woman or get deeply involved in politics or something like that.

Thus, we have a dream, as we see, on delicate matters, on forbidden love. In one English edition, the translator primly chose to render this passage in Latin, and even the author himself made a round-about in the wording of this private note. Johan Arckenholtz, who is mentioned in the dream, was a historian and Cap politician and a morose opponent of Sweden's alliance with France, urged by the Hats. Imprisoned for his opinions, Arckenholtz had been released in 1743, at the conclusion of peace with Russia. At the time this entry was written, he was on a journey abroad. Can the two men have met at The Hague?

In Swedenborg's dream, the man is transformed into a woman and an object of desire, yet not quite attractive. The toothed open-ing of the vagina prevents penetration or at least makes it im-mensely hazardous. In the moment of writing, Swedenborg cannot understand this dream. Is he to devote himself to politics, like Ar-ckenholtz? Or is the dream a warning against the wrong kind of love or commitment?

He can only sharpen his question. As we have already seen, he had almost certainly opposed the war against Russia. As early as 1734, he had warned, in writing, against such hostilities. On the other hand, the French alliance desired by the Hats had its risks too: no one knew whether in crisis the French would keep their promises. Sweden, therefore, had everything to gain from remain-ing neutral. If its economy were allowed to develop peacefully, Sweden could soon enough expect to get good compensation for its lost Baltic provinces. Swedenborg had most certainly advo-cated this policy on the eve of the Swedish attack on Russia, in 1741.

Thus, his ideas had been in line with Arckenholtz's, and the dream is a reminder of this fact. The dreamer knows very well that the career before him is not one of a political nature, that he is not to be a *mordant* politician, to use his own imagery in the entry. But the waking Swedenborg, who makes a note of this, seems quite be-wildered. As in so many other places in the diary, a dream's pur-port, or its real consequence, only transpires when linked up with preceding dream sequences. Here it is a question of something that he has earlier sympathized with, but with which he would not have intercourse—which brings us, once again, back to his questioned scientific work and his career.

121

I was all day in equivocal thoughts, which tried to destroy the spiritual by contemptuous abuse to the extent that I felt that the temptation was very strong. By the grace of the Spirit, I managed to focus my thoughts on a tree, then to the cross of Christ, and on to the Crucifixion; and as often as I did so, all other thoughts fell flat to the ground, as of by themselves.

122

I pushed this thought so far, that it seemed to me I was pressing down the tempter by means of the cross and driving him away; and then, after a while, I was free. Afterwards, I had to fix my thoughts upon it so intently that, whenever I let it slip out of my thoughts and internal vision, I fell into temptation-thoughts. Praise be unto God, who has given me this weapon! May God of his grace keep me in this, that I may always have my crucified Savior before my eyes. For I dared not look upon my Jesus, whom I have seen, because I am an unworthy sinner; but then I ought to fall upon my face. And it is Jesus who lifts me up to look upon him, and, therefore, I must look upon Jesus crucified.

We have here two entries about Swedenborg's state of mind during the day. In order to rid himself of his split state of mind and resolve the struggle between body and soul, he forces himself to concentrate on the Savior and the cross. His torment abates. In his struggle, we seem to hear echoes of the Stockholm Moravian revivalism and their Songs of Zion:

> Thus draw our heart and longing
> forever to abide with thee.
> Let our eyes behold thy passion,
> Thy Crucifixion see!

Forever thou now let us lie there
with our faces in the mud;
courageous watching, waiting, yearning
praying, thanking for thy blood

Thy pain may us console and strengthen
so let us share thy endless ending;
With thy dear wounds curing us
vigor, solace, brashness lending.

[April] 14–15

123 _____

It seemed as if I were racing down a stairway. I touched each step only a little and came safely down all the way without danger. There came a voice from my dear father, "You are making such an alarm, Emanuel!" He was said to be angry but would calm down. This means that I made use of the cross too boldly yesterday, but, by the grace of God, I passed through this out of danger.

The bishop had a secure and confident faith that rested deeply in the biblical word. Crises of the kind his son describes in his diary were probably foreign to his temperament. Swedenborg, who often had his father on his mind, was no doubt aware of this. Now Jesper Swedberg, living in the afterlife, obviously has witnessed his son's fall downwards, vividly gesticulating with the cross. This becomes too much for the father, who chimes in, reproaching his son for making such a racket.

However, that intervention has no soothing effect upon the son:

124 _____

I climbed a shelf and broke off the neck of a bottle, from which some thick fluid came forth and covered the floor and then flowed down. I believe [this signifies] that yesterday, by the

grace of God and not by my own power, a mass of evil was eradicated from my thoughts. I sat on that which has been written, which refers to that which I am still to do.

125

I heard a bear growling but did not see him. I dared not remain in the upper floor, for there was a carcass that he might scent. I therefore descended to one of the rooms of Dr. Mors[us], and shut the windows. This signifies temptation, as well as avarice, perhaps also other things, and that I am engrossed in my anatomical speculations.

The alarm is raised, and the noise becomes even stronger. In the middle of the roar lingers the crucial question of vocation. Swedenborg is at the crossroads but cannot remain there too long, since he is being chased. What kind of books is he going to write? He finds himself on one story, chased onward by a bear, which roars at him. Bears being attracted to the smell of decay, the dreamer dares not stay where he is. The stench of corruption can only be coming from his own sinfulness. Fleeing, he takes refuge in a room belonging to a certain Doctor Morsus, who might be identical with his cousin, Dr. Johan Moraeus, district medical officer in Dalecarlia, son of Bishop Swedberg's sister Barbro and father of Sara Elisabeth Moraeus, the wife of Carl von Linnaeus. He is moving in the rooms of his cousin, with whom he had at one time contested certain inheritances, attacked by temptations; by greed, perhaps; and "perhaps also other things" as well. That Moraeus should have appeared in his dream he thinks may be interpreted as signifying medicine. Anatomical speculations play an important role in his work *The Animal Kingdom*.

In the passage with the closed windows, signifying temptation, we meet yet another element in his dreams and visions. Image and thought hang remarkably closely together and possess a kind of inner logic of their own. In the diary, shut windows—we have already come across them in entry 3—are an image of temptation or of a demand that he abandon "experience"—empiricism and the analytical method—in favor of synthetic assessments and intuition.

126

> Dr. Morsus seemed to be courting a pretty girl. He obtained her
> consent and had opportunity to touch her wherever he wanted.
> I teased her, saying that she was quite willing to say Yes, etc.
> She was a pretty girl and swelled and became ever more beauti-
> ful. It meant that I have to inform myself on the subject of mus-
> cles and study these.

Dr. Moraeus is courting a girl who is willing in all respects. Swedenborg dreams of being mixed up and cuddling her too. At the moment of excitement when the blood is up, he is, typically enough for
his sphere of associations at this time, reminded of something he
ought to examine and write about. Probably this refers to the drafts
of his work *De sensu communi*, intended as part of the Animal Kingdom
series but which was posthumously published.

127

> I had a preternaturally good and long sleep for twelve hours.
> On awakening, I had before me Jesus crucified and his cross.
> The spiritual came upon me with all its heavenly, almost ecstatic
> life, and I was ascending so high and permitted to go higher and
> higher, that had I proceeded, I would have been dissolved by
> this veritable life of joy.

The long sleep is, as often, followed by this fruitful state of vision at
the moment of awakening. He is inspirited and faced by *vita coelesti
quasi exstatica*, he perceives a *vita gaudii* that is too much for a mortal,
and the author turns from Swedish to Latin in handling these terms.
This latter fact may be due to one of his father's favorite hymns, *In
dulci jubilo*, where *vita gaudia* is equaled to *coelorum gaudia*, the joy of
heaven. With a reference to the next verse, the bishop said that he
recited this hymn whenever he heard the church bell ringing:

> *UBI SUNT GAUDIA, in the Holy City,*
> *where angels sing NOVA CANTICA*
> *and the bells ring IN REGIS CURIA.*
> *Would we were there! Would we were there!*

128

> It then appeared to me in the spirit that I had gone too far; that in my thoughts I had embraced Christ on the cross, when I kissed his feet and that I then removed myself thence, falling upon my knees and praying before him crucified. It seemed that the sins of my weakness are forgiven as often as I do this. It occurred to me that I might have the same idol before the eyes of my body too, but I found that this would be far from right and, indeed, a great sin.

In this blissful state, Swedenborg knows he is going too far, and the idea of a crucifix merges with a sensualist Christology, which he feels is wrong. Once again, he is close to the Moravian cult of the cross and the blood.

In the following entries, Swedenborg observes the opposites prevailing inside him: science and theosophy, the sacred and the profane, guilt and forgiveness. The notes to entries 129–133 refer to the night between April 15 and 16, together with his interpretations. Later, probably on Friday, April 17, he has again been pondering the implications of these experiences. In entries 134 and 135, we find more detailed accounts.

[April] 15–16

129

> I seemed to be climbing a ladder from a great deep; after me followed other women, whom I knew. I stood still and willfully scared them, and then I went up. I reached green grounds and lay down; the others came after me. I saluted the women, and they lay down beside me. One was young and the other a little older. I kissed the hands of both and did not know which one of them I should make love to. It was my thoughts and my mental

work, being of two kinds, which finally came up with me, and which I regained and saluted and reclaimed.

Out of the depths arise the dreamer and women. By and by, only two seem to be left: one younger and one older. They lay down in the grass uphill, and he kisses their hands, not knowing to whom to turn.

The women are his thoughts and his *ouvrage d'esprit*, he writes, now switching to French for a moment. In entry 134, he deliberates a bit further: the women represent two roads, one being philosophy, which he of old prefers, the other being spiritual studies, which demand his attention. This question, which is the leitmotif of the diary, is answered in the final entries.

130

Afterwards, I came to a place where many men were assembled, a great crowd of handsome young folks in one place in a flock, others joining in, among them Henning Gyllenborg on horseback. I went to meet him, kissed him, and stood by him. It means that I have returned to the things of my memory and imagination and am once again greeting them; consequently, that I am returning to the upper and the lower faculties.

The consciousness of his sinfulness, so intense in his earlier entries, seems temporarily to have evaporated. In a lovely crowd, he sees the Hat politician Henning Gyllenborg in the saddle, the nephew of party leader Fredrik Gyllenborg, in whose circles Swedenborg moved on the periphery. The dreamer approaches him, kisses him, and joins the crowd. His first interpretation seems to link up with his final thoughts in entry 121. He sticks to his *res memoria*, the matters of memory, as well as to his *res imaginationis*, matters that appear to his inner eye. We may assume that he means the time has come for him to take at least a temporary farewell to staunch one-eyed empiricism and take on a more comprehensive, synthetic view. This he accordingly does in the before-mentioned prologue to the second part of *The Animal Kingdom*, referred to in his interpretation of March 25 above.

In entry 134. he modifies this generous interpretation. The purpose of the whole scene with Gyllenborg and the young people had quite simply been to remind him of how worldly his temperament still is and how inclined he is to boast of his own achievements.

131

> Afterwards I returned home and was in my own house, where I received many visitors. I knew that I had hidden away a pretty little woman and a boy and kept them hidden. There was, moreover, only a slight store of provisions, and I was not yet willing to bring out my table silver before I should treat them; nor was I willing to lead the guests into a magnificent inner chamber that was well furnished. This signifies that I have come home to myself again, that I have acquired the knowledge I have now written down here, and that, in time, I may make use of it and bring out the silver and show them all into the beautiful chamber.

Once more we are confronted with the theme of peaceful coexistence, or temporary settlement, between high and low, past and present, the inner and the outward. Of special value to Swedenborg is the hidden silver, a hidden treasure, as is the concealed magnificent chamber. The guests do not know of the woman and the boy, nor do they know about other precious things he is hiding.

The time has not yet come, he seems to think. Later, his secret knowledge will be revealed, the silver will be shown, and the door to the inner chamber will be opened.

132

> It seemed that I was accusing someone, but I do not remember how; in the end, however, I crossed out and excused something, because he himself had said so, but the words were buried. It signifies that I accused myself but excused myself because I had admitted everything.

133

It was said: *Nicolaiter,* and *Nicolaus Nicolai*—if this refers to
my new name, I do not know. The most remarkable fact was
that I now represented the internal man and was as another than
myself, as if I saluted my own thoughts, frightened them, my
res memoriae, and accused another one. So now there has been
a change: I represent the internal man, who is opposed to another person, for I have prayed to God that I may not be my
own, but that God may please to let me be his.
This has now been going on for twenty-one days.

The meaning of *Nicolaus Nicolai* will be discussed under the next
entry.

This is the *peripeteia* of the night's drama. Relinquishing his easy
compromise, Swedenborg now makes up his mind, choosing the
"internal man" and siding with him, dissociating himself from the
external. The women, Gyllenborg, the feast and the party, the ex-
culpation—now he sees all this at a distance, separate by far from
the sphere where he now is. Personifying his thoughts, he greets
his ideas from above, "scaring" them, accusing them. There will be
more such experiences.

The clarity of the dream must have struck him. Now he counts
the days: this has lasted for three weeks. Strengthened by the new
clarity, he revises the interpretation:

134

Later, I realized that most of this had another meaning: (1)
The two women signified that I would rather remain in philosophical studies than to be in spiritual ones, as rather showed
my inclination. (2) My kissing Henning Gyllenborg and seeing
so many people meant that I not only delighted in being in
worldly society but also wished to boast of my work. (3)
Nicolaus Nicolai was a philosopher who every year sent
bread to Augustus. First by this, I found it my duty to recon-
cile myself again to our Lord, because in spiritual things I am
a stinking carrion.

The first seems to refer to what he thought he heard in entry 133. "It was said: *Nicolaiter*, and *Nicolaus Nicolai*—if this refers to my new name, I do not know. " The interpretation he now accepts conforms to the idiom of the remainder of the diary.

Nicolaus Nicolai was a *philosophe*—in the original meaning of the term, a "lover of wisdom"—who used annually to send *panes*—bread—to Caesar Augustus, at first to pay off his debts; and this is the symbol of debt Swedenborg now realizes.

To Swedenborg the dreamer, monarchs are symbols of the sovereign, and so it is with this Roman emperor. The notion of debts and their repayment is another of the diary's recurrent themes (see entries 63 and 186) and synonymous with his scientific working method, based on reporting facts, being a large-scale statement of account. The predicament of his dream philosopher is his own. Shall he not pay his due to the emperor?

Swedenborg contrasts his working sphere, belonging to the world of the senses, with another, that of spiritual matters. But to pursue that research, he must first be reconciled with the Lord. His worldly activities make him resemble a nauseous corpse—the same as he feared that the bear could smell in entry 125.

Looking ahead on his future writings, we can also intuit the presence here of a biblical figure, the leader of "the Nicolaitans" in the Book of Revelation. In the second chapter of that book, we learn that their deeds were hateful. In *The Apocalypse Explained*, Swedenborg tells us why: they belonged to the solifidean fanatics of faith: "Those who separate charity from faith are called 'Nicolaitans' chiefly from the sound of that word in heaven, for its sound is from truth or faith, and not from good or charity."

135 _____

For this reason, I went to the Envoy Preis; and on my account, he called upon Pastor Pombo [Pambo], that I might again receive the Lord's Supper, which I was also granted. I met him at the envoy's house and went in with him. This was the providence of our Lord. I dined the same day with Envoy Preis, but had no appetite.

Swedenborg seems to have been a reserved personality, in the sense of rarely or never talking about his deeper personal problems; never, as far as I know, did he discuss his worries or anxieties with anyone. In view of this, the present episode is unique. Suffering from acute anxiety, Swedenborg goes to an old acquaintance at The Hague, the seventy-eight-year-old Swedish envoy Preis, who, obviously alarmed by his guest, drives in his carriage to Pastor Pambo and brings the clergyman back to his official residence, where Swedenborg is waiting for them and receives Holy Communion. This was indeed God's providence, he notes in his diary.

Earlier, I discussed the identity of "Pastor Pombo," who was probably a follower of Zinzendorf's doctrines. In the *Spiritual Diary* which Swedenborg started writing a few years afterward, he was seized by misgivings and wrote of seeing "a clergyman at The Hague" who believed in the doctrine of salvation through faith alone. That clergyman, a true Nicolaitan to be sure, then appeared to him in the guise of a dragon.

Can this have been Envoy Preis' clerical acquaintance seen in another light? According to the archives of the Evangelical Lutheran churches, the pastor of this German-speaking congregation was Johann Gottlieb Pambo, and we also know from the records that Envoy Preis had been chairman of a commission mediating a dispute between Pambo and another clergyman of that congregation.

[April] 17–18

136

I had horrifying dreams. I dreamt that the executioner roasted the heads he had cut off; and for a long time, he put the roasted heads one after another into an empty oven, which nevertheless was never filled. It was said that this was his food. He was a big female. He laughed and had a little girl with him.

137

Afterwards I dreamt that the Evil One carried me into various depths and tied me up. I do not remember all of it. Pinioned, I was thrown about in hell, everywhere.

As we have already seen, his nightmares display features reminiscent of alchemist symbolism, as applied during the seventeenth and eighteenth centuries to the human purification process. One's head, or thinking, must be purged in heat, really be "cleansed" as Swedenborg writes on this purgation of the head in entry 282. This clearing is a process that never ceases and is part of "The Great Work."

Who is this androgynous headsman? Is it Swedenborg himself? In alchemist literature, hermaphroditism is an image of wholeness, rebirth. In Swedenborg's mineralogical library, there were several alchemist works; in this context, one should bear in mind that, in the Age of Reason, alchemy was not abandoned. The dreamer must have been aware of that sphere of imagination, where biological bisexuality was a metaphor of atonement and fulfillment.

And what of the child, then? "We should be like children," he writes the next day, in entry 152. And he concludes, "Much of what I have seen agrees with this, and perhaps even that so many heads were roasted and thrown into the oven and that it was the food of the Evil One."

Most dreams either reveal or hint at a dichotomy: analysis-synthesis, purity-impurity, joy-torment, alienation-access, etc.; so it is here. The scene is infernal, yet the executioner has a little girl with him. Further in the diary, in entry 232, we shall meet this girl again, as an image of the right path. By constantly presenting and representing these dichotomies, Swedenborg reveals his own optimism and conviction of the possibility of choosing, of the existence of free choice. This is going to form the basis of his eschatology as well as of his doctrines of life.

138

On how a great procession was arranged, from which I was excluded, and that I should have got out of there. Still, I labored to get there and sat down; but they advised me to go away, and I went. Nevertheless, I found another place where I could watch everything, but the procession had not yet arrived.

In entry 29, Swedenborg seemed to witness a "procession of men," which was "magnificent." He seems to have interpreted it as a symbol for his own works, based on experience "which is now in full bloom." The procession recurs, but this time the dreamer finds himself ousted, his admittance refused. However, he has access to another place, from where he can view the procession when it passes by.

The import is quite clear. Swedenborg, the empiricist who believed it possible—or at least compelling—to seek for the human soul by collecting data from scientific observations made by means of autopsy, probe, and microscope, had to change methods. His plans for a long series of volumes on the animal kingdom had to be relinquished. He turns to another field, theology. He is going to view the scenery from another outpost, from another angle.

In September, the procession turns up again (entry 229), cast in the image of "beautiful horses, beautiful teams." This occurs at a moment when he feels his investigations are making progress. Horse sense is advancing in four-in-hands.

Entries 139 and 140 are a new reminder of his labile and highly strung state of mind. Perhaps his unnaturally prolonged periods of sleep, going on for half a year, are due to mere exhaustion and are part of the purification process.

139

I am certain, however, that God grants grace and pity to all poor sinners who are willing to be converted and who are willing in steadfast faith to take refuge in his inconceivable mercy and in the merit of the Savior Jesus Christ. I therefore assure myself of his grace and leave myself in his protection, because I firmly believe that I have received forgiveness for my sins. This is my consolation and may God confirm it for the sake of Jesus Christ.

140

I was this day by turns in interior anxiety and sometimes in despair; nevertheless, I was assured of the forgiveness of my sins.

Thus, at intervals, a heavy perspiration broke out upon me until 10 o'clock, when, with the help of God, I fell asleep. Then it seemed to me it was said that something will be given from within. I slept for an hour and a half, although, during the night, I had slept for more than ten hours. By the grace of God, I have had a preternatural sleep and this for an entire half year.

This long entry is introduced by a series of dreams with partly different themes. The main part, entries 148–153, consists of reflections addressing the problem of faith and knowledge.

[April] 18–19

141

It seemed to me that we were laboring for a long time to bring in a casket, in which were kept precious things, and this for a long time, as at Troy. Finally, they went below it and scraped it off; afterward, it was carried in as if in triumph, and they kept on sawing and sawing. It signifies how we must labor to gain heaven.

The casket with the precious things is surrounded and beleaguered, as was Troy. Finally, they set in from the underside, filing and planing it down; and the treasure is triumphantly carried in, while they keep sawing, endlessly.

The strange picture presumably represents the highest good, the heaven he is looking for. Swedenborg's search has been going on as long as the siege of Troy: for ten years.

142

It seemed I had a plain watch with me, although at home I had precious ones that I would not exchange for gold watches. This implies that I will obtain sound and noble knowledge, on which I may use my time.

Once more Swedenborg feels he is likely to attain proficiency of an exalted art. The watches symbolize learning. At the moment, he is carrying a simple item—*The Animal Kingdom.* "At home," he has something better in store.

143

> It seemed to me I was being girded down below in folds of blankets, which were wound around in various ways, and at the same time there came as it were . . . . This signifies that I am being continually protected, so as to remain with the right aim.

His loins are girded up in biblical fashion, the loincloth's being fastened with a girdle or belt around the thighs—as in St. Paul's Epistle to the Ephesians: "Stand now having your loins girt about with truth." Swedenborg's girdle consists of pleated coverlets, *stratis lamellatis.* Is it also a coat of mail? The chief thing is that he is "continually protected," that he is going in the right direction and has chosen "the right aim."

144

> There was a dog following me; he was quite well-mannered and of dark brown color. He rose up when any animal approached; when near water, he went into it to explore its depth. Perhaps this refers to the dog of Tobias.

The good-natured dog is of another breed than those who appear elsewhere in the diary. Is it Tobias' dog? The pious hero of the Apocrypha's Book of Tobit, Tobias, sets out on a long journey, guided by a person hired for the purpose, the archangel Raphael in disguise. Tobias is also accompanied by his faithful dog, who keeps running on ahead. Here we probably meet a first variation on the theme of the two factors that guide the true Christian: *amor* and *caritas,* love and charity. It will be alluded to in a later entry and achieve its final form in the diary's closing passages about the worship and love of God. A Christian is guided and governed by his love "on his side," its universal support being "ahead" of him (entry 278).

145

I saw a strange animal in a window; but it was quick and was also of dark-brown color, and it dashed in through another window. It had something on its back, which was rubbed off and turned into a handkerchief. I looked for the animal and could still see it a little but could not show it to anybody else. There was an apothecary inside. I asked if I should shoot the animal. This might signify that I am going to be instructed as to what may serve for improvement, etc.

146

Afterwards, it seemed as if it would be shown to me that I should be told or given to understand when I would be in danger of going astray.

In Swedenborgian emblematics, windows are openings of the vast sensory world. Here some strange creature appears, whose movements are swift. It slips from one opening to another, rubbing its back as it does so. A piece of skin remains, the size of a handkerchief.

The squirrel-like animal, quick as a flash, may be the dreamer himself. His experience seems to imply yet another disapproval of his scientific endeavors: his outlook and prospects so far have not yielded greater results than a piece of skin off his own back. He sees himself from above, seeking repentance. Yet the animal within him hinders him from seeing another path, another shape. With reference to later entries, we may guess that he has in mind a higher, divine knowledge. Once again, it is a question of sticking to the right purpose. The image of the pharmacy is Moravian, as the Songs of Zion proclaim, "Sanguineous is the dispensary of Soul."

147

I saw König and Prof. Winbom approaching, meaning that I was going to live with them: on weekdays with those who are not Christians, for König was said not to be a Christian; Winbom approaching means Sundays.

In the fifth and last dream, the thought of a "both/and" recurs. In Swedenborg's view, Johan Fredrik König, the Swedish consular agent at Hamburg, appears not to be a Godfearing person, whereas Professor Anders Winbom, a theologian at Uppsala, undeniably is a churchman. In Swedenborg's life, the children of this world have a place, as do the children of God.

After this follows the diary's deepest penetration of the problem of faith and knowledge:

148

This day too I have been somewhat unruly in my mind, because involuntarily the thoughts flew for and against, and I could not control them. I went to divine worship and found that the thoughts in matters of faith, respecting Christ, his merit, and the like, even though they be favorable and confirmatory, nevertheless cause unrest and allow contrary thoughts to come in, which cannot be kept out when a man desires to believe from his own understanding, and not from the grace of the Lord.

149

At last, it was granted me by the grace of the Spirit to receive faith without reasoning, a real assurance of it. Then, I saw my own confirmatory thoughts as it were beneath me and smiled at them in my mind, and still more at those thoughts that offended and opposed them. Faith then appeared to me far above the reach of reason. Then at last did I receive peace. May God strengthen me in this, for it is his work, and mine so much the less since my own thoughts—even the best of them—destroy more than they promote it. We may verily smile at ourselves when we argue against faith, as well as when we desire to confirm the faith with reason. It is therefore something higher—I know not whether it be the highest—when a person receives the grace no longer to mix up his own understanding with matters of faith.

150

It seems, however, that our Lord in the case of certain persons permits assurance to precede that which concerns the understanding. Blessed are those who believe and yet do not understand; concerning them I have written clearly in the prologue, numbers 21 and 22; yet, by myself, I could not have recalled this or discovered it, but it was the grace of God that brought this about without my being aware of it, which I afterwards found from the very effect and the change in my whole interior being. It is therefore the grace and the work of God, to whom be everlasting glory.

151

From this, I see how difficult it is for the learned—more, indeed, than for the unlearned—to attain such faith and thus to overcome themselves and be able to smile at themselves, for the adoration of one's own understanding must first be abolished and thrown down; and this is the work of God and not of man. It is, moreover, the work of God to keep a person in such a state. Accordingly, this faith becomes distinguished from our understanding and is superior to it.

152

This is pure faith [*pura fides*]; the rest is impure as far as it blends with our own understanding: we must make our understanding captive to the obedience of faith. We should believe because it has been said by him who is God over all, the Truth itself. This is perhaps what is meant by the teaching that we should be like children. Much of what I have seen agrees with this, and perhaps even that so many heads were roasted and thrown into the oven and that it was the food of the Evil One.

153

That confirmations becloud the faith may also be seen from the fact that the understanding never reaches further than

probabilities, in which there is always a trial of stronger or weaker arguments. For that reason, confirmations from private inquiry are always subject to doubt, which darkens the light of faith. This faith, therefore, is purely the gift of God, which an individual receives if he lives according to the commandments of God and diligently prays to God for it.

These six entries, numbers 148–153, are variations on the same theme: faith must be separated from knowledge, and blessedness is the reward of the one who has learned to distinguish between them. Two separate spheres of knowledge are in question. The one is a gift from above; the other is based on sensory perception.

Many early Enlightenment scientists appear to have maintained that science and theology are two sides of the same thing. Greater knowledge of nature yielded greater knowledge of God. Linnaeus, a relative of Swedenborg, seems to have been an enthusiastic proponent of this point of view, as were also his "household gods," the physicians Swammerdam and Boerhaave. Their scientific field of research was in reality—to employ a term from the philosopher Christian Wolff, another cherished authority—a *physico-theology*, a "natural theology."

Indeed, for a very long time, Swedenborg had thought that progress in knowledge meant distancing oneself from divine truths. Some time between 1736 and 1740, he noted down a few reflections on this subject on a manuscript cover:

> *The more the world is perfected in the sciences and in learning, the more it is estranged from God. . . . We ought not to inquire into the arcana of his nature in order thereby to acquire an intellectual faith. . . . The Lord demands an ignorance of things, full of faith and his praise . . . wherefore also he addressed himself to fishermen and shepherds; because the rest could not understand anything of the kind. . . . That philosophy and its departments and the physical sciences seduce us is clear, because they can extend only to visible and intellectual things and cannot penetrate to higher things, which they regard as paradoxical.*

This thought is repeated in the sections of *The Animal Kingdom* referred to in journal entry 150. When he had conceived that work, however, Swedenborg thought he might convert lukewarm believers by scientific means. The purpose of *The Animal Kingdom*, "that which drives and leads me," he maintains in his introduction, is to get skeptics to believe with the aid of "truths demonstrated by the scientific method" and disperse the "humiliating shadows or clouds which darken the holy temple of reason: so that in the end, with the help of God, who is wisdom's sun, an opening will appear, and a road to faith be opened up." Now, however, Swedenborg abandons this plan. The two worlds are wholly distinct and must not be confused.

The question of faith and knowledge would later appear to Swedenborg in another light. He was convinced that his own divinely inspired interpretation of Scripture revealed the spiritual meaning as distinct from the literal meaning of its texts and, furthermore, as concordant with human reason. *"Nunc licet,"* "now it is permitted," he was to observe and proclaim in his late work *True Christian Religion* (1771) "intellectually to penetrate into the glory of faith." In 1744, however, that insight was still far beyond his reach.

The sharp distinction drawn between faith and science the previous day seems to have lent him fresh confidence, an almost euphoric fighting spirit we have not seen before in the diary. With the exception of the following entry 154, all entries under the date of April 19–20 are colored by this new confidence.

[April] 19–20

154

I experienced a totally different kind of sleep. I dreamt a great deal, after which shivers came upon me; but I could not recollect anything, for, each time I tried, it escaped me.

155

I held my hands clasped; and, when I awoke, it seemed to me that they were pressed together by a hand or a finger; which by the help of God signifies that our Lord has heard my prayers.

156

Afterwards in a vision, which was neither one of sleep nor wakefulness nor ecstasy, it occurred to me that King Charles had fought in vain the first time and that, afterwards in his second battle with the Saxons, he had won and was covered with blood. And afterwards I dreamt that the muses [*Camaenae*] were victorious too, which signifies that, by the grace of God, I have gained the battle and that the blood and merit of Jesus have helped me and that, in my studies, I shall gain my object.

Swedenborg's exaltation is as grand as ever. He feels that his hands are being pressed together and takes it as a sign that God listens to his prayers.

The vision described in entry 156 primarily draws on three circumstances. At first, Charles XII had been defeated; but, in a second battle, he has been victorious, "covered with blood." After that, victory was gained with the help of the nine muses.

As usual in the dream diary, King Charles is a symbol of God. The defeat and adjacent victory in his combats against August the Stronger and his Saxon army symbolize the Passion and final victory of Christ, when "he shed his precious blood," to quote one of Bishop Swedberg's hymns. This victory has afterwards been represented and glorified by the arts of the muses. All in all, this says to Swedenborg that Christ's blood and merit support him in his struggle, a struggle that now also involves his studies and his writing.

The phrasing regarding the nine muses echoes the concluding words of the prologue to *The Animal* Kingdom [§23], where Swedenborg emphasizes, in a strikingly jubilant note, that the wealth of humanity and the glory of God are the aim and lodestar of all striving: "Let us then gird up our loins for the work. Experience is at our side with a full horn of plenty. The nine virgins are present also, adorned with the riches of nearly two thousand years: I mean, all the sciences, by whose abundance, powers, and patronage the work is constructed."

This juxtaposition of divinities, of myth and religion, recurs even in the diary's last entry. Swedenborg sees himself as a servant of the muses, a *famulus* of the Virgins of Wisdom. To those who love them, and who love God, they reveal their secrets.

157

I now arose as a whole God: God be thanked and praised! I do not wish to be my own, I am certain and do believe that thou, oh God, wilt let me be thine in all the days of my life and wilt not take away from me thy Holy Spirit, which strengthens and upholds me.

158

This day I was in the most severe temptation, so that, when I thought of Jesus Christ, there came at once ungodly thoughts, which I thought were not my fault. I beat myself, but I can confess that I was never of better courage than this day and was not in the least downhearted or pained as on previous days, although the temptation was most severe. The reason is that our Lord has given me the firm faith and confidence that he will help me for the sake of Jesus Christ and on account of his promise, so that I then experienced the workings of such a faith.

159

My heart was indeed such that I was so angry with Satan that I wanted to fight with him with the weapons of faith. From this may be perceived the efficacy of the right kind of faith without reasoning or confirming by means of one's own reasons, but it is the grace of God alone. If this temptation had taken place previously, I would have become altogether downhearted. Yet I was afraid that I had offended our Lord by forcing him as it were to set me free, on account of which I asked his forgiveness

with all the humility of which I was able. This probably signifies Charles XII who was covered with blood.

The first sentence in entry 157, "I now arose as a whole God," is a bit ambiguous or contains a slip of pen. Apparently, Swedenborg wakes up in a godly mood, "with God," and is ready to take his courage in both hands. Again, we read his *symbolum* or motto, albeit this time with an addition as humble as it is confident: "I am certain and do believe that thou, oh God, wilt let me be thine." All day he is in "the most severe temptation." His new insight into unreasoning faith gives his fight with evil an almost sanguine and positive character. In entry 159, Swedenborg suggests that he may have gone too far in his parallel between the bloodstained Charles XII and the crucified Christ, "on account of which I asked his forgiveness with all the humility of which I was able." Thus, the dreamer is the one who has wounded the Savior. As soon as he forgets the necessity of unconditional surrender, it becomes evident that his own human nature once devoured Adam's pernicious apple of sin, and the evil heritage surfaces.

The notes taken down from the night of April 21–22 contain something of particular weight, and the last paragraph is of special importance. Here Swedenborg for the first time puts his idea of justification by deeds into words, a dictum basic to his later theology. This unconditional demand for *praxis* will be a constant theme.

The first sections deal with straying and erring, a failing control of thought.

[April] 21–22

160

It seemed to me that I was lost in the darkness and had not gone out in company with others. I groped for the walls; and, after a

while, I came out into a beautiful house where there were people who wondered at my coming that way. They met me and said that this was not the way. I said that in the attic there is supposed to be an opening this way, which they denied. It signifies that this day I had gone astray very far.

The motif of wandering returns, this time in connection with an edifice. The charmed building represents, as houses usually do, a system or a doctrine. As we see, Swedenborg has entered the wrong way—repeating the epistemological predicament. It is noteworthy that the house is inhabited or has many visitors. Seen from the viewpoint of his later spirituality, this house takes a shape similar to the transcendent abodes of his inward journeys, where different spirits or angels group according to their moods and minds, experiences that will later be transmogrified into knowledge in Swedenborg's grand theological system.

"Isn't there any attic window that leads to this place?" Swedenborg asks, but the answer is negative. In the discourse of the dream, there might be a trace here of his earlier theory on how heavenly influence flows through a skylight of the brain—the garret—but it is now dismissed by the insight into the necessity of good works to achieve enlightenment: the right path is an active one without shortcuts. Now, Swedenborg sees the crucial importance of deeds to a Christian.

161

Then there was a big dog that came in beneath the cover of the bed where I was lying, and he licked my neck. I was afraid that he would bite me, but he didn't, and it was said he would not do so. This refers to my subsidiary motives, which shut me out from thoughts of the sacred.

162

Subsequently, I was in company with comedians. One of them said that a Swede had arrived who wished to see me. We drove in, and a large staircase was made ready for him. It was a dog

swaddled up, with a pup suckling. It signifies my terrible thoughts. Something similar was hanging from a fishing rod and could not be removed; finally, in another room, it was torn off. It signifies I will be liberated.

The actors, the staircase of fame, the dogs: once again, we are confronted with images of the "sensuality, wealth, and arrogance" of temptations. In entry 165, Swedenborg's own interpretation has its counterpart in the dreams of temptations during the night of April 5–6.

Swedenborg's struggle against temptations would never end. In work after work, he was to describe their persistency and forcefulness. He chose the life of Christ as his example, as seen in this extract from *Arcana Coelestia* §1690:

> . . . that the Lord's entire life in this world from his earliest boyhood years was a continual temptation and victory, the last of them being when he on the cross was praying for his enemies. . . . All temptation is an attack on the love in which man has his being: to the same extent as love is, to that extent also is temptation. . . . The Lord's life was love for the whole human race; against this his life was exposed to constant temptations. . . . Since this love was not human but divine, and the temptation as great as the love, from this can be seen how severe were the struggles and how great the ferocity of hell. This I know for certain.

163

In a vision, it seemed to me as if something was torn to pieces in the air. It may signify that my double thoughts will be torn asunder.

As I was waking up, there were heard the words "all grace," which signifies that everything that has taken place is grace and for my best.

164

Afterwards, I came into a state of hesitation because I seemed to be so far estranged from God that I could not yet think of him in a living manner, and whether I should not turn my journey homewards. There came a mass of complex reasoning and motions of the body, but I gathered courage and concluded that I had come here to do my very best and to promote the glory of God, that I had got the talent, that everything aimed in this direction, that the spirit had been with me from my youth unto this end, and I considered myself unworthy to live if I do not stick to the right way. And, accordingly, I smiled at the other seductive ideas.

165

Thus, as to pleasure, wealth, and rank, which I had pursued, I perceived that all was vanity and that he is the more happy who is devoid of such things and is nevertheless contented than the one who does possess them. And, therefore, I smiled at all confirmatory reasoning, and thus by the help of God I came to a resolution. May God help me.

I seemed to hear a hen cackling, as she does when she has laid an egg.

After having assumed that the persistent "double thoughts" eventually have been torn asunder and hearing that this is "all grace," Swedenborg ponders the nature of these experiences and the conclusions he should draw from them. He thinks of returning to Sweden—perhaps he could concentrate better in his native country, he thinks. But other ideas occur to him, too, accompanied by spasms of some kind. He perceives that his life follows an already established plan. Some years later, in *The Word Explained*, he returned to this notion and penetrated more deeply into the immanent teleology of his predicament:

> *What the acts of my life had involved I have been taught afterwards as to some of them, nay, as to many of them, from which I could at last clearly see that the tenor of the divine providence has ruled the acts of my life from adolescence itself, and thus has governed, so that at last I arrived at this end: that I could thus understand through the knowledge of natural things, and could thus, of the divine mercy of God Messiah, serve as an*

instrument for opening the things which lie inmostly concealed in the Word of God Messiah.

Swedenborg's reflections in the ensuing entry are of cardinal importance to his subsequent development and his life after the period of the dream diary:

166

I furthermore noticed that faith does indeed consist in an assured confidence that is received from God but that, nevertheless, it consists in work, that people are to do what is good to their neighbors, each one according to his talent, and this more and more; and that this has to be done from the faith that God has thus commanded, without further reasoning, but to do the works of charity under the obedience of faith, even though it may be against the lust of the body and its persuasions. Therefore, a faith without works is not the right kind of faith: one must really sacrifice oneself.

During the past month, Swedenborg has almost daily been concerned with a personal relation to God and with his own unworthiness, impurity, and faithlessness in the process of establishing such a numinous connection. At the same time, he felt assured of divine support through the agency of Christ. Essentially, this approach is much on the same lines as the decreed communion with God according to Lutheran orthodoxy. A sincere and personal faith and contrition result in justification and deliverance channeled by the Church. Luther's revolt was partly against the Roman Catholic stress on acts.

As pointed out in my introduction, Bishop Jesper Swedberg had his entire life been against what he called *solifidianism*, the doctrine of justification by "faith alone." One must believe but also act accordingly. This was a point Swedberg had stressed all his life, one that, for his practical-minded son Emanuel, concerned with function, purpose, goals and workings, was easy to accept. This entry will be followed by innumerable similar reminders emphasizing the importance of our actions for our redemption, a thought

Swedenborg would subsequently present in various ways in work after work.

The idea of "the works of love under the discipline of faith" will recur and will be varied and clarified in the following entries. Here is the journal's main question, one which, at least during his time in London, was highlighted by his intensive contacts with the Moravians. For them, as we have seen, good deeds had no direct bearing on salvation. However, after a break with the Brethren, which will be indicated by Swedenborg in October, to live and act as a true Christian seems to become one with worship and love.

Swedenborg liked to transpose the idea of the importance of good works to a person's relationship with God to the practical level, where they become objectified as *usus*, usefulness, as defined in *Arcana Coelestia* §997:

> *for love of mankind is nothing without works. Humanity consists in its exercise or usefulness. He who loves his neighbor as himself never experiences the pleasure of human love otherwise than in its exercise or usefulness, for which reason a life lived in benevolence is a useful life.*

This applies not only to the ethical level of individual life, but to all society, even the neighborhood. Goodness means active social usefulness, a loving and efficient neighborliness, so to speak. Even in this respect, Swedenborg was influenced by his father's actions. In his *Spiritual Diary* §4182, Swedenborg tells us how the family often wondered where the bishop was, that he was often away from home and nobody knew where he had gone:

> *but he always returned with a certain air of gladness about him, from which it could be inferred that he had been sent out to perform various uses among his fellowmen, now here and now there . . . since his joy consisted in an active life. It was furthermore pointed out to me that without an active life, one cannot be joyous.*

[April] 22–23

167 _____

> Obnoxious dreams, about dogs who were said to be my compa-
> triots and who licked my neck but did not bite; with other
> things, as that I wanted to do something with a couple, but
> nothing happened. In the morning, I fell into appalling
> thoughts, as also during the day, that the Evil One had taken
> possession of me, yet with the trust that he was outside and
> would soon let me go.

This is still another description of his horrid afflictions during
these days and these nights. We recognize the main elements:
Swedes, dogs who lick him, sexual vacillation. The components
themselves are shadowy; later, they will become more clearly
outlined and form a pattern.

The dream language forms layers and is stratified in a way that is
difficult to define even for the dreamer. The expression "I wanted
to do something with a couple [or two persons]" probably is sexually pointed and may refer to a situation similar to that alluded to
in entry 129 or be vaguely related to his being doubtful and being
of two minds, his constant theme. The wording is actually repeated
in the notes of the next day, in entry 171. The incomplete sexual
action is at the same time connected with the unfinished work *The
Animal Kingdom*. He tries to serve two lords, God and the world, and
fails in this pursuit.

168 _____

> When I was in damnable thoughts, the worst that could be, I
> was in that very moment strongly presented with the inward
> sight of Jesus Christ and the operation of the Holy Spirit set
> upon me, so that eventually I knew that the devil was gone. The
> next day I was now and then in a state of infestation and in dou-
> ble thoughts and in strife; after dinner, I was mostly in a calm
> mood and thought of God, although I was busy with worldly
> things. Then I set out for Leyden.

Swedenborg's world becomes increasingly polarized. The opposites—purity-impurity, grace-sin—put their stamp on the pale yellow linen pages of the dream diary. The dogs depart, and Christ appears clearly before his inward eyes. The diary's author is saved from the toils of evil, at least for the time being.

As mentioned in the introduction to this book, Swedenborg's metaphysics were based on an idea of series and degrees. Everything in the universe is connected, stratified in levels whose hierarchy is determined by their universality: the more universal, the higher they are. Components, degrees at each level, are related. The brain, for example, is a degree in the human series yet, at the same time, is itself a series that comprises within itself a long series of interrelated degrees.

Although series and decrees at various levels are essentially different in nature, they answer and correspond to one another. Here we meet Swedenborg's celebrated doctrine of correspondences. Its crucial content, as it appears in 1744, is his view of human nature in all its forms as utterances or as an echo of the Divine, a kind of structural concordance.

In all essentials, the entries made at Leyden are a practical application of this developing doctrine of series and degrees. Entries 169 and 170 mark a new beginning:

[April] 23–24 in Leyden

169
_____

It seemed that I was fighting with a woman in flight, who forced me into a lake and up; at long last, I struck her forehead with the plate, as hard as I could and pressed her face, so she appeared to be overcome. These were my vexations and my struggle with my thoughts, which I had overcome.

170

> It seemed to be said *Interiorescit* [he is becoming more internal], *Integratur* [he is being made whole], which signifies that, by my infestations, I am becoming more purified.

The opening fight, remarkably violent considering Swedenborg's well-known peacefulness, pictures the attenuated fray with his brawling thoughts. As we shall see in a moment, it may be related to his longstanding difficulty in striking a balance between his own powers and divine inspiration. The victory comes with his turning inwards on himself and with his becoming increasingly whole: he is getting more *interior* and *integrated*, according to the Latin terms used.

171

> Throughout the night, something was dictated to me, something holy, which ended with *sacrarium et sanctuarium*. I found myself in bed with one. She said: if you had not said *sanctuarium*, we would do it. I turned away from her; with her hand, she touched me and it got big, bigger than ever. I turned around and applied it; it bent, yet it went in. She said it was long. Meanwhile, I thought that a child must come out of this, and I got off *en merveille*.

The last of the sacred words dictated to him are *sacrarium et sanctuarium*. In the Hebrew Bible, the sanctuary was the Temple's innermost and most arcane room. The sacrarium was the Ark, the sacred chest preserving God's promise to the children of Israel. At the holy word *sanctuarium*, the irresistible woman at his side shrinks back; but union nevertheless takes place. To the dreamer, it all ends up in a wonderful way.

Swedenborg's interpretation immediately follows, and it is significant that the first and foremost English translator, Carl Theophilus Odhner, chose a Latin wording of this sexually explicit passage and the succeeding paragraph: *Significat amorem sancti maxime ultimum, omnis enim amor . . . .* It goes on, in a well-turned Latin. The original text, however, is in explicit Swedish.

172

> This signifies the utmost love of the Holy One, for all love orig-
> inates from that source, constituting a series, in the body mani-
> fest in its seminal projection; and when the ejaculation is there
> and is pure, it answers to the love of wisdom. The former was
> on behalf of truth; but since somebody was listening and noth-
> ing was done until that one was away, it implies that this should
> be kept to oneself and no one hear about it because, according
> to worldly reason, it is considered impure, although in reality it
> is pure.

From the highest quarters and at the highest level, a teaching on
the most holy has been dictated to him in symbolic form. On his
own earthly and bodily level, Swedenborg's love of God and his
longing for knowledge reach an acme in the language of a dream.

In considering these diary notes, one should bear in mind that
many mystics, both before and after Swedenborg, have described
their absorption in God in terms of a quasisexual relationship or
wedding, a *raptus*, rapture, reminiscent of erotic ecstasy. Of
course, this is merely a simile or metaphor for the ineffable experiences of *unio mystica*, a mystical union with the Divine beyond
the sphere of earthly gender. This is true of Swedenborg's expressions, too. However, in this transcendence, he goes a step further.
His imagery becomes mirrors of different layers of reality, answer-
ing to one another, forming a series of levels. All turns into symbols and signs, pregnant with meaning. Other Christian mystics
describing this peculiar kind of experience, have concentrated
wholly on their relationship to God and the meaning and implications of this relationship. To Swedenborg, however, dreams and visions are also vehicles for understanding the universe, in whole as
in part, all seen is a stratified manner.

It is well-known that Swedenborg was to pay an unusual
amount of attention to marriage and marital love. As it happens,
this is still another focus he had in common with Zinzendorf and
the Moravian Brethren. To the followers of Zinzendorf, marriage
was not merely instituted in heaven but was also an image of the
union between Christ and humankind. The very sexual act was

accordingly considered an almost liturgical act. This aspect was especially emphasized in the 1740s, during the sect's so-called Age of Sifting, when the Zinzendorfian sensual enthusiasm reached a climax, the excesses of which the count himself later regretted. At that time, Zinzendorf was as outspoken on sexual matters as Swedenborg was in his diary. But whereas the count expressed himself in public, Swedenborg confessed himself to his private diary, with no one listening. Swedenborg knew that these images would not be understood properly. To the pure, however, all creation is pure. All is linked together, Swedenborg observes, it is forming a whole, but all cannot be shown nor said straight away.

173

> **Then, I dropped off a little, and there seemed to be a flow of oil with some mustard mixed with it, which should be my future life, where there appears to be some amenity blended with adversity or something that is healing to me. This happened in Leiden, in the morning of April 24.**

The imagery is profoundly biblical. The Good Samaritan poured oil into the wounds of the man he aided, and the grain of mustard seed is a prominent New Testament metaphor of devoutness and the kingdom of God. Like the latter, the mustard seed grows into a huge tree, "so that the birds of the air come and lodge in the branches." Or, even if one's faith is no bigger than a mustard grain, one can say to the mountain, "Remove hence to another place, and it shall remove"!

Oil and mustard were common images for deeds and faith: Zinzendorf, for instance, founded a secret and flourishing order entitled "The Order of the Mustard Seed," and oil was a central ingredient of his cult of Christ's wounds.

Disregarding if there be any Moravian tinge to Swedenborg's dream and his rendering, the meaning of the strange picture is quite clear to him. It is about the future—on happiness, difficulties, health.

[April] 24–25. In Amsterdam.

174

I was all the night, for some eleven hours, neither asleep nor awake, in a strange trance-like state, being aware of all I dreamed, my thoughts being tied up tensely, which intermittently made me sweat. That kind of sleep I cannot describe, during which my double thoughts were separated as it were and torn to pieces.

175

Among other things, I dreamed that I talked to Charles XII a couple of times; and, indeed, he talked to me, which surprised me, but in a broken French, which I did not understand at all. And when I spoke to others and did not think he heard that, he was at my side, and I was embarrassed by what I had said. This signifies that God talks to me and that I do not grasp anything, because it is all representations, of which I yet know very little, and that he hears and notices all that is said and knows every thought as well. Indeed, not a single thought can escape his perception, penetrating ten thousand times deeper than mine.

In an extended, lethargic state of sleep or drowsiness, Swedenborg's thoughts revolve endlessly around a theme he cannot leave. He notes the same phenomenon as in dream entry 163, where he was in "double thoughts" which were "torn asunder." He fancies he is conversing with the late King Charles but does not understand his language at all, which seems to be a poor French. On the other hand, the king understands everything Swedenborg says and can even read his thoughts. Yet, the dreamer is obviously aware that the king is an image of God. The apparent obscurity of the messages is due to their figurative language, to which he lacks the key.

We immediately see how perspicaciously the dreamer decodes his dreams, the outcome being logical and consistent with other entries in the diary. Interpretation, hermeneutics, will also be his task to fulfill in the years to come. The interpretation of dreams will be transformed into Old Testament exegetics. The Hebrew of the Word of God was like the alien French spoken by the king. By divine initiation, he was to be granted the key of that tongue.

25–26 [struck out]

176

It appeared to me that women and men were sitting in a ship, ready to depart. One man was holding my dog, which I took back. He showed me the way home and into a beautiful chamber, where there was wine. Maybe this means that I shall send my work to England and that, on that very day, I would be led to a place where I ought to enjoy myself, which actually happened at Mr. Hinr. Posch's [Pasch].

The date of this entry has been crossed out. Probably, this entry was written on April 26, before Swedenborg made the subsequent note, entry 177. After having dated his entry, he evidently remembered that he had this dream in the night between April 24 and 25 and immediately corrected himself.

The ambiguity of the dream language is explicit to an extent that it almost attains pedagogical clarity. The elements "women" and "men" are sent off on a ship. Someone is holding his dog or his hand—in the manuscript, the word is *hud* (skin) or *had*, a misspelling that in a peculiar way links the words *hand* (hand) and *hund* (dog) to each other, and the context points onwards to a lead or guidance associated with the phrase "hand-in-hand." This is an instance where different layers of meaning appear to upset or confuse the spelling of an individual word. Whoever is guiding him and wherever he goes, wine is served in the pleasant room where he sits down to celebrate that his work is on its way.

His interpretation of the dream introduces us into the "superficial" level. The dreamer will be shown to a place for amusement; and, more closely examined, this is the house of a certain Mr. Hindrik Pasch (Posch). All details of the dream can then be seen in this perspective. The men and the women en route are his work, to which he now says good-bye, and the wine symbolizes social life and a spirit of community.

On a deeper—or higher—level of interpretation, we have a few hints but no particulars. Seen from the viewpoint of his dream language as a whole, however, another picture begins to emerge, one of profound consequence. He is struck by a presentiment of a passage to Britain, encompassing his manuscripts and himself as well. There, he will catch hold of a hand extended from above and be guided to a magnificent chamber—with Swedenborg, always an image of inspired work. The wine, then, is the communion with God.

[April] 25–26. At The Hague.

177

A delightful and rich sleep for almost eleven hours, with several representations; how a woman who was married was pursuing me, but I was saved. This means that the Lord is saving me from temptations and persecutions.

178

A married woman wanted to have me, but I liked an unmarried one. The former got angry and chased me, but I nevertheless gained the unmarried one and was with her and loved her. This may signify my thoughts.

179

There was a woman, who had a very beautiful estate in which we walked about and whom I was going to marry. Was *pietas*, and moreover, I believe, *sapientia*, which owned these possessions. And I was also with her and loved her in the usual manner, which seemed to stand for the marriage proper.

As usual, Swedenborg's dreams of women are in reality about his future work, the direction it must take—his methods and subject matters. As might be expected, the answer lies in the embrace represented by piety (*pietas*) and wisdom (*sapientia*), for which Swedenborg uses the Latin terms. Throughout the journal, the same idea recurs: knowledge is to be found through God.

The last section of this date's entry in a certain way links up with the three preceding:

180

It also was represented in a certain way that I should not contaminate myself by reading other books on theological and related theses, because this I have in the Word of God and from the Holy Spirit.

Thus, for the future, Swedenborg will stick to the Word of God, as the Holy Spirit may inspire him to read it. Has he not already concluded that he has received all he needs for his instruction (see entry 31)? This will now hold true not merely for methods and data but also for religious collateral works. Altogether, as we read in one of the diary's last entries, he is not to make use of *annars kram*, "the trash of others."

Here it should perhaps be pointed out that Swedenborg will long afterwards invoke this dream's ban on theological studies in other contexts. Thus, on one occasion, he would declare that this prohibition was the reason that he, for instance, never studied the writings of Jacob Boehme—remarkable enough considering the great interest paid to Boehme among Dippel's followers in Stockholm and among the Bohemian Brethren in London. That may be, but a central tenet of Boehme's writings incidentally had already begun to unfold itself on Swedenborg's inner horizon: the likeness between God and man when the Son appeared in human form.

His six dreams of the night of April 28–29 seem to revolve around two themes: the line Swedenborg should follow in his work and his conviction that he must aim at and, for the future, draw on a higher, divine sphere. Knowing the final results, we see clearly that, even at this stage of his development, he is turning himself toward a kind of writing totally different from all that he has done before.

[April] 28–29

181

> Last night, I thought I saw King Charles XII, to whom I had formerly dedicated my work; but it now seemed to me that he had risen from the dead and that I went out and now wished to dedicate to him, as if he were someone else.

Here, as before, Charles XII has been transmogrified into a symbol of the divine power that decides over life and death, now being "someone else," to whom Swedenborg ought to dedicate his new work, as he once had dedicated his work to the king. It is in that transcendent direction Swedenborg must now turn.

182

> I was walking along a road, and there was a side-road upwards, which I was advised to take. I went up that road, but it seemed to me there were only a few days left, so I went back into the plain where there was a lot of people. I wanted to leave and was pressed hard in the crowd.

The dreamer chooses the right way, "upwards"; but hesitating, as if pressed for time, he returns to *planen*, the plain or the plan—this is still another ambiguous word, pregnant with meaning. Then, he finds himself in a crush and wants to escape, pushing his way forward, but the throng of people presses in upon him. In his vacillating mood, he changes his mind and decides to get back on the right path, which is the only alternative.

183

I gave some fruits to a gardener to sell, and he sold them and returned two carolines to me. But it was said that he had kept thirteen dalers for himself, which I did not care about.

Swedenborg has given the gardener some fruits to take to the market, but he is poorly recompensed. We may suppose these fruits to be his own work, *The Animal Kingdom*, which, at this time, was coming out in Amsterdam and being distributed to book shops. In a broader context, "the gardener" as well as the king may be looked upon as the power proper directing his work onwards. Behind the *Regnum Animale*, there were years of hard work, the results of which now might appear to him meager. He had chosen the wrong track from the beginning.

184

It seemed to me I urinated and that a woman in the bed watched this; she was buxom and rosy. Afterwards, I took her by the breast. She did not withdraw herself much. She showed me her secret parts and something nasty. I did not want to have anything to do with her.

A scene of temptation: the seductive woman, here as elsewhere, is an object of scientific scrutiny. He says no to her with disgust; he has another destiny.

185

All this seems to me to bear upon the idea that I ought to employ my remaining time upon what is higher and not write about worldly things, which are far beneath, but about that which concerns the very center of all and concerning Christ. May God be gracious and enlighten me further regarding my duty, for I am still in some obscurity as to whither I should turn.

All these dreams tell Swedenborg one and the same thing: that he must renounce worldly things for God, for Christ, the center of the universe, and write of higher matters. In a manner typical both of the dreamer and his diary, this thought appears in various guises. It is suggested in entry 171, will later be repeated in the dream of July 7–8, and becomes a leitmotif in the concluding part of the diary. Divine love emanates from the center, on which Swedenborg must now concentrate his whole attention. He has been chosen to clarify and show the ways of divine love. Nevertheless, he is still in doubt as to what attitude he should take. He needs guidance and prays for it.

186

Appeared to be one who had written briefly to King Fredrik, who thought it was short and commanded some persons to call upon that one, who at first seemed to be a woman and then a little man, to vex that one in various ways with love-intrigues and the like. They did their best, but I saw that they had not hurt him or done him any harm. He said that now, between the thirty-sixth and thirty-seventh day (which was the day since my temptation), he wished to borrow a lot and go to heaven, without paying those from whom he had borrowed. This I told to Swab, that he should report it to the king. All this seemed to signify that, if I go on with the other, which I have proposed to myself, I have borrowed a lot from what is spiritual to get to heaven, which I was not willing to pay for, unless at length.

This dream about King Fredrik, the loan, the temptations, and his colleague and relative Swab is one of his most complex and, taken out of context, among the most difficult to comprehend in the entire diary. For the sake of clarity, I shall divide it into six segments.

(1) "Appeared to be one who had written briefly to King Fredrik." The indefinite pronoun "one" or "someone" usually is a self-reference. To "write briefly" to a king is the equivalent of having divine intuitions, inspired syntheses, without lengthy "notes" (see entry 32). As we have already noticed, this problem goes through the diary like a *basso continuo*.

(2) The king indeed "thought it was short and commanded some persons to call upon" the inconstant sender, who appears now

as a man and now as a woman, and to worry that person in various ways "with love-intrigues and the like." Evidently, Swedenborg is depicting his own situation. Although he is at last on the right path, busy writing down his divinely inspired intuitions "briefly," in the right way but as yet insufficiently, the ruler is putting temptations in his way, in order, we understand, to put him to the test. The envoys did their best in these trials, but they did not hurt him.

(3) In his dream, Swedenborg says—still speaking of himself in the third person singular—that he is at the thirty-sixth or thirty-seventh day after the temptation. This is the third time we meet this great tribulation, which seems to have been a turning point in the development of his ideas (see entries 17 and 40).

(4) "He wished to borrow a lot and go to heaven, without paying those from whom he had borrowed." Obviously, we here come across the same line of thought as found in entries 32 and 134. The loans refer to the sources of his knowledge. Swedenborg is to receive it from above, liberate himself like Faust from the prison of facts—"dusty moth-eaten treasures."

(5) "This I told Swab, that he should report it to the king." The person in question is most probably the same Anders von Swab we met on April 8–9, the owner of the licking dog. I have already given an account of Swedenborg's relationship with Swab, a remote relative who had died early, in 1731. Later on, after his dream diary period, Swedenborg would see him in hell, where Swab, due to his evil and libidinous nature, felt very much at home. In *The Spiritual Diary*, we read that Swab's spirit tormented him: "obscures my outlook." Even so, Swab is sent by the king, by God. Temptation has its place in the universal order of things.

Perhaps it is also this same Anders von Swab who is the small gentleman in the entry's first lines. Perhaps it is he, or rather his spirit, that has instigated the great temptation the diarist calls "my temptation"—explicitly, "voluptuousness, wealth, vanity" (see entry 40).

(6) "All this seemed to signify that, if I go on with the other [work], which I have proposed to myself, I have borrowed a lot

from what is spiritual to get to heaven, which I was not willing to pay for, unless at length."

To sum up the sense of the first five points, Swedenborg has been writing about matters told him by God. Thirty-seven days before his dream, the powers of this world had vainly tried to tempt him. For the future, too, he intends to restrict himself to higher knowledge. His work will be done without delay.

This should be related to his scientific work. The printing of *The Animal Kingdom* was no doubt in full swing. The first week after his great Easter vision, Swedenborg, to judge from entry 105, was busy going through part two of that work. On April 16, he had been writing its epilogue. This epilogue is in highest degree "synthetic." To a great extent, it is an encomium of intuitively grasped and divinely inspired knowledge, which supersedes all other forms of knowledge. After this, he had begun working on a longer section treating "the senses in general," which was to appear in the posthumous work *On the Five Senses*. This too is "synthetic" in character, building a bridge between the two approaches.

In Swedenborg's world of ideas, the spirits of the departed appear in the form of the good or evil promptings of our own minds, as malignant or angelic beings who seek us out. Whether we will or not, we take the dead with us. And whenever we, by an effort of will, liberate ourselves from evil thoughts, the evil spirits lose their grip on us, without realizing it. Swab's appearance as a rebuffed tempter is presumably a first indication of what Swedenborg would afterwards explicitly articulate as a detailed doctrine of spirits.

To reiterate, the dreams are a series of more or less coherent *tableaux vivants*, where there is only room for a limited number of actors. In the middle of the scene is the dreamer himself, sometimes masked and disguised, yet recognizable for the most part. With exaggerated and over-explicit gestures, the co-actors recreate his inclinations and attitudes in the theater of life.

It is time to move on; and, once again, Swedenborg sails for the British Isles. Why England? In his notes of April 25–26, he indicates that his scientific work should perhaps be sent to England, where a "beautiful room" with wine might be waiting for him. Was he weary of The Hague and of his acquaintances there? Did he suppose he could get better illustrations for his work in England? Some phrases in journal entry 125 seem to suggest this, so the main reasons may be strictly practical. The matter is probably irrelevant to our understanding of the diary.

Before leaving Holland, Swedenborg makes a number of annotations, all of which seem to refer to eating and drinking.

[April] 30–May 1

187

I saw someone on guard with a rapier; it was pointed and sharp, and there was something sticking out of the sleeve of his coat. I was in danger from him, for I saw that he was somewhat drunk and consequently might do harm. It signifies that, on the previous day, I had drunk a little more than I should, which is not spiritual but carnal, and accordingly sinful.

188

After this, it seemed to me that I had with me Eliezer, my deceased brother, who was being attacked by a wild boar that held him fast and bit him. I tried to drag the animal down with a hook but could not. After that, I went up and saw that he was lying between two boars, which were eating his head; I could not get anyone to help him. I ran past. This means, I believe, that, on the previous day, I had indulged my appetite and had partaken too freely of the necessities of life, which is also a work of the flesh and not of the spirit; for such is the life of swine and is forbidden by Paul: it is called *commessationes* [exaggerated feasting].

189

On the following day, I was more on my guard, but I came into a rather strong temptation—that now and henceforth I must forcibly govern my appetite. This brought me into a strange condition and, as it were, into a state of chagrin; but I was

quickly released after I had prayed and sung a hymn, particularly since I do not wish to be my own, but to live as a *novos homo* in Christ.

Perhaps Envoy Preis and other acquaintances in Amsterdam had been excessively hospitable before his departure, throwing bon voyage parties. Furthermore, it happened to be the eve of May Day, which is prominent feasting time in Europe. Swedenborg has drunk too much—in the original, he uses a Swedish mixture of French and Latin, *curerat pelliculam*, meaning that he has been feasting. Nightmares accordingly follow. Next day, forced back to a frugal regime, he is in "a state of chagrin"; a slightly depressive mood ensues. After prayer and pious singing, however, his melancholy evaporates.

Excessive eating and drinking are swinish, he explains, alluding to St. Paul. And we may note in passing that his conscience seems to regret these kinds of excesses more than his visits to low places. This circumstance may be connected with the Lutheran idea of sin: its size and specific gravity are proportionate to how far it alienates us from God. When Swedenborg, a year after these Walpurgis Eve celebrations, receives what he regards as his definitive call, it will be introduced by a warning against overeating. Sitting in a private room in a London tavern, he is having dinner. Suddenly, he hears a voice reprimand him: "Don't eat that (so) much." It is then he sets out on his new path through life.

We meet his younger brother Eliezer, who died young in 1716. Later, in entry 191, his youngest brother, Jesper—a farmer, who would die one year before Swedenborg—will also appear. Both are obviously synonymous with Swedenborg himself. And it is certainly not by pure chance that Eliezer is attacked by *two* wild boars who "were eating his head," nor that Jesper, as we shall see in a moment, is condemned by judges who are holding *two* documents in their hands. These, we may well assume, refer to the two parts of *The Animal Kingdom*, which right now are causing him such harsh mental torment and headache.

190 _____

> Then, for a number of days in succession, I was usually for
> some hours in a state of spiritual anxiety, without being able to
> tell the cause, although I seemed to be assured of the grace of
> God. After dinner, however, I was quite happy and enjoyed
> spiritual peace.

Once again, Swedenborg's simultaneous feelings of worry and assurance are yet another example of his divided mind. The soul—
our divine organ—only has to become aware of the
incompatibility between goodness and human imperfection to be
seized with anxiety. On several occasions, Swedenborg will raise
this point in *The Five Senses*, the work that will keep him busy late
May and all of June of 1744.

191 _____

> When I started on my voyage from The Hague in the
> Maaslandsskuiten [with Trekschuit from Maasland], which took
> place on May 13, it seemed that my brother Jesper had been
> put in prison on my account and also another person. I had put
> something into a carriage and imported it, for which I seemed to
> be responsible. There came judges who were to sentence him,
> holding in their hands two written papers. In the meantime, I
> saw birds flying towards me, but I hit them on the neck with a
> sharp knife so that they died. Then the judges came and re-
> leased my brother Jesper, whom I kissed and rejoiced over. It
> signified that I had been running wild in my thoughts but that,
> with the help of the Spirit, I had killed them and that I therefore
> was declared free.

On May 1, as Swedenborg wrote, he left the city of The Hague by
horse-drawn canal boat. The dating is wrong, most probably a slip
of pen for May 13: it was many years since that the Dutch had
adopted the Gregorian calendar, which put them ten days ahead of
the English, where, as also in Sweden, the old-style Julian calendar
was still in force. According to entry 192, he reached Harwich on

May 4–5, using the Julian calender as did the English in the town. Consequently, he must have left Holland about May 13.

192

In Harwich, on my arrival in England, I had only a few hours sleep. Then appeared to me many things that should bear upon my work here. This took place on May 4/5, according to the English style.

193

(1) How I lost a bank note, and the person who found it got only nine stivers for it, which also happened to another person who had likewise found such a bank note, and which was bought for nine stivers only. I said, jokingly, that this was *pietasteri*. It probably showed what is the case with England, partly honest, partly dishonest.

194

(2) There were some who admired my copper pieces, which were very well done, and who wished to see my sketches, as if I could conceive them as they were finished. It may mean that my work will gain approbation, although that they do not believe that I was able to make it.

195

(3) I received a little letter, for which I paid nine stivers. When I opened it, I found within a large book with blank paper. In the middle, there were many beautiful drawings, but the rest was blank paper. A woman was sitting at my left hand; she moved over to my right side and began to turn over the pages of the book, and the drawings appeared. It seemed to me that the meaning of the letter was that, while in England, I should order many such designs or patterns to be made. The woman had a rather broad neck cloth but was altogether bare on both sides all the way down; her skin was shining as if glazed; and, on her thumb, there was a miniature painting. It may signify that, with

the help of God. I may execute a lot of handsome designs in my work while in England; and that afterwards speculation will turn *ad priora*, which before it has been *in posterioribus*, as seems to be signified by the change of spatial position.

196

(4) It seemed as if I had received orders to accompany Bergenstierna on a commission and that money had been granted for the purpose. The commission, with which I was quite pleased, seemed to be well beyond Sicily, but I thought that I would have to be on guard against scorpions there. This might denote something that will be committed to me after my work is finished; that perhaps I am going to do it at some other place, and perhaps to some other cause.

The first thing we notice is the recurrence of the number "two" and his self-criticism apropos of *The Animal Kingdom*. Its two volumes are transformed into bank notes of very small value, further diminished by the *pietastery* of fraudulent exchange, confusing piety with piastres of silver in a toying way. Then come two paragraphs, entries 194 and 195, with a curious description of the work he thinks he is planning to carry out in England.

The pieces of copper are in all likelihood the copper plates on which the illustrations to his new work are to be engraved. They win approval. Although as yet unwritten, the work exists as an idea, a thought that is developed in the section about the blank book.

Swedenborg dreams he gets a letter containing an unwritten book. He pays nine stivers' postage—the same amount his lost bank notes had been worth. We may surmise that the unwritten book is the task awaiting him.

Beside the book sits a scantily clad, big-breasted woman, who moves from left to right. In his dream-language, she stands for his research subject. Now she changes sides, showing him remarkable *desseiner och mönster*, "designs and patterns," to be executed in England. On her thumb nail is a painted miniature.

Swedenborg interprets both woman and book in terms of the

problems facing him. Up to now, he has tried to work analytically, describing empirical facts that gradually form the basis of comprehensive conclusions. To use the expression in the drawing, he has worked *in posterioribus*, with externals and their implications. His dream augurs a change. The woman changes sides—Swedenborg's thinking is passing from analysis to synthesis, from "intuition," *a priori*, to what is primary and immediately given. As a confirmation, the woman has a miniature painting on her thumb. This is precisely how intuitive reason operates; comprehending within itself the particular, it fits it into broader contexts.

Swedenborg's dreams of the future continue in entry 196. Together with Johan Bergenstierna, one of his colleagues at the Royal Board of Mines, he has been sent out on a mission to a foreign country. Declaring himself content, he interprets this dream as referring to the work he is to write after finishing *The Animal Kingdom*. Perhaps it will be written far elsewhere, be about other matters, he thinks. Perhaps he intuitively realizes now how radically different in character his future work is going to be.

5

MAY 1744

————◆·►|◄·◆————

May 5–6. In London

197
_____

I was beaten up by a big man, which I put up with. Then I was
going to mount a horse to ride with the carriage, but the horse
turned his head and got hold of me and held me. What this signifies I do not know at all. I may have done something wrong to
a certain shoemaker who was with me on the journey and with
whom I was then lodging; or it may mean that I had not been
thinking of my work.

Without damage to our understanding of the diary, we may share
the perplexity of its author and leave the entry at that. In a way,
it is enough for us to see in this sequence still another piece of
evidence of his qualms of conscience and his pangs of self-reproach. We can, moreover, note that he has taken lodgings in
London with a certain "pious shoemaker": the fellow-believers of
this landlord will make frequent appearances in the diary from
now on. The dream seems to augur an experience he will have
later, of occupying a post as secretary "in Java," August 8–9. As
transpires from the commentary on entry 232, _Java_ is the Hebrew
word for those parts of Asia Minor that were colonized by the
Greeks. In Swedenborg's well-documented interpretation of the
Book of Daniel, _Java_ has to do with the Bible's "inner meaning,"
which, in turn, if it is to be accessible to the dreamer, seems to
demand a knowledge of the Hebrew he yet lacks. What is in
question in this later passage is thus a "commission . . . beyond
Sicily," for which money is being allocated.

198

Summa summarum: only grace can save us. (2) The grace is in Jesus Christ who is the throne of grace. (3) It is the love of God in Christ by which salvation is effected. (4) And that one then allows oneself to be led by the spirit of Jesus. (5) Everything that comes from ourselves is dead and is nothing but sin and worthy of eternal damnation. (6) For nothing good can come except from the Lord.

Swedenborg's pithy maxim, which he had arrived at during the three weeks of crisis, might have been written by Zinzendorf himself. God's stern law and humankind's duty to obey it by right living are far away in this summary. As in the *Songs of Zion* and in the Moravian confession generally, we are instead confronted with grace, the opposite of law. Grace, the forgiveness of sins, is gospel, "the glad news." Using a term that was common in Moravian teachings, Swedenborg calls Christ "the throne of grace." The concept is derived from the golden lid of the Israelite's Ark of the Covenant in Exodus, that *sacrarium et sanctuarium* we have already come across in journal entry 171: the holy shrine in which God revealed himself.

By the throne—Swedenborg writes *stol*, "chair"—of grace is meant the authority of love, its empire. This grace, we read, comes to us through "love of God in Christ." Here too is a Moravian key. Bliss is a state, a salvation that becomes the lot of Swedenborg and all humankind, both on this earth and after death, provided that we approach God—Christ—lovingly. Continually, we meet in Zinzendorf, as in Swedenborg's later writings, the idea that bliss, joy, and security are always potentially present, here and now: "the paradisian state does not constitute heaven, but an inclination to what is heavenly."

The Moravian confession stressed the will. Insight into one's own sinfulness and selfishness should be followed by a forsaking of one's own willfulness to be absorbed into and adapt oneself to the Divine. This is the thought we meet in his apothegm: one must let oneself be "led by the spirit of Jesus." A human being must concentrate completely on the Divine. Swedenborg has already touched on this theme in journal entry 55; and, as the diary proceeds, it becomes ever more important. There, however, the demand for an intense direction of the will is complemented in a way as typical of Swedenborg as it was alien to Zinzendorf, and this is of utmost importance: guided by "the spirit of Jesus," the individual must act. Love must be complemented by, be led toward worship, which is *caritas*, the works and deeds of love.

As will become evident, the following entries refer to a longer period of time than their heading would suggest, and their content is less about dreams than states of mind and "real" experiences.

[May] 19–20. In London.

199

On the twentieth, I had intended to go to the Lord's Supper in the Swedish Church, because recently I had fallen into many pernicious thoughts, and I observed that my body is constantly rebelling, which was, moreover, represented to me by scum that must be taken away. On Sunday morning, there came quite clearly from the Spirit into my mouth that this is the manna that comes from heaven. I was neither in a state of sleep nor of wakefulness, but it came quite clearly into my thought and mouth that it signifies Christ in the Lord's Supper. On the previous day, I had been so prepared that I enjoyed an interior tranquillity and peaceful contentment with the Lord's dispensation; and the whole time I felt the powerful influence of the Holy Spirit, a joy and an earthly kingdom of heaven, which filled the whole body.

200

Nevertheless, I could not restrain myself not to look for sex, although I did not have any intention to proceed into effect; yet, in the dreams, that did not seem to be altogether contrary to the dispensation of God. I was in the company of Prof. Oelreich in

some places, against which I had not been warned, as I had been warned against other things that I had done. Still, it had been represented to me some days before in a dream that, in one and the same day, I would twice be in danger of my life, as also happened, so that if God had not then been protecting me, I would have lost my life in two places. The particulars I will not describe.

Having arrived in England, settling down there with the aforementioned shoemaker, and walking the streets of London, visiting various places, Swedenborg has relapsed into "pernicious thoughts," that is, thoughts of more or less immoral or depraved nature, according to his own judgment. His mind is agitated, and his body is continuously rebellious, seething with excitement. He is faced by the revolt of the flesh, *rebellio carnis*. Yet, on Saturday, May 19, he seems to succeed in repressing these evil influences and feels himself embraced by God's love. In this frame of mind, the world turns into heaven, and he is filled with beatitude.

Toward the evening, this peace is gone, sorry to say. He cannot control himself and, as it would seem, goes to a brothel, albeit without "any intention to proceed into effect," as he puts it. He is going out in company with the same person who appears in an undated entry at the end of the diary, his compatriot Professor Niklas Oelreich, the teacher of Count Axel von Fersen and later the director of Swedish censorship. Swedenborg appears to indicate that, strictly speaking, this risky excursion was not that remarkable, the less so as he had in a dream earlier seemed to understand that divine judgment of escapades of this kind was lenient. Even so, his conscience is perhaps not quite unclouded: there is a tinge of defensiveness in his remark that he did not get any premonition—normally he has monitory intimations of future or imminent transgressions.

However, Swedenborg has been informed in a dream that he would be threatened by two lethal dangers—a reference, presumably, to the experiences reported in entry 197. These dangers had occurred, precisely, on the Saturday evening when he had been to "some places" together with his friend. He desists from recalling the details.

In spite of what he assures us in the diary's introductory entries, we may marginally note that Swedenborg still seems to have his old "inclination for sex," and this moral relapse is a major concern of the diarist. On Sunday morning, having withstood these perils, he ponders his having gone astray. The lusts of the body, he thinks, are like scum that must be skimmed off. Now he is again able to keep control of his thoughts, and "the Spirit" comes upon him. He is to attend divine service and take communion at the Swedish church, in London's East End. It strikes him that Christ's presence in the sacraments corresponds to the manna the children of Israel received from heaven in the desert. This Sunday thought, sticking in his memory, will later become one of the "correspondences" in his biblical exegesis. The Israelites, fleeing from Egypt, did not take the manna at its proper worth. Naturally not, he wrote: ignorant of Christ, they could not set a proper value on their heavenly nourishment.

Having noted down his debauches of Saturday, he is concerned to give an account of what he regards as his basic mood or frame of mind at this time. Presumably, the "mornings, evenings, days" in the following entry refer to the period after his arrival to London.

201

Yet the internal joy was so strongly awakened, particularly when I was alone, without company, in mornings, evenings, days, that it may be compared to a heavenly joy here on the earth. This I hope to retain as long as, by the grace of our Lord alone, I walk in the pure path and have the right intention; for, if I turn aside to seek my pleasure in worldly things, it vanishes. God knows best whether the internal principle, which is the influx of God's spirit, is there. Every least degree of exaltation is that of which it is sensible; therefore, I thought that, since I have this heavenly joy, why should I seek for worldly pleasure, which by comparison is nothing, is inconstant, hurtful, opposing, and destructive to the former.

Swedenborg's words about a heaven on earth will constitute one of the main lines of thought in his later writings—in the draft he is currently composing for the continuation of *The Animal Kingdom*, as well as in his religious works. We should not live as "prisoners of nature, but under the influence of the supreme reason or God's spirit," we read in *The Five Senses*, the work Swedenborg was preparing at this time. Instead, we shall have our share of "heavenly joy."

The concluding words about the intensity of celestial delight makes the dreamer think of the close Moravian Brethren.

202

> By various providential dispensations, I was led to the chapel of the Moravian Brethren, who claim that they are the real Lutherans; that they are conscious of the operation of the Holy Spirit, as they tell one another; that they look only to the grace of God and the blood and merit of Christ; and that they work in innocent simplicity. Concerning this, I shall speak more fully another time, but I may not yet be permitted to join their brotherhood. Their chapel was represented to me three months ago, just as I afterwards saw it, and all who were there were dressed as clergymen.

As in entry 201, this entry appears to have a recapitulative character, being an account of Swedenborg's connections with the Moravians since his coming to London. We have seen how, during the sea crossing to Harwich, the port northeast of London, he had met with a "pious shoemaker," John Seniff by name, at whose house he had temporarily taken lodgings. Mr. Seniff had in turn introduced him to John Paul Brockmer, an engraver living in Salisbury Court, off Fleet Street, in the immediate vicinity of the Moravians' church in Fetter Lane, Holborn. Probably it was Brockmer who, during this first London period, had taken him to "the church of the Moravian Brethren."

Obviously, the Moravian doctrine appealed to Swedenborg. As he understood it at that time, the Moravians ascribed all merit to God's grace and Christ's vicarious suffering. With this in mind, "they work in innocent simplicity." He seems to be contemplating joining their congregation, but he "may not yet be permitted to join their brotherhood." The question of joining them, or remaining an onlooker, was to remain one of the diary's central themes.

Swedenborg had dreamed about the Moravian Brethren, he says, three months earlier. In that dream, they had all been dressed like priests: an image of the Lutheran ideal of an earthly priesthood, where all try to live in Christ. This *representation*—this is the word he uses—must have occurred in Amsterdam or at The Hague, still another indication of his early familiarity with the evangelical Brethren and their preaching.

It may be added that the Moravians did not regard taking the sacraments in the Swedish Lutheran Church as incompatible with attending their own services. Zinzendorf's idea was that his evangelical congregations of brethren should put new life and fire into Christians of all confessions. Adoption into their congregation, with the right it conferred of participating in Holy Communion there, was another question of more than formal significance. A higher authority than the consistory refused sanction.

6

JUNE 1744

[June] 11–12

203

I was thinking about those who resist the Holy Spirit and those who leave themselves at the mercy of his government.

There appeared to me a man in white, carrying a rapier. Another set upon him and was wounded by his rapier; he renewed the attack but was wounded quite severely about the ear and the temples. Still another came to charge him, but he also was run through, drawing blood. I had a long spear and was thinking that, if he would go against me, I would hold the spear in front of me. But just as he was not far from me, I saw that he threw down the rapier and went away.

As I was wondering at this, I noticed that someone was walking before me and that he had reversed his rapier to give to him and surrender unconditionally, which was the reason for his reversing his rapier.

This vision seems to be a variation on the theme of longing for innocence and true childlike piety. A man in white—Christ—wounds and punishes with his sword all who oppose him. Swedenborg, watching the fight, thinks he will protect himself with a spear, should the man in white attack him. Instead, the latter throws away his rapier and walks off. Someone in front of Swedenborg makes him understand that one must surrender unconditionally to the man in white.

Unconditional surrender, a childlike belief in God, love's total absorption into the Divine—all these notions refer to the same state of mind. In *The Five Senses*, Swedenborg constantly stresses the effacing of self-love as a condition and preparation for receiving truth and wisdom, which is the Godhead's influx into our mind.

June 15–16. The sixteenth was a Sunday.

204

My past life was represented to me and how afterwards I walked where there were precipices on all sides and how I turned back. Then I came to a very lovely grove, planted everywhere with the most beautiful fig trees in fine growth and order. On one of them, there seemed to remain dried-up figs. The grove was surrounded by moats, except on the side where I was. I wanted to pass over a foot bridge, which was high and with earth and grass on top, but I dared not because of the danger.

205

At some distance from it, I saw a large and quite beautiful palace with wings, where, it seemed to me, I desired to take lodgings to have the prospect of the grove and the moats always in view. A window was open far down in one of the wings, and I thought I would like to have my room there. This means that on Sunday I should be in what is spiritual, which is meant by the lovely grove; the palace may mean the plan of my work, which looks toward the grove, whither I intend to look by means of it.

All these musings are, at least in some sense, Sunday thoughts. They occur in an "inspirited" mood, although the dating is erroneous; June 17, 1744, was a Sunday, indicating a retrospective character of the note proper. Now the time of perilous peregrinations is apparently past. He is walking in safety through a grove of fig trees, surrounded on three sides by a moat or ditch. The grove is beautiful; its figs are ripening on all trees but one, where they are withering. Wishing to go on, he must first cross a footbridge, covered with earth and grass. But he dares not, "because of the danger."

As we know, groves and gardens formed part of Swedenborg's

symbolic language, as well as of his life. The words signify spirituality, bliss, and paradise. Yet in this dream-grove is a tree that is not
fruitful. The dreamer tries to go on but is held up by the bridges or
plank. Again, this symbolizes a question of access or exclusion. To
use an expression coined by a later religious philosopher of the
North: Will he dare to lose his foothold?

Put off by the difficulty and danger, the dreamer glimpses, not
far away, a palace with wings. This is the true doctrine he has yet
to formulate. Behind a window far out in one of the wings he wants
to have his room. He is to be part of his own plan, his own *dessein*,
his design, in direct connection with "the spiritual."

[June] 20–21

206

> It seemed that a deliberation was going on whether I should be
> admitted to the society or to one of their councils. My father
> came out and said to me that what I had written about provi-
> dence was the finest. As far as I could remember, that was only
> a small treatise. Afterwards, one night, I found myself in the
> church, but I was naked, having nothing on but a shirt, so that I
> did not dare to step forward. This may mean that I am not yet
> clothed and prepared as I need to be.

From this entry on, the concepts "society" on the one hand and
"admission" or "be elected a member" on the other, or other phrases
to the same effect, will become one of the diary's recurrent elements. In all probability, Swedenborg is referring to the Brethren
congregation in Fetter Lane. After their break with John Wesley
and his Methodist followers in 1740, the London Moravians had
called themselves "The Society of the Moravian Brethren," only
two years later constituting themselves as a "congregation" or
"church," whereupon their official name became the "Moravian
Brethren of the English Communion." As a missionary center, active in England, in America, and on the European continent, they
called themselves the "Society for the Furtherance of the Gospel."

Looking at the diary's entries as a whole, we have every reason to make assumptions along this line. Nevertheless, we need not totally identify a "society" with "the society of Brethren." Dream-language is always ambiguous, having many possible interpretations; and one does not exclude another. The "society" can just as well be paradise. Perhaps it is from paradise that Jesper Swedberg appears to compliment his son on a minor work, one no longer extant, on providence.

This dream and Swedenborg's interpretation of his nudity in church link up closely with a common piece of Moravian imagery. Clothing, for Zinzendorf and his followers, makes up the imagery of the "old man" and the "new man," the *novos homo* of journal entry 189 above.

Conversion calls for purification. The sinner must clothe him- or herself in the Savior's "holy and undefiled garment of righteousness." Swedenborg's thinks his own interpretation places him somewhere in a middle position: he has taken off his old clothes but has not yet put on the new ones.

Some of those who have speculated about Swedenborg's mental health have indeed supposed the last part of this particular entry to refer to a real event. The reader is referred to the introductory chapter on Swedenborg's state of health (pages 52–59); but, even from a superficial point of view, the embarrassing situation outlined is certainly recognizable by almost any dreamer.

[June] 26–27

207 _____

I was in a place together with many persons. I went past my garden, which looked quite bad, no doubt in comparison with the heavenly. Then, for a long time, I heard the roar of cannons being fired against the enemy in various directions and imagined that the enemy was being defeated. There also came a message that the Danes were attacking with ten thousand men. The battle was mostly with sword in hand, and they were altogether beaten. There was also [a battle] in another place, and I wanted

to go out to view the battlefields. Where I was, there were a number of persons who wanted to run away because they were of the Danish party, but I advised them to stay, being in no danger as there was no Danish soldier.

In the spring of 1743, Swedenborg had bought a house at Hornsgatan, a street in south Stockholm. For the rest of his life, he would devote incessant care to his garden. But in his dream world, the state of a garden has a wider and higher significance. As he saw it, well-trimmed earthly gardens were images of salvation, bliss, and paradise. His own inward garden, however, is badly kept. As he has stressed in the previous entry, he is not yet "prepared as I need to be."

Like the garden, the hostilities between Swedes and Danes are deeply rooted in reality, although they too have a higher meaning. The successor to the Swedish throne, Adolf Fredrik, was elected in the spring of that year [1743]; but the Danish crown prince, supported by the so-called Danish party in Sweden, had been a serious rival. Immediately upon the Parliament's electing Adolf Fredrik, the Danes had prepared an attack on Sweden. That threat remained. It is probably this abortive war of succession that Swedenborg now dreams about.

Clearly, however, the battle also has to do with his own state of mind. The war reflects the skirmishes going on inside the dreamer, the strife "lengthwise and crosswise" between faith and science, with guns firing on all sides and hand-to-hand fighting.

208

Then I saw something like a large screen that preserved me—that there was something wrong with my left foot, which I had not noticed before; it was bandaged but would soon be all right again. In a large cage, there was a little bird, which had been concealed for a long time; but it still lived, had food and drink, and went in and out of the cage. I saw Eric Benzelius wearing a wig with two curls behind; he walked about, tired and old. I went with him and saw that he walked into a church and sat down in the very lowest place.

In a later note, that of October 10–11, it seems to Swedenborg that he is applying for a post with a gentleman, "having lost my fortune by the war." Now he draws four dreamy tableaux, all connected with "the war."

Swedenborg is protected by a screen rather than projected on it. For this dreamer, screens, curtains, and sheets are not merely physical protections. They also shut out the confusing world of the senses and facilitate knowledge on divine conditions. We have seen this before, and we will take up this thread again in connection with a somewhat similar scenery in journal entry 225.

Unknown to the dreamer, something is failing (*fehl*) with his left foot. It is bandaged, though, and is getting better. On April 5–6 (entry 43) Swedenborg had described himself as a "Jacobite." Is this weakness in his foot a reminiscence of his special warfare, his wrestling with God? As we know, Jacob had received a blow on his hip muscle, causing him ever afterwards to limp. Perhaps this is also reminiscent of one of his earliest entries, where his inability to achieve agreement between theology and science had expressed itself in the inability of a "black image" to use its foot (dream entry 26).

A little bird in a cage, though long hidden, is still alive. It has food and moves freely in and out of its habitation. Despite all the uproar of battle, Swedenborg's longing for God remains unchanged, still has the breath of life to it. His call? Insight into "right knowledge?"

Eric Benzelius appears, "tired and old." This is his brother-in-law, thirteen years his senior, who had played an important role in his life. Gradually, however, disputes over inheritances, temperamental differences, and Benzelius' coldness toward Swedenborg's religious ideas led to strained relations. Long after Benzelius' death, Swedenborg was to write in his *Spiritual Diary* that what Benzelius had refused to understand was that all truth is revealed in the Holy Scripture and is not to be said by rote but lived. The intellectual had let himself be governed by vaingloriousness, trusting his excellent memory more than his heart. Thus, Swedenborg meets him, *post mortem*, in the other world, merging truth with falsehood in an abyss specially designed for the purpose. Everything there is on fire, even those who dwell there. Still, Benzelius does not notice anything of this: he had come to this place of his own free will, being perfectly adapted to it.

At the time of this particular dream vision, Benzelius had been dead for a year. Swedenborg saw him, old and worn, entering a church to sit down, humbly, near the entrance. The dreamer follows him. Was the old man with the wig Swedenborg himself, who had "lost all in the war"? And whose trust and confidence, shaken and weary but still vibrant, in humble assurance reposes at the far end of the church?

7

July 1744

Swedenborg was now approaching the end of the long section on "senses in general" that was to form the central part of the third volume of *The Animal Kingdom*. His main problem appears to be the relation between the body and the soul. The soul in this context is conceived as being composed of our preferences, our bents, our *amores*. In fact, an automatic and simultaneous interconnection between body and soul is established, a harmony of another kind than that proposed by Leibniz, however.

This agreement or concordance immediately posed a problem when the ability to distinguish between good and evil was to be accounted for. Using a biblical reference, Swedenborg referred to it as "the separation of spirits." We are blinded by our tastes and perceive only what we want to see. The soul runs the errands of the body. The basic problem is freedom of will, a freedom that is the *conditio sine qua non* of Swedenborg's ethics. Swedenborg appears to find the deep-sounding solution to the problem, as can be seen, for example, in the *Spiritual Diary* §§4757, 5074, and 5751, in a comparison between our will and the destiny decreed by God, or in the following excerpts from *The Five Senses* §97, 4–7:

> To ascertain the causes, we have to ascend . . . towards the eternal, and from there descend to the effects, if we are to clarify the causes (of our thoughts and actions) by analysis.
>
> In this manner we might, as rational beings, behave like angels. When truths are discerned, when we are in truth, we can be among them. Here is a way to heaven, the original state, to perfection.
>
> There we are met by . . . a superior power . . . (which)

introduces us into truths—through the senses we go amiss. Therefore: to a right understanding of one thing, knowledge about all is necessary. The whole must be grasped, if the part shall be realized.

When penetrating this problem, he has a vision:

July 1–2

209

Something strange happened to me: I got strong shivers, like those I had when Christ granted me his divine grace, one after another, ten or fifteen in a row. I expected to be thrown on my face like the last time, but this did not happen. At the last shiver, I was lifted up; and, with my hands, I felt a back. I touched the back all over and the chest underneath. Soon, it lay down, and I saw on the front a face, but quite obscurely. At that moment, I was on my knees and considered whether I should lie down beside, but this did not take place because it was not allowed. Shivers permeated my body from below upwards to my head.

210

This occurred in a vision, when I was neither asleep nor awake, because all my thoughts were composed. It was the inward human, separated from the outward, who experienced this. When I was wide awake, such shivers came over me several times. This must have been a holy angel, since I was not thrown on my face. What this means, our Lord knows best. At first, it seemed to tell me that I would get something for my obedience or other things. God's grace is shown both to the inward and outward human in me; to God alone be praise and honor!

What Swedenborg is now going through testifies to his passionate devotion. He—and the reader as well—recognizes the course of events he previously experienced at Easter: shivers and the experience of physical contact with a power that guides him. This time, too, and even stronger, he senses a presence—he feels a backbone, a breast, and gets a glimmer of a visage.

He is neither awake nor sleeping. His internal man is distinguished from his external being: he is apparently completely absorbed by the divine passion, the sense of numinous encounter. This is a phenomenon similar to the features of his "double thoughts" described in entry 69 (April 7–8) and later, when he is torn between pain and joy, as if an inward war is raging.

The difference is that the union here is almost complete, and the alarm of the outer world is far away in this silent scene. This is the pious ecstasy, the blessed *cultus*, quite different from the fatal distraction of the priests Korah and Dathan later described in entry 247.

211

From the following and other things, I notice that this means that I would perceive *veritates de sensationibus internis* [truths of internal sensations], but from behind and obscurely on the front, since, before it occurred, I seemed to be told that it was an annunciation of what I have been working on so far, and it also seemed to me that I had exchanged my plain stivers to some better coins and got some gold, alongside with some copper, however.

As we have seen, Swedenborg was contemplating the truths of internal perceptions when this note was made. He immediately saw the connection with his vision. This was a revelation: he had, or was to obtain, the capability of describing this evanescent phenomenon—only superficially, however, "from behind." Its profound nature was to remain "obscure."

The vision left a deep impression. In the manuscript of *The Five Senses*, Swedenborg refers to this vision. In §592 of that work, he acknowledges that he has "in a wonderful way been informed" about the matters he is treating. He returns to the vision even on later occasions. He repeatedly mentioned also the obscurity that remained, even after the enlightenment. The visage he vaguely saw

in his vision corresponds in his manuscript to circumstances perceived "as in a shadow." He did not doubt the possibility of eluci-
dating these matters; in his metaphysics, this was to be done by the
doctrine of divine influx in the world.

We may also note that he thinks he has encountered a "holy
angel" here, a conclusion he draws from *not* having been prostrated
this time: the body before him is not that of Christ. This is the second time an angel appears in his interpretations. The first one we
came across was in connection with entry 17. Later in his life, angels were to accompany him every day.

July 3–4

212

**With a special tenderness, I took leave of her, as it were, kissing
her, when another [woman] was seen at some distance. The outcome was that, when awakening, I was in *continuo oestro
amoris* [in a continual burning of love]. It was said, however,
and regretfully so, that this is incomprehensible, which means
that I have now managed to write *de sensibus in genere* [on the
senses in general] and *operationi facultatum interiorum* [the
operation of the internal faculties], which cannot be comprehended in its present sketchy form, and that I am now going to
the next, which is *cerebrum* [the brain].**

A sweet farewell to a woman, with another waiting in the background, awakening in transports of love and a voice intimating that
what he has written can not be understood: the features of the
scene concur with the dialectical pattern that pervades the dream
diary, which translated itself in a variety of forms and images. A
new love is awaiting him—"another was seen at some distance"—
and he leaves his first love. He bids farewell to his work on "the
senses in general," which was printed posthumously as *De sensu communi* (The Five Senses) and includes parts treating the functions of
internal bodily and spiritual faculties (*operationi facultatum interiorum*).
He is told that this is an incomprehensible piece of writing—

which is true. The text is rhapsodic, with frequent references to facts that remain to be examined. Now, he was to leave that work, and he leaves it with obvious regret. He says goodbye with a special tenderness and turns to the next project, the text on the brain. While in Stockholm, Swedenborg had completed a comprehensive work on this subject, entitled *De Cerebro* (On the Brain) and would later in the summer of 1744, while he was in London, make additions to that manuscript. As transpires from the following entry of July 7–8, he seems to begin with the eye and the sight, a section that was to be printed in *De sensu communi*.

The number of drafts, rewrites, and additions this industrious man produced on his way forward are difficult to fathom. For clarity, I will recapitulate the situation. When Swedenborg left Sweden for his long journey abroad, he brought almost final manuscripts of the two first volumes of *The Animal Kingdom*. These were printed at The Hague in 1744. The manuscript of the third volume was probably written in London and was printed there in 1745. The draft version of that volume is the text of the posthumous *De sensu communi*.

At the same time, among his luggage was the huge manuscript on the brain—and much more. According to his original plan, that work was meant to form a part in the long Animal Kingdom series of volumes; "a procession of horses . . . in great numbers . . . large and beautiful, adorned with handsome harness" (as expressed in entry 229). As things turned out, however, he never published that manuscript; It was posthumously published as *De Cerebro*.

July 7–8

213

I saw how everything in an elliptical sphere concentrated itself upward in the highest part, since, in the lowest part, there was something like a tongue from which it spread out. This means, I think, that the innermost was *sanctuarium*, as a center of the globe above, and that such things indicated by the tongue shall be conceived. I believe I am destined to do this, which was inevitably the meaning of the *sanctuarium* I was dealing with and which

was, moreover, confirmed by all *objecta scientiarum* represented to me by women, as also that there was a deliberation whether I would be admitted to the society where my father was.

All in an oblong globe or ellipse is concentrated in its highest point. Beneath, in the low center, there is something like a tongue or flame that spreads up to the top or is diverged upwards. From this, Swedenborg construes that the center is *sanctuarium*, the most holy. The blazing tongue is to be described and explained. That is his task.

The idea of the sanctuary goes back to Genesis. As pointed out in connections with entry 171 there was in the tabernacle, the moveable shrine of the Israelites, a closed inner room—the Holy of Holies—where the Ark of Covenant was kept, containing God's promise to the Israelites. Swedenborg's task is to find out its meaning for posterity. The Old and New Testaments completed each other and were logically connected. Because of the coming of Christ, the Ark of the Hebrews, containing God's promise, now concerns all humanity: from the sanctuary, the flames of divine love reach out to embrace all the world. In the Swedenborgian worldview, the celestial center of gravity has its counterpart in the human soul. That is the most holy of our organs, the nexus of divine inflow. If it is allowed to take on command, the soul reigns in the kingdom of the flesh. Then, and then only, the end of existence is fulfilled, and all is subsumed to the angle of agape.

In the interpretation of the dream, an aspect of Swedenborg's call is clarified: to investigate the workings of divine love through the human soul. That this is his assignment is further testified by the apparitions of the sciences in loving female forms.

The main problem, however, still remained: how to tell good from evil, in practice as well as in theory. In the preceding paragraph, Swedenborg appears in a somewhat dejected mood; the physiological-anatomical aspect of the problem proved too difficult for him. Certainly, it is this very problem that is alluded to in the words on the tongue from which something was spread out. In his previously mentioned draft on eye and sight, the posthumously published *De sensu communi*, he treats this particular propagation. To understand how the perceptions are received by reason and soul, he must apply "philosophical principles," he writes. These principles are largely the doctrines referred to in the introduction to the present book—on correspondences, divine influx, and series and degrees. In fact, Swedenborg already has the instruments of understanding at hand: all can be explained step by step and understood, and not only be seen "obscurely" and "from behind" as he stated in entry 211. In the chapter on the eye and vision in *The Five Senses* §262, he expresses himself with marked confidence, based upon his recent dream experiences:

> *According to what I have been urged to observe, I should use my philosophical principles to consider lightness, weight, and activity in relation to purity. It must be pointed out, that in this way it is possible for me to fly wherever I want.*

We will return to the question of weightlessness and ability to fly when we read about his dreams during the night of July 14–15.

Swedenborg's growing awareness of his call is evident. But there are other points worth noting. A few weeks earlier, he had realized that his admission to a "society" was considered. That society or congregation might have been earthly as well as heavenly (see entry 206). The final sentence of entry 213 unambiguously refers to a heavenly admission, however: it concerns the place where his father, the bishop, now is dwelling. In other words: shall the dreamer, who is about to explore the nature of heavenly love, get access to the world of angels? According to his own words in the contemporaneous manuscript on the senses, he intuits a future transcendent activity, an ability to "fly wherever I want."

214

There came to me also the assuring thoughts that God's Son is love and that he took all sins of mankind upon himself and atoned for them up to the maximum penalty, since, if justice was to be done, there had to be *misericordia per amorem* [compassion by love].

The theological content of these assuring thoughts of his youth echoes the confidence of Arrhenius's hymn (see entry 37), which was ever-present in his mind:

For my sake he suffered, made up for the past:
a new life began that forever will last.

In the foregoing entry, Swedenborg described a dream about a globe generated by a propelling force, contained in the Holy of Holies. In *De Cultu et Amore Dei* (The Worship and Love of God), the work that takes its starting point from the moment when he closes the dream diary, Swedenborg outlines this sphere as the source of "intelligence, wisdom, righteousness, and honor." In this context, he perceives his task as an analysis of divine emanation. In this way, he hoped to establish a firm philosophical basis for moral distinctions, to illuminate truth, and to clarify the ontological status of our inner philosophical concepts.

Swedenborg is filled up by the profundity of the scope of his mission—this is evident from the notes of early July. From the notes of July 3–4, we see that he had finished the part treating the senses and was about to embark on the section treating the brain. He then wrote the section on the eyesight, which, in fact, considers the heavenly radiance.

The introductory lines of that section indicate that something important has happened. Swedenborg announces that he is to describe the different layers or auras that exist between the Divine and the human being. In doing so, he can "fly wherever he wants." The account given by his landlord Brockmer indicates that Swedenborg at this point has fallen ill, probably from mental exhaustion and over-excitement, and has been laid low under the burden of a task of superhuman dimensions, a final scientific proof of the soul's eternity, laid down in seventeen tomes, according to his published plan.

When he recovered and composed himself—and became aware of his real mission in life—he realized this himself. In *The Worship and Love of God,* he wrote that God punishes the one who faces God's glory without shielding his eyes, and a state of giddiness accordingly follows. Nor is that enough: "Our intellect . . . is struck by a fit of swoon or lunacy."

Swedenborg knew what he was talking about. He had boldly approached the glory of God without shielding his eyes.

[July] 9–10

215

I was together with the king and spoke to him, who was afterwards in a chamber, and then I talked to the princes and got to know them. They talked to each other about me; I said I was modest in amour and veneration. When I wanted to leave, I saw that the table had been set by the queen. I was not properly dressed since I had taken off my white sweater [woolen jacket]. I went upstairs to put it on again and talked to my father, who kissed me for having reminded him not to swear. Then the queen ascended with her retinue. This means that I will get to know the children of God because, the day before, I had chosen a new lodging.

This dream is peculiarly interesting since it can be related to well-documented realities. Many details in Brockmer's memorandum, which is discussed in the introduction, pages 54–57, date the dramatic episode of Swedenborg's alleged breakdown to July 9. Thus, we can compare dream and reality in the course of a single day and closely observe the operation of Swedenborg's dream language. For clarity, I will recapitulate some of the main features of the Brockmer–Mathesius account, limiting the account to elements later verified by Brockmer himself.

(1) Swedenborg's removal from Brockmer's lodgings was preceded by a strange confusion: Swedenborg saw himself as called to a divine assignment and was to be crucified on behalf of the Jews. Brockmer called upon an acquaintance of his, a doctor—apparently a member of the society of Brethren also—to give Swedenborg

medical care. Swedenborg at the same time went to the Swedish legation.

(2) At the legation, Swedenborg was not received by the minister himself, who was busy with the mail that day. After the visit to the legation, he got to a place called Gully's Hole. Here he took off his clothes. Some delegation employees saw this and chased him.

(3) At Brockmer's suggestion, Swedenborg was housed by a friend of the doctor who was caring for him. The new landlord was probably also a Moravian brother.

(4) When Swedenborg came to his new lodgings, he began washing his feet manically. When he settled down there, his health gradually improved, although he continued to behave strangely. Around July 19, during the "the dog days" according to the English account, his condition changed for the worse again.

We will return to some features of Brockmer's account in connection with dream entries 218 and 224 below, which add to the strange resemblance between Swedenborg's notes and contemporary eyewitness reports.

It seems probable that the meeting with the king and the conversation with the princes in the dream refer to the visit to the legation. The king's being in "a chamber" corresponds to the fact that the minister was busy with the mail. According to Brockmer, the minister was busy because that day was mailing day. In the National Archives of Sweden, we, in fact, find letters written by the Swedish minister in London, Casper Joachim Ringwicht, dated on that very day, July 10 (one of them being a request for higher wages). The princes were apparently Ringwicht's staff, who was concerned about him: "they talked to each other about me."

Seen from a wider angle, taking into account the full scope of the dream diary, Swedenborg's somewhat defensive declaration that he was "modest in amour and veneration" is interesting for another reason. That may well have been his motto when, three months later, he started writing *The Worship and Love of God*, the thesis of which is that the adoration of God means active love. In this mood, the low and worldly are transformed in us, and we become considerate and modest, "humble, meek, and polite." This is what he probably surmises Ringwicht's staff is saying about himself.

The prepared table, where the queen is waiting, represents something that Swedenborg is well aware he is still not prepared for, not yet pure enough for, or not worthy of. As we have earlier observed, *queen* denotes "wisdom" in Swedenborg's figurative language, an insight into divine order. The table is ready, but the guest is not.

The apparently unconnected reprimand to his swearing father, while on his way upstairs to put on his white sweater, fits in somewhere in the evasive logical structure of the dreams. To Swedenborg, it was becoming increasingly clear that all knowledge is available to the one who in love and worship turned his mind to God, to the prepared table of the queen. In the *Arcana Coelestia* §9166, written just a few years later, he observed that all depends on a pious acceptance of this fact and that true devotion is enough. The insight does not have to be confirmed by various oaths. The apparatus of annotation in his father's books appeared superficial to the son (compare entry 32 above!). According to Matthew 5:34–37, in Christ's Sermon on the Mount, we shall indeed not swear oaths, neither take an oath on heaven nor swear to the earth: "Do not swear at all, either by heaven, for it is the throne of God or by the earth, for it is his footstool. . . . Let your word be 'Yes, Yes' or 'No, No.'" This means, Swedenborg tells us, "that divine truths should be confirmed by the Lord and not by humans. This takes place when they are interiorated, and not external. Because shallow people confirm by swearing oaths, whereas inwardly directed people do that by adducing arguments. Those who are deeper in spirit do not confirm at all: they just state the facts.

[July] 14–15

216

I talked with Brita Behm, who seemed to give birth to a son; but, as Sveden had died long ago, I wondered how this could

happen. The baby was dead, however. In its place were the two Rosenadlers. She brought me to Count Horn in a large and costly carriage, the magnificence of which was extravagant.

Brita Behm, the Rosenadlers, and Count Horn are all main figures in a brilliant world to which the seer of visions also belongs; regarding these personal histories, please see the note for entry 216, pages 343–344. In the present dream context, they, like Swedenborg's brothers Eliezer and Jesper, should be regarded as masks or images representing something very distant from their earthly existence. Brita Behm, Swedenborg's forceful aunt, the widow of Johan Schwede—who obviously was nicknamed "Sveden"—appears to be reduced to a stand-in for her nephew. She/he has given birth to a still-born infant, replaced by the two Rosenadlers, grandsons of Brita Behm. We may suppose that they represent the two remaining parts of *The Animal Kingdom* series—on the senses and on the brain—the disappointing remainder of Swedenborg's still-born research project, which he now was about to give up. She/he now travels in a splendid coach to the famous Arvid Horn, president of the government offices and, for many years, a leading figure in Swedish politics.

217

There a meal was prepared. I went away but would come back later; flew all the time; came to a beautiful city, which I viewed; noticed I flew amiss and turned back. This refers to my work on *sensibus internis* **[the internal senses] and [De]** *cerebro* **[on the brain], which are likened to the offspring of Brita Behm; that I went in a costly carriage to Count Horn, as president of the government offices, and** *primas regni* **[principal regent/prime-minister], and went to another city, perhaps means that I had spiritually gone too far.**

In the vocabulary of the dream journal, the journey of nephew and aunt to the foremost office of the country is an approach to the Almighty and to the highest knowledge. A meal is being prepared for him—to acquire the knowledge of the Most High that is awaiting him—but, while there, he retreats, determined to come back later, and flies far away. The present reader, who has access to Swedenborg's posthumously published works, is reminded of the manuscript on the eye—he can now fly "wherever he wants." The dreamer apparently gets lost, sees another city, turns back. He wonders if perhaps he had in his excursions ventured too far from the soul or had wandered from his subject. Indeed, in the work he is writing at this time, *De sensu communi*, Swedenborg has by now made very far-reaching digressions to heavenly spheres, which at least formally, are loosely connected to the topic discussed.

218

> I crossed a footbridge over water. A ship was alongside. I came to a hole; then, I thought of bread, that every day bread is brought there, both large and small loaves. I suppose that this his refers to the Lutheran congregation. Christ is likened to the spiritual bread.

In his dream, Swedenborg now seems to have returned to London. There are four external points: (1) he passes over water (2) on some kind of wooden bridge or plank (*spång*); (3) there is a ship nearby; (4) he finally arrives at a hole or hollow in the ground. The ship he perceives as the church, where the heavenly bread is received.

The ship, the water, the footbridge, the bread—all these concepts have their proper places in this dream world. The only strange and unfamiliar element is the hole in his way. Perhaps, in his dream, Swedenborg is now back to his walk from the Swedish legation, five days ago, and Gully's Hole, where he is alleged to have undressed and rolled himself in the dirt. Gully's Hole was a huge drainage ditch not far from the legation.

The notes from the night of July 21–22 concern his relation to God and to "a congregation," probably the society of Moravian Brethren.

[July] 21–22

219

I saw a congregation where everyone had a little crown on his head, and two of them stood out front with quite large and magnificent crowns. One of them spoke joyfully, half in French and half in German. *This signifies those who have received the crowns of martyrs*, which I thought about the day before; but who the two were, if one was Huss, I do not know.*

In which congregation are crowns worn? We may assume that Swedenborg is imagining heaven, the society of the blessed. He sees two persons standing before the congregation, "with quite large and magnificent crowns." In his attempt at an interpretation, he recalls having thought of martyrs and martyrdom during the day. The fact that he thinks of Jan Hus in this context, is, as Inge Jonsson has pointed out, a memento. From Arvid Gradin's history of Moravianism, published in London in 1743, we know that the Moravians regarded Hus as a saint. He suffered martyrdom in 1415, when he was burned at the stake for his faith. Gradin remarks that "Jerome, a colleague, was honoured with the same martyrdom on 30 May 1416." Had Swedenborg the day before reflected upon Gradin's book? That little work is found in his library, no doubt procured during this stay in London. Whatever may be the answer to these questions, Swedenborg's reference to Hus nevertheless indicates that the Moravian Brethren, with whom he was apparently still lodging (although since July 9–10 with a different member), remained part of his world of imagination. This circumstance is of importance to an understanding of entry 221 below.

Earlier, in journal entry 47, we met with the concept of martyrdom, which meant the highest happiness. That this theme now recurs, or surfaces again, may give us a hint of the intensity of Swedenborg's longing for salvation, for spirituality. It may also hint

---

*The italics that appear in the following entries represent phrases or sentences that were underlined in Swedenborg's journal.

of an emerging awareness of forthcoming accusations and criticism of various kinds and of his reputation's being called in question.

The "right" rendering, however, may be quite different. Are the two leaders with the majestic crowns, the two standing front and center, Christ and Swedenborg? That Swedenborg saw his task as Messiah-like and thought he was going to be martyred are two of the traits pointed out by his friendly and much-concerned landlord in London.

220

A little child wanted to be attached to me, hugged me; but I seemed finally to refuse it. This meant that *one must be as a child towards our Lord*. This I then pondered, since children now had twice represented themselves, as in the preceding night. This means that you should not attend to the spiritual as if it were brought about by your own power or as if anything worldly would provide for it, but as a child who leaves all cares to our Lord.

The idea of being a child at heart with God is one of the dream diary's most important notions. In October, when the major themes of the crises come to a head, this becomes evermore clear. Swedenborg's confident and unconditional surrender, when he conclusively gives himself up to the Almighty, is the classical *Gelassenheit* of the mystics. To his inwardly directed but profoundly practically oriented mind, this process of wholehearted submission is not without complications: he is bound to adduce arguments. The basic problem that faced him was the following: if one's own efforts are left out of account or are considered negligible in comparison to the works of God, then one is back to the repudiated *sola fide* doctrine of journal entry 166, the "faith alone" confidence that had been dismissed by the dreamer as it had by his father, the late bishop. At this point, however, as can be seen in the next paragraph, the element of action is worked back into the equation.

221

> I pushed my way through a crowded congregation. I wanted to get out in time, but it was packed. I made my way through and came to an empty bench that had a cloth upon it, with which I wanted to cover myself. *This meant that I wished on my own to come into that congregation, remaining unknown,* as I had done the day before, but that effort should be deferred to our Lord.

Through his own efforts, the dreamer thus makes his way into a congregation. He stresses that he makes his way on his own. Furthermore, he wants to be incognito, to sit invisible in the church, covered, and leave in due time. When he considers his dream, he concludes that he has to rely on divine guidance in this case too.

Against the background of entry 219, it is not farfetched to conjecture that the congregation is the society of Brethren. As is clear from entry 202, Swedenborg paid visits to their ecstatic meetings. He probably got to know the leaders of the congregation and discussed theological matters with them. We know that such talks were very common in the circles where Swedenborg lived. We will return to this circumstance in a short time, when we consider entry 231.

The dreamer wants to join the group, yet remain unknown. We recognize the courteous distance of the court official and scientist Emanuel Swedenborg; in this respect, the religious crisis has not changed him. Here we also catch a glimpse of the unavoidable conflict between Swedenborg's reserved nature and the Moravian enthusiasts. Their superintendent was James Hutton, a friend of the leading Swedish Pietist Sven Rosén, who described Hutton as follows: "When he talked about the Passion of Christ, his heart was burning and his eyes were running." That was a mood and a temper completely alien to Swedenborg. From a superficial point of view, a spiritual affinity seems not very likely. When, in his dream, he is among the enthusiastic Brethren, Swedenborg recedes to an empty bench not far from the exit and hides under a cloth.

222

When I woke up, I had a vision, seeing a lot of gold before me and the air full. This means that our Lord, who disposes all things, gives me all that I need of spiritual and worldly things when, like a child, I entrust all care to him.

The vision of gold connects to the reflections on submission and true child-like piety of entry 220. In Swedenborg's special psychological-theological terms, this reads, "The highest reason promotes the victory of the soul and makes bodily states of mind vanish." When Swedenborg, in the May/June period, had written about this state of things, regarding the senses in general, he was struck by the profound theoretical implications of this idea. He realized that he was confronted with a completely new task, besides the one he was at work with. A new basis was required, "Yea, a new temple must be built." He added parenthetically: "This was symbolized by the gold I was carrying, by means of which the door could be opened, although with difficulty. Inside there would be a lot of gold on a table. This signifies that I will get access to spiritual things."

[July] 22–23

223

I seemed to take a quite high flight, but in such a circle that I came down duly when I felt faint. I saw a beautiful hall with a magnificent tapestry covering the walls; it was made all from one piece. This signified what the previous day I had in mind and heart: that we must let Christ take care for us in all that is spiritual and in all that is worldly.

The first sentence, on the his flying on high, is obviously connected with the next paragraph of the notes.

There are numerous halls, chambers, and rooms in his dreams. They are magnificent or disorderly, tidy or untidy, dark or lit up. Usually, they are metaphors of various states of mind, of the soul's readiness for the Divine. These rooms or spaces are found in houses and palaces, edifices built from truths, verities visible to the inhabitants of the clean and orderly dwellings. In this case, the room has a costly tapestry, all of one piece.

Swedenborg's interpretation of the two dream visions is not far-flung. All depends on trusting, body and soul, in the Divine. Knowing his present difficulties with the problems of sensory perception, he subordinates his scrutiny of the brain to a higher perspective from which all organs are seen as the compound materialization of a grand design. The tapestry is continuous, all cut in one piece. This state of things is evident from the previously mentioned studies on eyesight and visual perception.

224

I saw a boy rushing off with my shirt, and I ran after him. *This is supposed to mean that I have not washed my feet.*

Let us first consider the child and the shirt. Throughout the dream diary, children of either sex are images of purity and innocence. Seen against that background, the dreamer has been undressed by a force of innocence, and he tries to catch up with that. Loss of clothes, nakedness, certainly belongs to a universal dream world. To Swedenborg, his clothes are always connected with purity or impurity in a spiritual sense. We can follow this sense from the nightmare on the invitation to eat at the queen's table in entry 215, after he had taken off his white sweater or undershirt (*tröja*) in the royal palace. As pointed out concerning entry 206 above, vests, garments, and clothes are also part of a Moravian imagery regarding everything sinful a person must strip off to take on the shroud of righteousness. These sins were worn by Christ already. In one of his last entries, Swedenborg dreams that the king takes the burdens of others upon himself and wore them "like clothes" (see entry 274 of October 20–21). Again, we may recall the peculiar Moravian *Songs of Zion* of 1743:

I got a coat
and a pilgrim's staff
to my support
to my comfort
on my way,
and off I went.
When the need
made itself felt,
the cane bent,
fell off my hand,
The coat burnt,
was reduced to ashes
to the last fray.

A carnal stay
is useless in need,
wherever you head.
Be dressed in conceit
is revealing behavior;
laid bare you proceed
stark naked you go.
Nothing counts
and nothing will do
but the wounds of the Savior.

We cannot exclude the possibility that this imagery was, in some sense, universally Christian at the time. Nevertheless, Swedenborg's own interpretation, underlined in his manuscript, has Moravian connotations. We have earlier come across the ritual washing of feet of the Brethren (see entry 91 of April 9–10). A typical but significant trait of Zinzendorf's interpretation of Christ's *pedilavium*, adopted as a church practice, was that it was looked upon as a purification, not as an act of humility as in the Gospel of John. The boy in Swedenborg's dream runs away with his garment of sinfulness, but the owner pursues him. The reason for this theft, then, is that he has not washed his feet and thus is still defiled.

[July] 24–25

225

Beside other things, I seemed to be in company with many, and we made merry. I was to be the guest of one of them. I left there, was going to travel, then appeared to come back; but when I left, I went away from there, which was not my intention. I met with someone who told me that a canopy had been cut for my bed, without my knowledge. *If I shall choose another way in my work and another is being prepared, I don't know.* This is all dark to me.

The dreamer finds himself in a "worldly" environment. He is invited to another party. He leaves but then returns. Then, he unexpectedly leaves again. After the second departure, he meets someone who has a four-poster bed ready for him.

The pattern is easily recognized. Swedenborg had been working as a scientist for a long time. At the same time, he knew that his task was theological in the etymological sense of the adjective: pertaining to the Word of God. This awareness put its imprint on his work: we may divine that the dreamer refers to the *Economy of the Animal Kingdom*, where the Christian epistemology is already developed. In the *Animal Kingdom*, he had returned to the worldly. In the latter, giant research project, he aimed at proving the existence of God and the functioning of the soul by means of the "flowering" empiricism of eighteenth-century science (see entry 29 of March 30–31).

We know that Swedenborg planned a long series of volumes. His work was interrupted, however, "which was not my intention," and once again he leaves worldly reality. On this new track, he meets God. Without his knowing it, the Divine had prepared a screen for him, a protective curtain, that will screen off the world of the senses.

The purport of this dream sequence is knowledge and divine call, a variation on the theme of entry 31 of early April, where the dreamer, together with the king, drew the curtains of their room;

furthermore, it reminds us of the note on the marching soldiers outside the window, guarding the servant of divine wisdom (entry 35).

The canopy image belongs to a number of protecting elements
of divine origin—screens and curtains, for example. For the
bishop's son, well versed in the Scriptures, the screen metaphor was
natural. Since his childhood he had read and heard the words of
Psalm 31:19–20:

> O how abundant is your goodness that you have laid up for
>   those who fear you,
> and accomplished for those who take refuge in you, in the sight
>   of everyone!
> In the shelter of your presence you hid them from human plots;
> you hold them safe under your shelter from contentious tongues.

[July] 27–28 [changed from 28/28]

226

**I saw my father in a beautiful vestment before a congregation.
He spoke kindly to me and wanted to take me to a person in an
inner room, one who appeared to be asleep, to tell him about
me. I left, afraid of waking him up.** *This referred to the fact
that I began reading the Bible in the evening and that, on Saturday morning, I feared I was not prepared as I should be.*

Swedenborg sees his father in a magnificent surplice—perhaps, as
in the Easter vision, in a reddish attire. Jesper Swedberg is addressing a congregation and speaks amiably to his son. The bishop, who
according to his son's diary is now in paradise, wishes to tell somebody "who appeared to be asleep" about Emanuel. The context indicates that Christ is referred to in the guise of the sleeper. The
bishop also comforts Emanuel, who regards himself as impenitent
and unprepared for the Holy Supper. As we have already seen, the
Saturday preliminaries, when he was going to partake of Communion, were very important to Swedenborg.

The friendly words of the bishop are also seen as a sign of his father's satisfaction with his son's Bible reading in the evenings. Jesper Swedberg's contentment will not surprise anyone familiar with his pious habits and his unshakable biblical foundation.

[July] 29–30

227

I saw a big animal with wings; at times, it looked like a human being, but with a huge mouth. He did not dare to touch me. I dashed after him with my rapier, but I lacked skill and enough strength in my arms to hit him. Finally, he was standing in front of me with a rifle and fired a barrel at me with something like venom, but which did not hurt me because I was protected. Then, I presently ran the rapier into his gaping mouth, not with much force, however. I thrust it deeper, and it appeared to be said that he was killed. *The day before I thought of the woman and the dragon in the Apocalypse, and I wished I could be instrumental in killing the dragon; but that is not in my power but that of God alone.*

The mentioned Bible reading in the evening, so commended by his father, appears to have been the Revelation of St. John. As he was to do many times later in his life, Swedenborg stops at the twelfth chapter. There the reader is met with a wondrous woman in the throws of childbirth, "clothed with the sun, and the moon under her feet." She is faced by a red dragon, who stands before her waiting, ready to devour her child as soon as it is born.

Who is this woman in labor pains, and who is that child to be delivered? Who is the dragon? The monster is the discrepancy between what we believe in and what we do, between faith and behavior, insight and life. In Swedenborg's dream iconography, the woman signifies divine wisdom, the outcome of which is threatened by the ravenous solifidian beasts of blind faith.

Swedenborg asks himself whether he is the one finally to kill the monster. Here, we confront a clear sign of his emerging awareness of a future challenge and of his desire to play a principal part in the world drama.

8

AUGUST 1744

---◆◆×◆◆---

228

For a long time, I was in holy shivers and besides that in a deep sleep. I thought that maybe something holy was going to happen. I seemed to be thrown on my face, but I am not certain about that. Then, I was taken away from there and found under my back one who appeared to me familiar, and I was annoyed that he had taken me away from it and said when he left that he should not do that anymore. The shivers continued, but I did not see anything more. *This was that something holy had come to me and touched me, and I was brought to the work I this day had begun writing about the sense, and that I did not want it to draw me away from what is more important.*

The shivers are "holy." According to the hermeneutics Swedenborg was to develop, the shuddering, quailing, and trembling with fear are, as in the Psalms, a sign that the Godhead is close. One shakes as "the earth trembled and shook" when Jehovah comes down (Ps. 77:18). In *Arcana Coelestia* §8816, Swedenborg wrote on this holy tremor, distinguishing fear of God from terror:

> They who are in good do indeed tremble in the presence of the Divine, but it is a holy tremor which precedes reception. But they who are in evil are in terror at the presence of the Divine, and therefore flee away, and are then enveloped in their falsities as in a dusky cloud, and are hidden.

Swedenborg feels he is prostrated and has a presentiment of something holy. The sacred mood withers away, however; he then discovers that somebody is behind him and that he is acquainted with that person. We catch a glimpse of something he was to explain in his future teachings on spirits, an embryo of which we will see in his October notes. Evil influences approach us from behind. When a sinister specter sticks to our back, it takes on the identity of the possessed and believes it is us.

The tremors return. Swedenborg believes they bring him to his new work *De sensibus*; but, at one and the same time, this distances him from "something holy." It should be noted that the Divine appears to encourage him to go on with a traditional scientific work. Less than eight weeks afterwards, he is urged in a dream to stop that very work, to enter an enterprise of completely different character. Seen from Swedenborg's point of view, this is logical. It is due to his present work that he gradually realizes his call.

As has happened at many other times, the message received is corroborated by a subsequent dream:

229

> **Then I waited for a procession of horses, and indeed there came beautiful, big, white-yellow horses in a large number, then even more horses in beautiful teams, which came to me—fat, big, handsome, ornamented with magnificent harnesses—*which refers to the work I have now begun, the second [team refers] to the work on the brain. So now I find that I have God's permission for it and believe he assists me.***

The pageant scene appears for the third time. The ongoing work on the senses is represented by horses of yellowish white color. The others in the procession of splendid pairs or four-in-hands are his work on the brain. The precedence of the dun-colored horse may be a reminiscence of Swedenborg's reading of the Bible. In the Old Testament, Zechariah had put forth some abstruse prophesies in a related figurative tongue, the particulars of which were to occupy his thoughts for a long time afterwards. The equestrian scenery appears again in Swedenborg's tract *The*

White Horse, where the position of the cream-colored horse is accounted for.

August 4–5

230

> I saw a man approach me with his rapier drawn. I seemed to have a rapier with a silver hilt; but when he reached me, I had nothing but a broken sheath. He lay down on my back and bit my hands. I called for help, but there was no help to be found.

This tribulation resembles that of the preceding night; the form is similar. The dreamer is defenseless, while the temptation bullies him and hangs on his back, biting him. And the next dream is similarly connected to trespasses and penitentiary ordeals.

231

> Then I was dealing with a whore in the presence of As. B. I seemed to boast about it, that I was so strong. *This means that I have prepared myself against my God, every day, with thoughts that cling to me; that, from this, nobody but God can deliver me; and that I have boasted before J[?]. H. about my work.* I planned to go to God's table the next day, but thus finding that no human being but God alone can grant absolution, I gave up going; and on this account, it was also given to me to comment upon confession.

Swedenborg's inferior self forces him to commit sins. On his own, without God, he is a prey to temptations and pride. The editors of the original Swedish text, Klemming and Dahlgren, conjectured that the abbreviation *"As. B."* referred to the Assessor Elias Brenner, a well-known resident of Stockholm in the Age of Liberty. However, the figures in Swedenborg's dreams do not pop up accidentally; rather, the actors and galleries in this chamber of dreams are kindred and immutable, close to his waking life rather than distant. A coworker at the Royal College of Mines, Assessor

Johan Bergenstierna, is a more likely candidate for "As.B." Bergenstierna was married to the widow of Swedenborg's brother Eliezer, mentioned earlier in the dream diary in entry 196.

The dream about bragging and undue intimacy is not only a reminder of his sinning when he is left to himself but also states that he has boasted of his actions. Klemming and his assistant Dahlgren were uncertain as to the first letter of the initial and guessed that it was a "D." However, after a close examination of the manuscript, it can be inferred that the letter is a "J." Swedenborg probably refers to James Hutton, the leader of the London congregation to which his landlord belonged (see entry 221).

We observe that Swedenborg intended to go to the Lord's Supper but changed his mind. In this connection, he notes that "no human being but God alone can grant absolution," for which reason he was allowed to make some observations concerning the confession before Communion. These words become comprehensible when viewed against the background of the rituals connected with the Brethren's Communion. In his book on the Moravian Church, published in London by bookseller James Hutton, Arvid Gradin wrote:

> *Fjärde eller femte dagen före nattvardsgudstjänsten brukar varje broder och syster besökas av den äldste i sin kör, eller av deras gruppledare. Deras själars tillstånd rannsakas, och tillstånd ges att gå till Guds bord. All omsorg och försiktighet visas när det gäller dessa heliga ting. De medlemmar som befunnits brista i renhet eller hjärtats enkelhet blir uteslutna.*

> [Four or five days before the celebration of the Holy Communion, every brother and sister are usually visited by the eldest in their choir, or by their group leader. The condition of their souls is thoroughly searched, and permission is granted to the Lord's Table. Minute care and fastidiousness are shown regarding these holy matters. Members who prove deficient in purity and simplicity of heart are expelled.]

Certainly, Hutton wanted to get the presumptive communicant to confession, but Swedenborg resisted or stopped [afhölt] this. He probably also commented upon the matter.

Hutton's visit to Swedenborg need not necessarily have been caused by the Communion, however. This kind of visit was customary, a social routine within the congregation, and we should remember that Swedenborg was being housed by a member.

In his later works, Swedenborg argues against ritual confession of sins and sacramental delegation of absolution. Every individual shall examine him- or herself and ask the Lord for forgiveness for his or her trespasses. To enumerate one's sins to another human being is superfluous, Swedenborg maintains.

When later in the *Spiritual Diary*, written between 1747 and 1765, Swedenborg again noted down his dreams, reflections, and inspirations, he was critical of the Moravians. In particular, he objected to their belief in justification by faith. They also had another disadvantage for him: they were too inquisitive and for their own gain tried to collect as much information about their fellow-beings as possible.

[August] 8–9

232

I came to Sweden and saw that the kingdom was divided into two kingdoms: the larger one was at Upland, and the other one in the direction of Örebro. There were two kings, the second being minor, yet it was said that his kingdom extended toward Bohus. I was with him, and his kingdom grew. It seemed to me that I was commissioned to become a secretary in Java, but that I was unfit for this as I did not know the language; still, I acceded. Afterwards, I dreamed about small birds that settled down about my head and that had to be picked off. *It signified that I had not properly arranged and carried out the part on corpore reticulari Malpighii.*

The first part of this dream is a variation on one of the dream diary's main themes: Swedenborg's call and his feeling of insufficiency. The two kingdoms are certainly the heavenly and earthly domains, Swedenborg's own allegiance being to the former. Through a royal appointment, he is authorized to serve in a foreign country whose language he does not understand, and he thinks he is unqualified for the task, ("still, I acceded").

This dream is probably a reminiscence of Swedenborg's studies of the Book of Daniel. With its famous prophecy of the Messiah's appearance on earth, its dreams, and Daniel's interpretation of those dreams, that book must have appealed to Swedenborg in the same way as did the Book of Revelations. In the marginal notes to one of his Bibles (the Schmidius edition), Swedenborg commented on Daniel 11, where there is an account of wars between two powerful countries, the lands of the North and South. Swedenborg has the North stand for falsity, the South for truth. Part of their southern kingdom, or allied to it, was Greece. In the original Hebrew text, it is called the *Jawan*. Thus, he dreams, he is appointed to work there. The vital importance of linguistic knowledge is reflected in his commentary on the first verse of that chapter in Daniel:

> Greece *(Java)* symbolizes those who *(opposite to the people of the North)* never speak literally *(of heavenly things)*. Instead, they stick to the inner sense. Yet in their hearts they are at odds. Therefore, their princes war with each other, as when the salt of the New Church appears among the leaders of the old church.

When he made this entry in his dream journal, Swedenborg certainly did not yet have a clear idea of his future commission. We now see how, in his sleep, he approaches the future work in an interplay of meanings, a task at which he will later excel. For the time being, however, he does not interpret his secretarial commission, Java, or the words about linguistic abilities. Very likely he has just been reading that chapter of the Book of Daniel, and the context appeared self-evident to the only intended reader of his diary—

himself. We should bear in mind that we are dealing with private notes and not an account intended for publication.

This entry is particularly interesting since it illuminates his dream language. The implicit task of interpreting the hidden meaning of Scripture presupposes a knowledge of the tongue. As pointed out earlier in the introduction to this book ("The Call," 66–69), Swedenborg began his studies of Hebrew immediately after the dream diary period. The theme is indicated already in entry 196—in the extensive entry on various dreams, jotted down shortly after his arrival to London.

We recognize the birds in the ensuing passage. They are his erroneous or "ungovernable" thoughts, which must be eliminated. Instantly, he understands their relevance. Evidently, he has just written the section of *The Five Senses* that treats the anatomy of the papillae of the skin. These papillae are full of reticule or netlike bodies, first demonstrated and described by the famous seventeenth-century Italian anatomist Marcello Malpighi by means of the microscope. The problem Swedenborg here refers to is probably the one alluded to in entry 212, namely, how impressions from the outside—as sensations of touch through the tactile corpuscles in the skin—are transmitted as nervous impulses to the brain.

August 26–27

233

During the past days, I was quite troubled and as it were oppressed by my sins, which seemed not to be forgiven and which prevented me from attending the Lord's Supper the last time. Then, it seemed to me that I was relieved the day before; in the night, the soles of my feet appeared altogether white, *which signifies that my sins are forgiven* and many other things, that I was welcome back again.

This date is another Sunday entry with its significant features. Burdened by his wickedness, Swedenborg feels unworthy of partaking of Communion. This is a matter we have already met with in several contexts. On the "right preparation" for the Lord's Table, see entry 89 of April 9–10.

On this particular Sunday, the sign of purity was the whiteness of his *plantae pedis*, the soles of his feet. Here we come across another indication of the significance of *pedilavium*, the ritual foot washing, particularly as a means for purification and preparation.

[August] 27–28

234 _____

I seemed to take out a book from my father's library. Then, I went into a ship and was sitting with another where the helm usually is. Yet another person was sitting at my right hand. When I stood up, there was another man who sat down in my place; and when I wished to resume it, he sat higher up and made room for me. A woman was sitting on my left and another one in front of me. I arose and allowed her to sit there; she sat down, but then there was no fauteuil but only an armchair, and I was in front of her.

235 _____

Wine was brought in; it looked like oxlip wine and was served in rummers [a large, footed drinking glass]. A rummer was given to me, which I emptied at once. It was the most delicious I could ever taste and was taken in almost imperceptibly, as if it were heavenly nectar. The man by the wheel all the time sat in his place highest up. *This signifies how I shall receive help in my work from a higher hand, so that I am simply used as an instrument:* on this account, moreover, I had with me a companion, whose employment, I said, was to sweep clean. This, too, signifies me.

Swedenborg perceives that his dream is about the direction to be taken and the method he should use for his next work. It is related to the motifs of entry 232, taken down earlier in August, and it is also linked to his final entries of October 1744.

First, he borrows a book from his father's library. Can it possibly be the one he is about to write—the book he later (in entry 278) calls a *liber divinus*, a divine book?

Next, he is on board a sailing ship, sitting at its wheel. A man is seated to his right. The dreamer rises, and the scene changes. A new figure first takes Swedenborg's place, but then moves higher up at the helm. Two women are also on board: one is sitting on Emanuel's left, one in front of him. Again, he gets up and gives his seat to the woman who has been sitting in front of him. They exchange places. But, as she sits down, he notices that the easy chair he has been sitting on has been changed to a railchair.

To summarize these intricate movements, we have a helmsman, the dreamer himself, and two women. One of these women is always at his side, the other first in front of him, then behind him. Swedenborg is describing a paradigmatic situation that is deeply anchored in the Christian mind. The ship is an archetype of a congregation, with humankind perpetually exposed to Gennesaret's waves, threatened by storms within, by "roving Poles and hussars," to use Swedenborg's metaphor for intruding thoughts. In this vulnerable position, the human being has only one recourse: the three virtues of faith, hope, and charity or love. Each has its ritual place.

First and foremost of the three is love, *caritas*, which Swedenborg will later term *cultus* (worship). It is the deed, which is a "liturgy," in that word's original sense of a public act, in which everyone may take part. Action is central.

To one side sits faith, iconographically in the place of the heart, like the risen Christ beside his disciples on the road to Emmaus.

Hope is in Christ, the man at the helm—hope, for the forgiveness of sins, eternal life.

Shortly after his Easter vision, Swedenborg dreamed of arcane movements in the crypt of St. Peter (entry 84). In his journal of travel for 1738, he had described Bernini's basilica. Did he see Giotto di Bondone's fresco of the storm-tossed boat on Lake Gennesaret?

In his dream, Swedenborg is the ship's principal passenger. His task, precisely, is *caritas*, the action inspired by love. The shift from armchair to a more simple chair seems to indicate sacrifice and devotion, the work of love. The task of the woman by his side is to "sweep clean," and he adds: "This, too, signifies me." This cleansing is, in his dream language, a paraphrase of the love that purifies. He uses the same expression again in entry 282. Love purifies action, purging it of the self-love that has been tormenting him: *impurum—* all that might obstruct.

Highest on the poop is Christ. All hope rests with the pilot. The dreamer follows his orders.

As so often in Swedenborg's interpretations, his interpretation of this dream of a divinely steered ship relates directly to his own writings: *"I shall receive help in my work from a higher hand."* This dream is the first articulation of what kind of book he is now going to write. From now on, we shall be able to follow, stage by stage, how this task becomes clearer, up to the final instructions contained in the diary's last entry.

A golden wine is served. It tastes like nectar, the drink of angels. Is this wine a figure for his relation to God? Christ's blood?

More or less clearly, we glimpse certain recurrent motifs in the series of dreams. Gradually, the theme of divine worship—that is, divine love—emerges from his Easter vision and Christ's exhortation, "Well then, do!" What had first seemed to Swedenborg as a matter of method and form—of giving up his belief in his own capacity and submitting himself to the divine will—turns outs to be a complete transformation of content and aim.

9

SEPTEMBER 1744

——◆◆◆◆◆——

September 1–2*

236

On 2 Aug. [Sept. 2], I intended to go to God's Table because I
was assured, as far as I could understand, that I was relieved of
my sins; but then I saw a large dog that ran up to me but did me
no harm. I showed it to a person who stood beside me, and the
dog did not hurt him either. [This signifies] *either that, during
the day before, I wanted to boast of a visit or else that the others around me are flattering.*

This note was written down on a Sunday. Swedenborg intended to
go the Lord's Table, feeling freed of his sins. However, one of the
diary's many dogs turns up, those singular signs of pride and selfishness. Although the hound does not bite him, it is still a reminder
of his own depravity. The creature reminds him of his pride, now
in connection with his reception of a distinguished visitor.

237

Then, I seemed to perceive that Dideron had left his king, with
whom he had stood so high in favor, and that he went to the
Danes and died there; and that his wife, who was deceitful,
caused this and now was awaiting his corpse. *Now I hear, as if
he inspirited me, that I should not leave the church of Christ
and go for the Lord's Supper over yonder, since then I would
again become spiritually dead.* The rest I could not grasp, so
there is a mystery under this. I refrained from attending, and I

---

*Swedenborg mistakenly wrote "Aug. 1 x 2" as the date of this entry.

was kindled by the Holy Spirit, as is generally the case when I act according to command.

This dream about "Dideron" is most interesting as an example of the relationship between dream and interpretation. Lieutenant-General Johan Fredrik Didron, whom Swedenborg must certainly have known in the House of the Nobility in Stockholm, was a Cap politician who, like Swedenborg, had opposed the war with Russia. Indeed, at its conclusion, he had been condemned for his remarkable passivity in the war.

In Swedenborg's dream, Didron, although high in favor, leaves his king and, deserting to the enemy, is killed. Behind this desertion lies his wife, a false character. Now she is waiting for his stiff body.

A modern reader, examining this dream schematically against the background of Swedenborg's dream language as we know it, finds that it is about an act of treason, albeit not one of a military or political nature. Didron is Swedenborg himself, who, despite all the grace shown him, has abandoned his king: God. The general— the scientist—takes sides with all that turns its back on and is hostile to the Divine. Behind this act of desertion is a false-minded wife, a false love. This leads to his death and his false love's waiting for the arrival of his remains: his miserable existence and his corrupt humanity.

Whether or not Swedenborg himself, interpreting the dream, is explicit about this parallel, he introduces the special problem that seemed most urgent at the moment of awakening and that was also implied, on a higher plane, by his question of fidelity and apostasy. Instantly, he thinks he is hearing that his dream about Dideron bears on his own relationships with "the church of Christ," which might refer to the London Moravians. To abandon them would be like deserting to the enemy, and he decides to remain with them. A little more than a month later, he will note in his diary that he is still "there, but am not accepted" (see entry 264 of October 10–11). If this was the case, his reluctance to become a communicant was due to their strict ritual demands.

Didron had died as a refugee in exile. Dogged by the hound of arrogance, Swedenborg finds himself spiritually stiff. It is a Sunday, and he asks himself whether he ought to receive Communion, but, finding that he is not properly prepared, he abstains. According to Paul in 1 Cor. 11: 27, to take the sacraments without first having prepared oneself for it a sin: "Whoever, therefore, eats the bread or drinks the cup of the Lord in an unworthy manner will be answerable for the body and blood of the Lord." The Moravian Brethren laid particular emphasis on such preparation. Swedenborg did as he had been told. As so often when following instructions from on high, he is rewarded with spiritual lucidity.

September 16, on a Sunday afternoon

238
_____

During the night between the fifteenth and the sixteenth, I saw in my sleep two kings, the king of France and the king of Poland, who proposed sublime things. Then, I saw a little girl, who sang for me as I was going out. *This signified that what I had written was satisfactory, which was the conclusion of the first chapter on the tactile sense* [sensu tactus].

In his dream about Didron, there had been two kingdoms, Sweden and Denmark. Considering recent historical events, these naturally stood for good and evil: knowledge received from God and imperfect knowledge derived from the senses.

As Swedenborg's diary approaches its end, kings will often appear in its pages. Royalist symbols came naturally to Swedenborg: he was living in an age when kingship by divine right probably still seemed to have an objective content. Royalist symbolic values, furthermore, had appeared in the titles of his great works on the animal kingdom. Yet this title, "The Animal Kingdom," *Regnum Animale*, is ambiguous. In the language of that age, the words simply meant "the realm of the animals"—that is, the "realm of living beings." One of the three earthly realms explored by science, it was superior to the vegetable kingdom and the mineral kingdom. The Latin adjective *animalis*, however, can be derived from two substantives:

animalis, which refers to a living being or an animal, and *anima*, the soul. Thus, *The Animal Kingdom* meant the realm of life or the dominion of the soul. The sense must be determined from the context and by the reader: we have two realms in one, two kings. To this must be added Swedenborg's associations in connection with his reading of the Book of Daniel. Here, as mentioned in connection with entry 232, it was precisely a question of "kingdoms."

Accordingly when Swedenborg, in the final entries of the diary, leaves the animal kingdom, he, like Didron in his dream, is truly changing sides, escaping one kingdom for the another.

His vision of the two kings who "proposed sublime things" symbolizes his existential and scientific choice. Although he does not explicitly take sides on this particular Sunday afternoon, he says that what he had written toward the end of the week had been "satisfactory." And, as a sign, he thought he had heard a girl singing when he went out. He fancies this refers to the end of the work's first chapter, a part on the sense of feeling, found in *The Animal Kingdom* II, §519, where we read:

> *The outermost sphere, or sphere of the body, consists of and draws its nourishment from food derived from the earth's bosom. But the outermost sphere is nourished wholly by the ethereal and heavenly. This food is absorbed through the extraordinarily finely constructed mouths of the skin. . . . In this way, the coarser, undermost, and lower part of the human being is supported by and comes from the earth. But the better, purer part comes from heaven. But as long as this earthly connection is maintained, this better part of the human being is unconscious of the nourishment that comes from above.*

After the note discussed above, Swedenborg writes down a dream he had while taking a nap on this Sunday afternoon:

239

Immediately after the midday meal, when I was asleep, there appeared to me a woman, but I did not see her face; she was

rather stout and was dressed in very white clothes. I wished to buy something to drink from her, but she said she had nothing left. There was one person present, however, who yielded to me his right to get a glass from her, which she had concealed in her clothes. She was feeling for it, when I noticed how very stout she was, as if pregnant. After looking for it in the folds of her sleeve, she found what I was to drink. She thought it was chocolate, but it was wine. It seemed I was not willing to take it since it was chocolate. Immediately afterwards I awoke. It seemed to me then, as also once or twice before, that I perceived a very strong odor of wine. I wondered most at her snow-white garments. *I cannot know very well what this means*, whether she was the same woman *that I had when the word* sanctuarium *was uttered, for I did not see her face, and that she was pregnant, which should signify that I am now on the right path laboring on the work I will give birth to, whereas, that day, I found myself quite enlightened in the things I had in hand.*

This dream can be seen as a sequel to the "vision" that preceded it. As he writes, it is a confirmation that he is on the right path. The form it takes yields further insight into the Swedenborgian dream mechanisms:

(1) The woman in white has only one duty toward the dreamer: he is thirsty, and she must give him to drink. He asks for wine and is finally given some.

(2) It is not certain that his request for wine would be granted. Initially, the woman said there was none left. When she finally accedes, it is due to some other person present, who accords him his right to get a glass. There seems to be some confusion as it is served, and the dreamer declines it, believing he is being given chocolate instead. In the end, it turns out to be wine.

(3) The woman is fat and flowering, pregnant. She is dressed in shining white clothes, folded and pleated, in which she hides wine and glasses.

Swedenborg has no interpretation of his own request for wine or his refusal to accept anything else. On the contrary, he seems to regard this point as obscure. For us, however, with our knowledge of the full context, including entries still to be written, the matter is transparent. The wine is connected with the nectar in his dream of August 23–24 (entry 235), a heavenly drink. Or, in liturgical terms, the blood of Christ in the communion wine. Or, the "nourishment that comes from above," as he describes it in the section of *The Animal Kingdom* quoted above.

His dream of April 2–3 (entry 34) had a similar implication. There he had seemed to see a beggar, calling for pork. "They wished to give him something else, but he insistently called for pork." That beggar symbolized the dreamer himself. What he had demanded in that dream had not been wine but the transubstantiated Word, the body of Christ.

This time he insists on wine and is refused: "She said she had nothing left." Whereupon someone beside him intervenes. This other person lets Swedenborg have his own glass, his own portion. Thus, he is drinking someone else's wine.

The two realms, and the need to choose between them, are, as we have seen, paradigmatic. That also applies to the worship and the help from "someone" who is present beside him. Relation to the Divine can be said to have a dual aspect. On the one hand, one must turn to the Godhead in prayer and worship. On the other, neither prayer nor worship may have any result, may even be harmful, unless offered within divine love. This is suggested, as we have seen, in the dream about the ship and the wine (entries 234 and 235). Now it appears again. It will be further clarified in early October and finally become the central thought in his last diary entry.

Wine or chocolate? One of Swedenborg's major problems for the rest of his life is foreshadowed here: how to distinguish between spirits, between good and evil. We will return to this theme, which will become prominent from early October on.

Lastly, who is the voluptuous and commanding woman in white? She seems to be hiding both the wine itself and a glass in her generous snow-white garments. We may take her for an image of "right" love. The dreamer is surprised at her expansiveness, wonders whether she is not the same woman with whom he slept in his dream at Leyden in April (entry 171). If this is so, he thinks his relationship with pure truth has born fruit. This feeling he expresses in the last lines: "That day, I found myself quite enlightened in the things I had in hand."

[September] 17–18

240

I saw the king of Prussia and someone who said he was on his way to cause enmity between the kings of Prussia and France.

Swedenborg does not provide an interpretation here. To him the sense of this dream may have been self-evident. We have already become acquainted with the two kingdoms of his dreams, the realm of God and our earthly "animal kingdom." "Someone"— Swedenborg?—is to "cause enmity between" them.

Ratio naturalis does not agree with *ratio spiritualis*, he observed when starting his diary (entry 26). The existence of the kingdom of God can never be proved in terms of the animal kingdom. Faith is one thing, knowledge another. That conclusion changed his life. Before, he had not been aware of the incessant conflict, but now he finds himself called to evoke the strife. The experiences of the dream diary period had forever upset his scientific scheme.

[September] 18–19

241

I seemed to be walking on ground that was very rough, with an iron staff in my hand. After a while, it was not heavy to walk with, and I arrived at the end of the field and lay on a bed. A huge black ox approached me and looked as he wanted to gore me with his horns. I was afraid, but it was said to me, *"You will come through." I awoke: something will happen to me when I have finished the first chapter on the sense of touch* [sensu tactus].

The rough ground, the iron staff, and the bullock that is about to attack him with its horns are, of course, all images of his spiritual hardship. He seems to be faced by a difficult chapter of his book but is told all will end up well. The prompting dream voice, which again is heard here, consoles, warns, and exhorts the dreamer throughout the diary, leading him on his way forward.

[September] 21**

242 _____

> This was a Sunday. Before I fell asleep I was thinking very hard on what I am writing at the moment, and then it was said to me: "Shut up! Or, I'll beat you!" Then, I saw somebody sitting on ice, and I was scared, came into a vision as it were. I stopped my thoughts, and one of the common tremors came over me. This means that I should not persist in my work so long, especially not on Sundays, or perhaps in the evenings.

Swedenborg is evidently persistent in his scientific work and deeply involved in it, week after week. In view of his sickness in July, we can see how he himself seems to be afraid of working so hard that he will again be overwrought. Thinking about his work as he falls asleep, a voice is checking him, urging him under penalty to hold his tongue. The ice sheet is thin, and he is in danger of falling through, being badly beaten. He must go on with some caution, rest on Sundays, perhaps in the evenings too.

[September] 29–30

243 _____

> This was on Saturday night before Sunday. I saw the gable of the most beautiful palace that anyone could see, and the center of it was shining like the sun. I was told that it had been

---

**The date was corrected by Swedenborg; it was first dated "27."

resolved in the society that I was to become a member, an immortal one, which nobody had ever been before, with the exception of one who had been dead and lived; but some said
there were others. Then, the thought occurred to me whether
the most important thing is not to be with God and thus to
live. *This, therefore, was about that which I had just then
brought to a finish concerning organic forms in general and
especially the conclusion.*

This sequence begins with the dreamer's glimpsing the gable-end
of a magnificent, shining palace—that is, as always, a work or a
doctrine. As we see, he refers to his chapter on "Organic Forms in
General," which would later be included in the third part of *The Animal Kingdom*, printed in London in 1745. The last section of this
chapter is about the physiological processes involved when we
choose between what we call good and evil.

It is mostly this research at the worldly level that now causes
Swedenborg to dream of his being summoned, while still in this
life, to paradise, "which nobody had ever been before, unless one
who had died and lived again." Ever since his great Easter vision,
this is a thought we have seen sporadically in the diary, most recently in June and July (see entries 206 and 213). Does this make
him Christ's equal? Or, to use his later terminology, a "new Messiah"? As yet, it is only a dream. Later in life, he will regard himself
as having insights into the true meaning of the Holy Scripture, insights so decisive for our attitude toward life and death that the
thought naturally crosses his mind.

244

Afterwards, somebody said that he wanted to call on me at 10
o'clock, but he did not know where I lived. I replied that, as it
by then seemed to me, *I lived in the gable-end of that palace.
That signified that the things that I, with the help of God,
had written concerning forms [formis] were such that it
would bring me still further and I behold even more glorious
things.*

Again, Swedenborg is on his way securing his own immortality.

245

> Afterwards, I was in the company of women, but I was not willing to touch them, inasmuch as previously I have had to do with the holier ones. *With this, many things occurred to me, which I left to the good pleasure of God, because I am like an instrument with which he does according to his pleasure. Yet I would like to be together with the aforesaid,* but be not my will but God's. God grant I incurred no misdemeanor; I believe I did not.

What Swedenborg describes here can hardly be a dream altogether. As we shall see in a short while, in entry 248 of October 3 to 6, he has, in fact, been "in the company of women." This present entry concerns a Saturday; as we have earlier seen, he appears to have allowed himself such diversions on the weekends. This time, according to entry 248, he had been "in terrible danger," but escaped.

"God grant I incurred no misdemeanor," he writes. The Swedish verb *förse* may refer to the noun *förseelse*, "offense," but the verb has many meanings, particularly in combination with the objective pronoun "me," *förse mig*, as in this context. It means "procure," "catch," and "contract" and might as well refer to a contagion. In Swedenborg's day, it could mean "have been infected." Which interpretation is the right one cannot be determined with certainty. All we know is that some negligence is a cause of worries.

10

OCTOBER 1744

———◆◆◆◆◆———

October 3, in the afternoon

246

I had a little sleep, and it was shown to me how everything consists in its most inward parts of units [*unitatibus*], the reason of
the cause [*ratio causae*], and the end [*finis*], so that our
thoughts, considered also as units, carry within them no other
end and reason than that which comes either from the spirit of
God or of the body. If of the body, it is all sin from the innermost, for we aim at nothing but what strives against the spiritual. What governs us we may ourselves observe if we reflect
upon our loves [*amoribus*], which are always there.

This compressed entry might be rendered this way: I fell into a
light sleep where I was shown how within all units everything is
cause and purpose, so that, when we consider our own thoughts as
units, we find how, at their core, they are led by no other purpose
or other cause than that which comes either from the spirit of God
or from the body. If our thoughts come from the body, all is most
inwardly sin.

The first thought expresses Swedenborg's theologically tinged
psychology. In his dream, he seems to see human thinking as a unit
that, like all other units in the universe, comprises its own cause
and purpose. According to his way of looking at the matter, purpose at the psychological level is a function of the will, which is
dictated by love. Love can, in turn, be commanded by "the spirit of
God" or be geared by "the body." The human problem, the background of which Swedenborg does not develop in this entry, is

that the kind of love directed by God and the kind emanating from ourselves seem to us to be directed by the same source of goodness. Our love behaves as if it were inspired by the supreme good, yet our reason goes astray.

Swedenborg's second thought concerns the practical consequences of this masquerade. We must be able to analyze what he calls in his later writings *amor regnans*, the love that dominates us— what really lies behind our thoughts and doings. As we shall see, early in this month he will return several times to this problem. In Swedenborg's later writings, this issue is of great importance. Our existence after death will be a purified form of that very love that has dominated us during our life.

Later, when developing his doctrine of spirits, Swedenborg will perceive the inspirations of the dead behind all thoughts, whether good or evil; these spiritual influences may come from heaven, from the spiritual world, or from hell. This will turn the question of *amor regnans* into a problem of "distinguishing between the spirits," the subject of the following entry.

We have seen how, on a number of occasions, Swedenborg found himself divided, of two minds, in some cases split by conflicting feelings, as is shown in this quotation from the entry of April 7–8, number 79: "I perceived an interior gladness; but, still, there was a pain in my body for it was not able to bear the heavenly joy of the soul." Gradually, this conflicted state clears. He perceives his own thoughts, as it were, standing in front of him: he seems to greet them or scare them away (journal entry 133, April 15–16). By making the extraordinary ordinary, he can examine his situation and take his bearings.

Little by little, Swedenborg realizes that he is the battleground of opposing influences; that good and evil are struggling for his soul—a thought he has already presented in abstract form in the *Economy of the Animal Kingdom,* in *The Animal Kingdom,* and in *Rational Psychology;* which was not published during his lifetime. In the foregoing entry, he wrote that we are ourselves able to investigate "what governs us." This transpires from our *amoribus,* our loves. These loves, he figures, are governed by spirits. Therefore, it is important for each of us to find which spirits are really at work influencing our thoughts. For Swedenborg, this is a matter of greatest consequence, and so it will remain. Only the person who has God in his or her thoughts—is in the "right spirit"—attains happiness and wisdom.

Already at the time of the Easter vision of 1744, Swedenborg spoke of "trying the spirits," an expression he picked up from the first letter of John 4:1–3:

> Beloved, do not believe every spirit, but test the spirits to see whether they are from God; for many false prophets have gone out into the world. By this you know the Spirit of God: Christ has come in the flesh is from God, and every spirit that does not confess Jesus is not from God. And this is the spirit of the antichrist, of which you have heard that it is coming; and now it is already in the world.

[October] 3 to 6

247

A number of times I have noticed that there are spirits of various kinds. The spirit of Christ is the only one that carries all beatitude with it. The other spirits entice us in a thousand ways to follow them, but unhappy is the one who does. Once or twice, Koran and Dathan came before me and brought strange fire to the altar but were not able to offer it. Thus it is when another fire is brought in than the one that comes from Christ. I also saw something like a fire that came to me. It is therefore necessary to distinguish between the spirits, which is a thing that cannot be done except through Christ himself and his spirit.

For the third time, he addresses the question of inducements, the "spirits" behind our thoughts and actions. Here we have one of the anthropomorphic concepts so typical of Swedenborg. As mentioned, this notion of our being governed by spiritual beings, both good and bad, will become one of the basic notions of his later theologically based psychology. These spirits are the souls of men and women who once walked the earth.

Consequently, all depends on our power of discrimination. If we are not discerning, we are lost. To exemplify, Swedenborg refers to the two priests Korah and Dathan, who, according to Numbers 16, had rebelled against Moses in the desert. Afterward, while lighting the sacrificial fires, they were swallowed up by the earth. Their worship had been inspired by the wrong spirit, not by love of God.

With the passion for systematization so characteristic of the Age of Reason, Swedenborg would later arrange the spirits in groups and subgroups. The evil ones were divided into two categories: spirits and genii. The latter are particularly insidious since they instantly know what we most desire and infiltrate our will, as we see in this passage from *Arcana Coelestia* §5977:

> *If this be something good, then it is cleverly turned to evil. They are never so happy as when they have succeeded in turning evil to good, good to evil. . . . They serve lusts, disguising themselves as love.*

As is obvious from Swedenborg's persistent ransacking of his heart in his private diary, he perpetually doubts his innermost motives. His touchstone—used many times in his later writings—is whether a thought, an influence, or a "spirit" conforms to the love of Christ. The spirits dwelling within us can be tried by self-analysis, by scrutinizing one's own desires and true intentions; we see this expressed in the previous entry: We may observe what governs us if we reflect upon our loves, which always accompany our thoughts.

His insight into the existence of spirits and the importance of assessing their nature are confirmed by a vision in his dream. A fire comes toward him. Like other mystics, Swedenborg regards his experiences of lights, "photisms," as confirming signs.

248

The terrible danger in which I had been in the night between the 29th and the 30th was afterwards represented to me in sleep:

that I was upon ice that could scarcely bear me. **Further on, I came to a fearful chasm; a person on the other side could not come to my rescue, so I went back. But it is God alone through Christ that has helped me in this, and he is my Lord and my master, whose servant I am. Glory be to him and thanks, without whom no one can come to God.**

Swedenborg's dream takes him back to the night of September 30. He was, in "terrible danger," walking on thin ice, on the edge of an abyss; but God interceded. This probably refers to the "women" mentioned in entry 245. Those may have been the most severe temptations, overcome only with difficulty. Now, less than a week later, he feels that he has come out of this peril safely and unhurt.

In the entry for the night of October 6–7, we are met with the same ideas expressed in his earlier October entries: the seduction of the human being by spirits in the shapes of "earthly loves." These ignite our self-complacency and distance us from the Divine and God's design.

October 6–7

249

It was quite a lot, yet gracious. There was a shining black veil or skin, which was drawn over me, yet it had no permanence. It was said it did not hold together, and therefore it was folded up; and I was promised to be more enlightened. There also appeared some interior illumination. I wished to bring this about on Sundays. *That is, by my own understanding and imagination, I had entered into something that was comparable to the black veil, and which does not hold good. Again, I saw an abyss, which is the danger in which I am in my thoughts.*

The black veil is folded together. At the same time, the dreamer beholds an inner light and hears a voice promising him greater knowledge. He hopes he will attain such light and the spiritual enlightenment to be derived from it on Sundays—a pious hope and resolution, considering that the day of this note was a Sunday.

The veil, the black gauze, is connected with his work and life. In *Arcana Coelestia* §963, he expatiates on this material:

> Among punishments a frequent one consists in the throwing over the sufferers of a veil, and is as follows. By means of fantasies that are impressed on them, the sufferers seem to themselves to be under a veil that is stretched out to a great distance. It is like a closely clinging cloud that increases in density in proportion to the fantasy. Under this covering they run to and fro, more or less swiftly, possessed by a burning desire to burst out of it. . . . This usually goes on for some hour, and is accompanied by various torments according to how strong the desire is to work one's way out. This veil is laid over those who think they see the truth, but out of self-love refuse to acknowledge it. They feel constant indignation that the truth should be as it is. When under the veil some feel so anxious and terrified that they completely despair of their deliverance.

When unveiled, he is put into communication with higher sources of knowledge:

250

Furthermore something was told about my book. It was said that it would be a *Liber divinus de Dei cultu et amore* [a divine book on the worship and love of God]; I believe there was also something about *spiritibus* [spirits]. I thought I had something on the subject in my work *De Infinito*, but there was no answer as to that. Then I was wrapped up in thought and was informed that *any kind of love* [amor], *no matter for what it may be, as the love for my works on which I am now employed, if I were to love them* [for my own glory] *but not as a medium for the only love which is the love of God and N Christ Jesus, this would be a meretricious love. For the same reason, such love is always compared to whoredom in the Word of God; such also is the one that I have experienced. But when one has the love of God as the supreme, then one has no other love than that which one finds by devoting all to the service of God.*

Here for the first time Swedenborg receives words on his future work. This clarifying moment, in which the forthcoming work is named, connects with sporadic earlier insights into a concrete task recorded elsewhere in the diary, which will be developed in greater detail in entries 276–281 in the last days of October 1744.

Concerning his new book—"a divine book on the worship and love of God"—he seems to understand that it will be about "spirits" and will have points in common with his earlier work *De Infinito* (On the Infinite). The passage he seems to be referring to—the book had been written ten years earlier—is about the correct form of faith and its relation to scientific knowledge:

> *The qualities of faith are determined by knowledge . . . and when such knowledge exists it is inseparable from faith. However, we shall explore this matter further when we, in accordance with our plan, shall deal more particularly with the worship of divine.*

To achieve true knowledge, one must have the right spirit: the spirit of love and belief. Love must be focused on the Divine. Awake, or half-awake, Swedenborg takes the title of the prefigured work as the starting point for reflections on the nature of true love, and then he underlines his words and writes for safety *"nota bene"* in the margin.

All other love—to things of whatever kind, even of his own work—is considered as *meretriciatio*, forbidden, "whorish." In the biblical excerpts he is currently making, Swedenborg confirms this theory with quotations from the New Testament: "For all that which cometh not of faith is sin." "Love of God is the greatest." His desire to be absorbed in the Divine conforms with classic mysticism's demand for unconditional devotion, submersion in the Godhead. Yet it has a notable and quite marked active and intellectual aspect. To Swedenborg, devotion is the only way to higher knowledge, and that insight follows from a dynamic connection between God and the human being. This is the theme of his new book: an attitude and a theosophy, a "knowledge in God."

251

> I also thought I saw Czar Peter and other great emperors, who despised me because I had short sleeves; I do not know what party they were of. A number of times, I have been given lovely bread and other things. May God *grant that it is, as I believe, the spiritual bread.*

Recall that, at the time of Swedenborg's Easter vision, short sleeves—shirt sleeves without cuffs—had signified the clerical estate's renunciation of earthly vanities. His father had, with his own hands, attached cuffs to his sleeves, as a sign that he was not to take holy orders. Despite his father's gesture, he now is dressed as a clergyman and is mocked by the representatives of worldly power. It is no coincidence that those who mock him are the Czar Peter the Great and his princes. They are the leaders of a hostile country. Swedenborg persists and is rewarded. On several occasions, he is given "beautiful loaves of bread," something the dreamer usually associates with spiritual nourishment or insight.

252

> From this and the foregoing, it is found how soon and how easily a human being is seduced by other spirits, which are represented according to the love of each, since loves are represented by spirits, furthermore, in fact, by women in dra—

Thus, Swedenborg summarizes the experiences of the night, "quite a lot, but gracious." Obviously, he thought of describing how lusts can present themselves in the shape of women, but hesitated and let his pen rest.

His experiences and comments serve on the whole to clarify his dreams of the night between October 6 and 7. He had found himself entrusted with writing a "divine book"; and this entry, together with those that will follow during the rest of October, relate to this exalted task.

[October] 7–8

253

> It seemed to me that I was walking on a road. I was determined to proceed but met a little boy who walked on a path, and I followed him; but there was a fog. I thought I saw soldiers out there; I crouched and crept, afraid, but they did not seem to be enemies but [troops] of our people. Still, I did not find my way onwards. I turned back; came into an untidy room; asked for another chamber, which I got; and ordered water; but he said it was not fresh but muddy, so I then asked for milk. Then, I woke up. *This dream means that I have been on the wrong path and have followed my reason in a fog, where one is afraid even of one's own people, as if they were enemies; but when on the right track, one is afraid of no one. Water means that it [my reason] is still muddy, milk that it must still be strengthened.*

At first the dreamer feels lost, outwardly and inwardly. Finally, he gets a tidy room and a nourishing drink. He interprets this, again, as relating to the problem of "distinguishing between spirits." As long as he had followed his own reason, in the shape of a small boy, he had confused friend for foe. Now he has at last grasped the proper way of seeing and understanding his own questions and how he should handle them. A new domicile is now prepared for him. This idea is sharpened in his next entry—a brief vision and a long discursive passage in italics, in which we seem to feel his joy at what he at last has comprehended:

254

> Then I saw in vision a person who had a black coat, but it was taken off and he disappeared—*which means that the former blackness vanished, since such it is when one sticks to the way and trusts only God and Christ and nowise oneself, or*

depends on the strength of one's own arm and one's own understanding. Moreover it was found that we are soldiers to fight Satan continuously. And when one has the spirit and life of God, every day is a victory; but if contrariwise, there is daily discomfiture [clades], a falling from one defeat into another. For this reason, one should not despair but trust in the mercy of God.

In journal entry 249, Swedenborg's sight had been dimmed by a black veil. Here a black cloak has the same effect. It disappears, and there is no longer any hindrance to divine perception. He outlines two guiding insights. First, he must let himself be steered by the Divine and no longer rely on himself; he must renounce all reasoning based on his own limited experiences. Second, he must use this total reliance on God in an unceasing combat against evil. He draws on St. Paul's image of the Christian warrior and submits to the Lord of hosts. In this struggle, the Christian transmogrifies his faith into reality. Even if the warrior is supported by faith, victory (*victoria*) is certain as defeat (*clades*) as long as he relies on his own strength.

255

Last night, I think I saw myself commissioned to serve as captain, lieutenant, or something like that; but I called upon Secretary Bierchenius to say that I wanted to remain an assessor as before, which implied that I did not yet understand what it means to be a warrior and fight against Satan, since God sends angels to him [the warrior] to fight at his side. This is the black cloak that is pulled away, and God himself has condescended to inform me in this matter.

In the earlier dream he now recalls, the question of what his calling must imply for his civil position was dealt with for the second time in the dream diary. After the Easter vision, Swedenborg had been in doubt whether he ought to change his estate or not. Here, he declines a military appointment, preferring to continue as a mining official. At the same time, he perceives that this is too literal an interpretation of his dream. He must fight for good against evil in any task assigned him. God is sending angels—as he did to Tobias in entry 144—to fight on his side.

256

Moreover, I saw in a vision a heart full of blood; it was love.

As a seal and a sign, Swedenborg discerns a bleeding heart, confirming his call. It was love itself. The image is reminiscent of Zinzendorf and his marked blood mysticism. The trustful self-abandonment to God recommended by the Moravians does not suffice, however. Swedenborg sees clearly that a Christian must also actively fight evil. In this, above all, his call consists.

The initiation process continues, and particulars of the new duties emerge:

[October] 8–9

257

This night was the most joyful of all because I saw *Regnum Innocentiae* [the kingdom of innocence]. Beneath me, I beheld the most beautiful garden that can be imagined where, as time went on, white roses were placed in tree after tree. Then I came into a long chamber where beautiful white vessels of milk and bread were, so dainty that something more savory is inconceivable. I was in company with a woman, whom I do not remember very well.

The key words in this passage mirror the dreamer's predilections: the kingdom of innocence as a beautiful garden; an oblong room with exquisite vessels, milk and bread.; a woman. He is in the rose garden of innocence in paradise. The long chamber is his works and days, where rows of lovely vessels seem to suggest his future output. Vessels will later become a frequent image for disciplined reason and memorized knowledge; afterwards, they can be imbued with divine truth and goodness. The image has other ramifications too. When the blood vessels, *vascula*, are filled with pure fluid, the individual, according to Swedenborg's physiology, is healthy and open-minded. Impure fluids, however, have a contracting and closing effect. The vessel is also, we should recall, an alchemist symbol, a container in which the melt is transmuted into the great work.

Milk and bread were, at least in his later years, Swedenborg's favorite food. Here, as in entries still to come, they appear as tokens of life and power, figures of nectar and ambrosia. The woman—his love—is also with him in this setting, but, enthralled by the captivating scenery, he overlooks her.

258

So, I went back. A little child, beautiful and innocent, came up to me and said that the woman had gone without having said good-bye but asked me to buy her a book, which she would take up but did not show it to me. I woke up. Furthermore, it seemed to me that I was giving a feast at my own expense, to a crowd of people in a house or palace that was standing apart. There were some acquaintances, among them the Councilor-of-State Lagerberg, and, I believe, also Ehrenpreus and others. Everything was at my expense, and it seemed it was costing me a great deal: the thought kept coming continually that it was expensive; sometimes I did not care, for I observed that the whole expense was borne by that Lord who owned that estate or who showed it to me.

259

I was in the kingdom of innocence, and I was treating the others and worldly people without seeing them; perhaps it signifies my work, that it should not be like them, although I am giving them a treat by it, or something else. The child was innocence proper; I was quite touched by it and wished I were in such a kingdom, where all is innocence. I lamented that upon awakening I had to leave. As to that woman who left without bidding farewell, I do not know what is meant thereby.

Swedenborg's writing turns up again. An innocent child presents the woman's wish that he buy her a book, which she will accept. In entry 259, he observes that it all refers to his work. Knowing the future, we can see that the dream is an image of a state of mind he describes in *The Worship and Love of God*, about life and the struggle of love. Whether the dreamer himself understands the message, it seems he is now being told that the scene of his work is paradise, the garden.

Swedenborg has another dream: he is entertaining some high officials, among them two councilors of state, Sven Lagerberg and Carl Didrick Ehrenpreus. All this takes place in a magnificent palace that stands alone. According to his own explanation in entry 259, the words indicate that the dreamer was not himself present at the banquet. He is needlessly worried about the expense. All will be paid for by the great Lord in whose house he is giving a party.

Swedenborg's own interpretation (set in italics), although tentative, is consequently drawn. It signifies that he should write for the world yet keep at a suitable distance. He will receive all he needs from a higher authority. There is no need to worry about expenditures, since such things will be provided for by the owner.

260

The next day, the 9th, my eyesight was so sharp that I could read the finely printed Bible without the least difficulty.

The visit to the realm of innocence implies spiritual progress to the dreamer. As we will see in entry 268, Swedenborg felt it natural that progress and insight in the "order of grace" should also find its physical expression. Thus, now, his sight improves.

It may be added that the exquisite but small Bible print he now has no difficulty in reading was probably Castello's edition of the Vulgate, four duodecimo volumes printed in London in 1726, which was found in the posthumous list of books in his library.

[October] 9–10

261

In a vision, I saw, as it were, a fire in pit coal, burning intensely, which signified *ignem amoris* [the fire of love]. Then, I was together with a woman who had a set of teeth in a certain place where I wanted to get but was stopped by the teeth, *which means that, the day before, I had been busy with a work quite distinguished from the other and another love; and whether it would prevail and whether it would be regarded as mere words* [parlage] *or a plaything in comparison to the other, this I was then about to resolve . . .*

262

. . . when I woke up determined to abandon this work, which indeed I would have done had it not afterwards appeared to me in my sleep that I was sent to a certain place with a letter. I did not find the way, but my sister Hedvig saw the letter and said that it was addressed to Ulrica Adlersteen, who was said to have been longing for me for a long time. I arrived there and saw Schönström. Afterwards, I had continually before me the thought of sensory impressions, how they ascend to the brain and again descend, *by which I was strengthened to continue with the work.*

263

May God grant that this is not unpleasing to him, since I cannot take anything from the sleep without getting myself into a temptation to abandon it; but God helped me in this resolution and to God alone be praise and honor. Nevertheless, a child stumbled over my foot, was hurt, and screamed. I wanted to help it up and asked, "Why do you race about so?" *This no doubt referred to that I was carried away in this pursuit.*

The fire in the dream is the love of God, which, according to his doctrine of love, never goes unanswered. One of the more difficult dreams to interpret because of its obscure allusions, entry

261 implies that, on October 6, Swedenborg had been working on the continuation of *The Animal Kingdom*. But the enticing female—science—is incompatible with his love of God: the toothed vagina makes union impossible. His projected work on *The Worship and Love of God,* first mentioned on October 6–7, was to be inspired by "right" love, the divine *ignis amoris* of which he is now dreaming. That work could not, should not, nor would be regarded as diversion or toying. He must submit himself wholly to divine inspiration, he concludes.

In entry 262, Swedenborg describes his wavering between the two works. Waking up, he is determined to abandon the scientific work for the "spiritual." Falling asleep again, however, his decision is postponed. In a dream in which his cousin Albrekt Schönström's wife Ulrica Adlersten is the main figure, he seems to be exhorted to go on with *The Animal Kingdom*. In his dream, he envisions a concrete image of the solution to one of his main problems: how sensory impressions are disseminated throughout the body up to the brain and then downwards to influence our movements.

The heavy and ambiguous language of the last entry communicates that the dream has not yielded any final clearance as to the future direction of his work. "Why do you race about so?" he asks the child who has stumbled over his foot. The bishop, his father, had alluded to the same situation six months earlier: "You are making such an alarm, Emanuel!" (entry 123). To the dreamer, these words indicate that, if he would just be patient, clear instructions will penetrate the dimness and put an end to his vacillating mood.

[October] 10–11

264

It seemed as if I were in bed with someone, but I did not touch her. Then I met a gentleman whom I asked for employment, since I had lost my former position through the war, but he said "No." They seemed to be playing basset [a card game]; the money kept changing hands, but I was with them all the time. I asked my servant if he had said that I owned anything;

he answered "No," and I said that he should not say anything else. *It signifies the Moravian Church, that I am there yet not accepted and that I state that I have no knowledge of religious matters, that I have lost it all, whereas those who play basset win now and then.*

This entry marks a turning point in Swedenborg's lengthy dealings with the Moravians in London. He was faithful to his acquaintances, including the London Brethren, but his attempts to be accepted as a member of their congregation came to a close at the meeting here referred to. He was not to be assimilated in the movement but began turning in the other direction, outwards, choosing a way of his own.

At the beginning of this dream, he is in bed with a female, but does not "touch her." It is obvious from his interpretation of his dream or vision that, although he is *in* the Moravian congregation at Fetter Lane, he remains an outsider, a stranger.

The dream evidently depicts his religious standing. "Through the war," he has "lost my former position," words he interprets as meaning that he has "no knowledge of religious matters." Clearly, the "war" is the ongoing spiritual struggle reflected in his diary. We may also read the words in the light of an earlier entry, no. 180: in April, he had written that theology and dogma were not his fields, that he should stick to God's Word and the Holy Ghost. Now he is supposedly witnessing the dismantling of that theological outwork, the superficial facade. He is applying for a position with "a gentleman" or "lord," giving as his reason that he has lost all.

"They seemed to be playing basset," he writes. "The money kept changing hands, but I was with them all the time." He gives no further explanation.

Bringing these fragments together, we surmise that Swedenborg had indeed applied for membership in the London congregation, but in vain, not passing the trial. The Brethren were few, hardly more than a hundred, who, here as elsewhere, constituted a "sacred society." Zinzendorf's personal representative, Professor August Gottlieb Spangenberg, was known for his skepticism of new members and his loathness to increase his group. Hallmarks of the members's mutual relationships were to be love, absolute trust, and candor. Only "well-tried souls" could gain access to the rites, we read in a Moravian ceremony of 1743, at Västerås, in Sweden. The congregation was "the heart's link between those who have been redeemed by the merits of Jesus and are born of the one and same Spirit." At their meetings, everyone was obliged "mutually and without pretense or boasting openly to confess their infidelity and wretchedness. Not little depends upon this honesty among ourselves."

The same applied largely to the mother congregation. In a *Narrative about the Moravian Congregation* of 1739, Arvid Gradin tells his Stockholm friends that "no one is confirmed or adopted into the congregation and confessed a brother before we have sure proofs that he really partakes of Jesus' reconciliation and is in communion with Him." Gradin's words certainly applied in London, too.

Had Swedenborg been weighed and found wanting? Had the congregation showed interest in him but then rejected him? His reserved personality, the quasi-secret nature of his scientific work, his stutter, and his poor command of English must have made him seem a bird of another feather to this circle of brothers and sisters, all burning with the spirit, people whose social and economic circumstances were utterly unlike his own. The attitude of the congregation's leaders might have been different had they realized how well off Swedenborg was. That same month Spangenberg was being severely criticized for his way of leading the congregation. This criticism, which was also directed at his wife, may allude to his treatment of the Swedish proselyte. It is found in a letter to Zinzendorf from the leader of the Moravian Brethren in Yorkshire, Martin Dober:

> I must confess—and I have given the matter all due thought— that I am most dissatisfied with their way of drawing lots, with their appeals to the wealthy, their method of first showing interest in souls and then rejecting them.

The drawing of lots as an expression of the divine will, it should be stressed, was a Moravian characteristic. They used this method when choosing spouses, when selecting missionaries to send out to different parts of the world, and, not least, when in doubt whether to accept new members. The game of basset in Swedenborg's dream probably refers to this kind of spiritual lottery, at which Swedenborg may even have been present in person: "but I was with them all the time" when "the money kept changing hands."

Those who play basset win "now and then." Swedenborg had lost the game.

Is this dream unambiguous, referring only to one matter—the humiliating end to his relationships with the London Moravians? It may also be read on a more universal level—as a dream about someone who has not yet found his proper element, an observer who in "the war" has lost his ground.

[October] 12–13

265

> It seemed to me that someone was being beaten and scourged, and afterwards he preached with greater zeal and insisted upon the same from above and from below. *This means that, when a person has been chastised by our Lord, he will afterwards get greater zeal and spirit to persist in that which the spirit leads him to, so that chastisement and punishment increase it. I was wondering yesterday, when I was so happy and allowed my thoughts to run somewhat freely, whether correction would change it, whereupon this came as an answer.*

The dream is about someone who is "beaten and scourged." The maltreatment only makes him preach all the more forcefully, both from the pulpit and on the floor, from "above and below."

Obviously, Swedenborg has Christian martyrdom in mind. He reflects on the significance of divine chastisement, discipline, and correction. Perhaps the precipitating factor was his humiliation at the hands of the Moravians. Trials and tribulations, he considers, help to purify. Before this ordeal of correction had befallen him, he had been giving too free vent to his thoughts. Now, with the trial behind him, he can continue his quest for "that which the spirit leads him to."

This is another expression of his "spiritual" state of mind. In many important respects, as I have earlier emphasized, the dream diary has the power of illustration rather than of illumination. This is especially true of the spirituality that, as his journal nears its end, Swedenborg is seeking more eagerly than ever. Spirituality, he had written some years before the crisis, in his *Rational Psychology*, is the ultimate expression of the freedom of the human race. After turning seriously to God in prayer, we are endowed by providence in such a way that we are warmed by love and commitment. In turning to God, we turn away from whatever is bodily and physical. A new kind of reason is born, a "spiritual intellect" that makes up a complete change of our condition. Here we attain the perfection of freedom. Receiving intimations of the highest good, we willingly choose it.

This special form of consciousness will afterwards color Swedenborg's sphere of thought and constitute a point of departure. Within it, he was at long last to find a way to that *mathesis universalium*—universal knowledge—where pure truths emerge without any need for discursive thought. It is infallible and immediately recognizable: "for a certain correspondence, a harmony . . . give an experience of light . . . as if from a holy room," he wrote in *The Animal Kingdom* I.

266_____

Afterwards, I seemed to say to myself that the Lord himself wanted to instruct me; *for I found that I am in such a condition that I know nothing except that Christ should be all in all, or God through Christ, so that we ourselves are unable to do anything towards it, still less strive for it. Therefore, it is best to surrender unconditionally; and, if one could further be entirely passive in this, that would be perfect.*

267

Moreover, I saw in a vision how the beautiful loaves of bread were presented to me on a plate, which was a premonition that the Lord himself was going to instruct me, since I have now finally come into such a state that I know nothing, and that all *preconcepta judicia* [preconceived opinions, biases] have been taken away from me, which is the beginning of learning, namely, that one first must become a child, and then be nurtured into knowledge, as is now, I think, happening to me.

We read that Swedenborg has been relieved of all prejudices: a variation of his declaration in entry 264, that he has lost his previous position due to "the war." All preconceived ideas having left him, he is in that state where he "knows nothing."

This way of describing that state of mind would have appealed to Zinzendorf. All the Moravian congregations stressed the crucial importance of "childhood in God," of liberating oneself from burdensome knowledge, which poses the main hindrance of salvation. Unconditional acceptance of one's own childhood in God came to set its stamp, not only on the Moravian brothers' and sisters' whole attitude, but also on their mode of speech. Diminutives were encouraged, as was a pious simple-mindedness, styling a kind of religious rococo.

For the more grave and serious-minded Swedenborg, childhood in God was a purely theosophical attitude. He would let himself be led "in the spirit," free of all intellectual ballast, to ever higher insights. This is the domain of unconditional devotion. Perhaps it is in this passage that the dream diary most unambiguously depicts Swedenborg's existential experience of a path to knowledge of which he had previously been aware and been close to, but into which he had not yet made any serious attempt to enter, hesitating on the threshold.

[October] 13–14

268

Among other things, I was told that, a fortnight ago, I began looking much more handsome, being like an angel. God grant it be so, God stand by me in this and not take his grace away.

"Among other things I was told"—we do not know if he is dreaming or is inspirited. The information about his improved looks, taken together with what he notes in entry 260, reminds us of an aspect of Swedenborg's doctrine of correspondences: the idea of a harmony and concordance between body and soul, the material and the spiritual dimensions, where the latter is the propelling force. He would later develop the theme in detail in the *Arcana Coelestia*. Probably he has about this time, in September–October 1744, treated the subject in the forthcoming volume of *The Animal Kingdom* III, §537:

> *The human face gives a vivid picture and expression of these changes, because there is no affective perception, no enjoyment or strong feeling, no lust . . . no wish . . . no attitude to good and evil that is not reflected in the face.*

Later, in the *Arcana Coelestia*, he developed this theme extensively and explained how the inward is present in the outward, why states of mind reflect themselves physically in general and not only in facial expression. There is "a correspondence between the inward man and his face" and "there is a correspondence between thoughts and inclinations on the one hand, and action and patterns of movement on the other." Here Swedenborg outlined the body language of the soul.

Not unexpectedly, Swedenborg says the changes he observes in his own appearance had started around the turn of the month: at that time, his worry and feeling of having gone astray were being replaced by a sense of his true call. He began to glimpse his great future theme. He no longer raised "an alarm" but became more silent, taciturn. His later well-known serenity seems to be taking over. When, in the diary's last dated entry, he finds his "head is thoroughly cleaned and rinsed from all that might obstruct these thoughts," he follows this observation with a sentence corresponding to his angelic mood: "I seemed to be writing with a fine hand."

[October] 15–16

269

In a vision, there was a person who was carrying a heavy burden. He was carrying wooden planks and fell down under his burden. Another person came to his rescue, but in what manner he was helped up I did not see. In sleep, after a while, I was walking up a foot-bridge and saw depths and perils before me; afterwards, I climbed a rope after another one but did not see the top of the rope or how I should be able to get there. *This signifies that those who want to get to heaven on their own and strive on their own toward the higher work singlehandedly in vain and in constant danger, but this easily happens when one aims at God who is the helping hand, and*

In vision and dream, the same thought is expressed: Swedenborg is in a difficult and dangerous position, trying to proceed on his own. But he catches a glimpse of someone who is ready for rescue and assistance. This image is common in the dreams and may invariably be interpreted as a reminder of the impossibility of reaching any summit without the helping hand in the dark.

Even in its details, this entry exemplifies the repetitive elements of the diary. The too-heavy burden was first encountered in entry 31. The climbing of ropes or ladders—similar experiences appear in entries 20 and 29. Seen from the outside, Swedenborg's dreams and visions are imaginatively restricted. Only rarely does the dreamer, already 56 years of age, replenish this set of images; indeed, in his future writings, he will keep even more strictly to well-charted fairways. Certain "key moments" from the experiences of his youth, impressions from encounters with certain people, traces of studies, and recurrent reading will form a structure that supports the colossal edifice of his skyscraping inner experiences in the years to come.

October 18–19

270 _____

[I dreamed] how a big dog, which I thought was tied up, flew at me and bit my leg; somebody came and held his terrible jaws so he could do no more harm. *Meant that I had listened to an oration at the College of Medicine the day before and was presumptuous enough to expect that they should mention me as one who has a superior understanding of anatomy, although I was glad they didn't.* **In a night vision afterwards, [I saw] how a lame walker went away from me,** *which may mean that I, because of the bite, limped.*

Swedenborg attended a lecture in medicine and hoped to hear himself referred to as a prominent authority in the field of anatomy. In the dream, he is badly bitten by a hound, but a stranger comes to his rescue and gets hold of its frightful jaws. In a vision, Swedenborg sees a man with a crooked foot leaving him: it is, he understands, himself hobbling along, crippled by the dog's attack.

Vanity, "thoughts of my being more worth than others," is, as we know, one of Swedenborg's three besetting sins: "voluptuousness, riches, vanity." As several times before, his egocentricity takes the shape of a dog, whose owner on previous occasion had either been Broman or Swab. Before he had managed to control the beast; this time, however, someone helps him out. Now, in late October, the Divine is becoming the main protagonist of his dream play, protecting him from the ravenous jaws of egotism. The lesson left a mark on him: bitten on his foot, he imagines he limps. In July, Swedenborg had dreamed of a battle between Swedes and Danes. Although God had afforded him protection, afterwards he found there was something amiss with his left foot, which, without his knowledge, had been dressed (entry 208). He then felt assured it would soon be healed. Or this may be the same recurring image of Emanuel as Jacob, limping after wrestling with the angel.

[October] 19–20

271

> [I dreamed] that I saw one creature after another, which spread out their wings; they were dragons. I flew above them, away; yet I ran into one of them. *Such dragons signify amores spurios [spurious loves], which show themselves as if they were not dragons, until their wings are seen.* This subject I had now at hand.

Again, the main question is how to distinguish among spirits. Swedenborg has now learned to identify them: those that unfold their wings are counterfeit loves, disguising their nature, dragons that sink their teeth in their victims and devour them.

Again, we see how his dream life and his science agree. At this time, Swedenborg was writing about the influence of good and evil. In one section of *The Five Senses*, he admits that his analytical attempts could not arrive at the desired clarity. Very soon, he will fully grasp what he still only intuits: this question does not belong to science, despite his far-reaching philosophical scope, but to theology.

[October] 20–21

272

> *It was quite gracious and wonderful. The day before I had found myself unworthy of all the grace God deigned to show me, considering how deeply pride was rooted in me. I therefore prayed to God to take it away from me, since it is not within my power. In the evening, I found myself in a strange situation, new to me, as if I despaired of God's*

grace, although I knew how merciful God is. He has shown
me especially a greater grace than to others. It was an anxiety
in the soul, but not in the mind, so it was not felt except in the
sense itself and without pain in body.

Swedenborg's state of mind in October is very different from that
of early summer; he has traveled a long distance. Now he is far
from debauchery and the escapades with Professor Oelreich. "Anxiety in the soul, but not in the mind." When analyzing his feelings
in terms of their worth and divine grace, Swedenborg sponta-
neously thinks of his contemporaneous work, *The Five Senses*, according to which mind or reason can operate separate from the
feelings of the body and the perceptions of the soul. The soul is a
discrete center of affections and experiences, whereas the mind,
without being touched by the soul, can receive, record, and
process the signals from the external world independently. The
persistent pain that his egotism and vanity cause him has its center
in an "organ" he has for long tried to locate.

References to his philosophical-psychological theories are
hardly necessary, however. The field of force introduced here is the
polarity between sinfulness and grace that stemmed from Swedenborg's Christian upbringing, the urgency of which now had become acute. Israel Kolmodin, one his father's colleagues at Uppsala
University, wrote in the Swedish Book of Hymns (1695):

> *None but Jesus our Beloved*
> *Nor in Heaven nor on Earth*
> *Bring the Burdened Levity*
> *And Make the Gloomy Avid.*
> *With Him is Thy Prosperity*
> *Wipes Vice from Eternity*

In the history of mysticism, the spiritual state Swedenborg describes here parallels one of the "stations" or passages we go
through on our way to God: the dark night of the soul, where the
desires are to be restrained and the bodily fires extinguished.

273

> I then fell asleep again, and there appeared two dogs that fol-
> lowed me closely. After a long time, I got rid of them, and it was
> said to me in my thoughts that this strange pain was to cure me
> of them. *So there is such a pain, when the root is to be re-*
> *moved from that which is so deeply rooted. This is well worth*
> *remembering and keeping in mind.*

The ordeals of passage described here, his efforts to free himself
from the roots of sin, can also be related to *The Five Senses,* more
precisely to the section on "Senses in General," finished in June of
1744. With the aid of free will, we can let our soul, which comes
from God, govern our life. By doing so, the mental states that result from our imaginative world, affected by attenuated influences, are annihilated, killed off; and our whole outlook is
transformed.

Swedenborg now dreams of two dogs that follow him around,
representing the self-conceit from which he is cured. We have met
such pairs before: two wild boars, the two pieces of paper, two
bank notes (entries 183, 191, and 193), all images of hubris em-
bodied by the two volumes of *The Animal Kingdom.* This struggle is
so painful to him because it concerns the very roots of his personality. In the margin he puts a reminder: *Nota bene.*

274

> Later I saw a great king, the king of France, who went about
> without a retinue and had such an insignificant household that
> he could not from this be recognized as royalty. There was one
> with me who did not seem willing to acknowledge him as king,
> but I said that he is of such a character as to care nothing about
> such things. He was courteous towards all without distinction
> and spoke also with me. As he left, he was still without his fol-
> lowers and took upon himself the burdens of others and carried
> them like clothes. Thereafter, came into a very different com-
> pany, where there was much more splendor.

275

> Then I saw the queen; and when a chamberlain came and bowed before her, she made just as deep a reverence, and there was nothing of pride in her. *This means that in Christ there is no pride at all, whereas he makes himself the equal of others; and although he is the greatest of kings, he cares nothing for grandeur and takes the burdens of others upon himself. The queen, who is sapientia [wisdom], is of the same nature; she has no love of self and does not regard herself as more lofty because she is queen.*

King and queen return as figures of divine love and wisdom. Note that the royal couple, as here described, have certain traits that the dreamer himself is trying to adopt. "Nobody wants to be more polite and humble than I do," he exclaimed to himself in entry 93. He was "modest in amour and veneration" (entry 215). Indeed, Swedenborg's modesty was remarkable and his manners simple for a man of his social position in those days. He lodged with craftsmen and had simple habits. The ideal king he sees in his dream has no retinue, only a small court, and carries others' burdens as if they were his own garments. Swedenborg adds that later he came into a very different company, where there was much more pomp. That is another world, inferior or higher, depending on our perspective.

"There was one with me who did not seem willing to acknowledge him as king, but I said that he is of such a character as to care nothing about such things." The images may reflect Swedenborg's own reluctance to submit fully to divine power and God's forgiving tolerance. This does not exclude simultaneous reference to someone in Swedenborg's environment who takes him for another man than he is, or he wishes to be.

The next entry is chronologically the last one in the dream diary and both concludes it and summarizes its results. Swedenborg is to abandon his research project *The Animal Kingdom* and start work on something new. His task is no longer to clarify the position of the human soul but to describe the crucial elements in the experiences he has been recording in his notebook. *Regnum Animale* means not only "the realm of all that is animal." It is also, literally, *the realm of the soul.* This realm is constituted by—and is a consequence of—God's love for humanity and, reciprocally, humanity's worship and love of God. In that love, we are liberated from the bondage to self that prevents illumination and see everything from a completely differ-ent point of view, as Swedenborg himself has been doing during the past months when he has intermittently been "in the spirit," been an "inward" man.

October 26–27

276

I had been told that the 27th of October would return: then I undertook the cultum et amorem Dei *[The Worship and Love of God]. It seemed as if it were Christ himself, in whose company I was as with another, without ceremony [Sw. fazon, "manner"]. He borrowed a little money from another person, about five pounds. I was vexed because he did not ask me. I took up two pounds, but it seemed to me that I dropped one and likewise the other one. He asked what it was. I said that I had found two and that one of them might have been dropped by him. I gave them, and he accepted. In such an innocent manner, we seemed to live together, which was status inno-centiae [a state of innocence].*

Swedenborg states that he has already received a message that, on October 27, the very day of this entry, he is to work on *The Worship and Love of God.* Perhaps the reference is to October 6–7. Now the day has come, preceded by a dream where Christ is the chief personage.

This third and last encounter with Christ recorded in the diary is quite undramatic. Dreamer and Savior associate as friends, quite informally. The "loans" they make each other, as elsewhere in the dream journal, may stand for knowledge. Christ accepts a few coins from "another person," of whom we are not told further, but from Swedenborg he borrows nothing, which baffles him.

Who is this "other person"? Swedenborg does not tell. Can it be the last dream reminiscence of Count Zinzendorf of Berthelsdorf? Pronoun ambiguities in the following lines make several readings possible. One reasonable interpretation is the following: the dreamer picks up two pounds, one of which he has lost, the other stemming from Christ. After an exchange of views, Christ accepts Swedenborg's gift.

The dreamer and the Divinity associate without particular manners of courtesy, in an everyday way. Once again, we seem to hear an echo of the Epistle to the Hebrews and the subsequent Moravian idea of a brotherhood in Christ, stressing the human aspect of Christ and the understanding Savior's fraternal readiness to forgive his fellow-beings.

277

Afterwards, I was in my chamber with some other acquaintance or relation, and I said that I wished to show him I had better lodgings. I therefore went out with him, first into an adjoining room that extended far, chamber after chamber, but they did not belong to me. Someone in the bed asked what he wanted; I went out with him, into my parlor. When I opened the door I saw that a whole marketplace was lodged there: right in front of me there was a lot of notions, and beyond it, there appeared the flank of a great palace, but this was taken down. In front and at the sides then appeared plenty of beautiful vessels, porcelain ware it seemed to me, recently put up there; on the side, everything was still being arranged, and then I went into my own little chamber, which was shining too.

278

This refers to all the work I now enter upon in the name of God, first of all de cultu Dei, *on the side* de amore, *and that I should not draw upon others' notions* [Sw. kram, "small wares,"

"junk," "lumber," or "trash"], *but of mine, as it was in the par-lor I rented, my chamber, and beside it was the other work, and the rooms at the side did not belong to me.* May God lead me the right way! Christ said that I should not do anything without him.

In entry 277, Swedenborg's new attitude and working methods are presented in concrete images. First, in his dream-idiom, he characterizes the now-abandoned *Regnum Animale.* His great room, the hall, resembles a marketplace with its variety of merchandise and superfluous goods. A wing of a palace symbolizes his science. But then insignificant merchandise and the edifice suddenly vanish, and instead appear the "beautiful vessels" of the night of October 8–9. These, already in place or being carefully set out, will be useful for his future labors in the little study.

"Others' notions" are irrelevant to his new way of achieving knowledge. His own love and that of God will suffice, and a main theme of his new book will be an account of this devotion. After detailed paraphrases of the biblical stories of Creation, it describes Adam's and Eve's innocence and their love of God and each other—in other words, their condition before the Fall. In that prelapsarian state, the first human being appeared as an embodiment of divine love, the bearer of *caritas,* an *amor Dei* that overshadows all other love.

After the first sin, human love obviously no longer sufficed but must be supplemented and retained by "worship," directed by love, which is also divinely inspired good deeds. We celebrate God's omnipotence and force back our own love of self. This will be a recurring theme in Swedenborg's later writings. The self-searching implicit in worship is a discrimination between good and evil, a tool of crucial distinction.

It is *cultus,* in this sense, that Swedenborg from this time on is going to describe in epic form, as a drama of creation, a piece on loving ardor now "in front" of him, "before" him. Divine love is to be his lodestar as he proceeds.

The first entry concerning his new book, appearing in the entry of October 6–7, is foreshadowed by the fate of the two priests

Korah and Dathan in Numbers, who, to the diarist, are examples of the danger inherent in a worship not permeated by love and, to use his expression, not directed by a "right spirit."

De Cultu et Amore Dei was to remain unfinished. It would go no further than to describe the emergence and love of Adam and Eve in the Garden of Eden. Several years later, Swedenborg would, in another context, elaborate his idea of divine worship, its true form and content.

279

I mounted a fine black horse; there were two of them. He was bold, ran first astray and then back. This refers to what I am now about to do, which is still too much in the dark, but I will get on the right way.

280

While I went with my friend through a long tunnel, a beautiful girl turned up and fell in his arms, but she was whining. I asked if she knew him, and she did not reply. Then I drew her away from him and led her by the arm. *It was my other work to which she addressed herself and from which I took her in this way.*

281

In the morning, there appeared to me in a vision the market held such as Disting in my father's house at Uppsala, in the parlor upstairs, at the entrance, and everywhere. *This means the same, that it should take place, and even more certainly.*

The three passages confirm for Swedenborg what he now obviously regards as his call. The horse on the right road after a detour, the girl, his love—whom he carefully takes from his friend ("Jesus is the best of friends")—whom he leads by the arm are variations on the same theme. In his last vision, he returns to the security of his paternal home, the professor's residence, whose "parlor," according to the doctrine of correspondences, also signifies "doctrine." There he overviews the market and all the notions of others being offered at the annual *Distingsmarknaden* in Uppsala, a market held until 1895. It was a feast of ancient heathen origin, the offering to the *Dises*, the Weird Sisters in Northern mythology.

282

> In the morning when I woke up, there came again upon me such a swoon or *deliquium* [fainting fit] as I had six or seven years ago in Amsterdam, when I began the oecon. Regni anim. [Economy of the Animal Kingdom]; but it was much more subtle, whereas I seemed to be near death. It came upon me as I saw the light and threw me on my face. Gradually it passed off, while I fell into brief slumbers, so this *deliquium* was more inward and deeper; but soon it ceased. *This means that my head is thoroughly cleaned and rinsed from all that might obstruct these thoughts, as happened last time, when it gave me the power of penetration, especially with the pen*, which this time too was represented to me insofar as I seemed to be writing with a fine hand.

Swedenborg's dream diary reaches its pinnacle and culminates in a vision of light, with prostration, fainting fits, and brief moments of sleep. He recognized the phenomena from the time he began his work on the *Oeconomia Regni Animalis*, but now all are intensified. The preparatory state for a major consequence, unleashed by his sense of setting out for something completely new, having a divine call, is so strong that he is dazed almost to unconsciousness. For a moment, he feels close to death, but he is not frightened. All he is going through implies purification, that his mind is being swept clean, and he is ready to receive the divine messages he is to put into writing.

The spiritual clean-up takes on physical expressions, as internal changes always do in the diary. As a living evidence of the analogies of life, it seems to Swedenborg that he is writing in "a fine hand," *en fijn styl*.

11

THE ELEVENTH NIGHT

The last words of October 1744, in neat handwriting, are written on top of page 99 in the manuscript; the rest of the page is empty. It is followed by six other pages in the notebook, which are likewise blank. On the seventh, however, page 101, appears a note, dated only with the figures 11–12. In his Swedish edition of 1859, G. E. Klemming suggested that the month omitted in the heading might be May 1744, a guess supported by the entry's theme and by the name "Oelreich," and also by comparing it with the entry for May 19–20 of the same year.

That may be so. In any case, in this entry, Swedenborg describes still another set of dreams, although not about real events, as it probably was in the two friends' desire of "the sex" in the mentioned entry.

Let us now look at this odd, last entry, dating presumably from late spring or early summer 1744. Does it supply us with yet another prediction in the form of dream sequences? Why was it put aside?

[May?] 11–12

283

It seemed to me that I was with Oelreich and two women; he lay down; and afterwards it seemed he had been with a woman. He admitted this. Then I recalled, and I told him so, that I also had

lain with one and that my father came by and saw it, but went and did not mention a word about it.

Swedenborg and Oelreich appear, each with a woman. Oelreich seems to have been intimate with one of them. It appears to the dreamer that he is telling Oelreich about how Bishop Swedberg once took his son unawares when he was having intercourse with a woman. The father walks by and sees what his son is up to, but makes no comment.

As so often before, several interpretations suggest themselves. The dream scene may contain an approval of the work he had on hand at the time. If so, it is one in a series of episcopal assents in the diary, the last one we have.

His father's silence may also concern the correct attitude toward extramarital relationships. To his son, who is a bachelor but strongly interested in women, the matter is obviously urgent, and these distinctions are crucial. In his later writings, Swedenborg will emphatically call adultery a grave sin. However, premarital relationships, or those entered into after the death of a spouse, or if love is dead, appear to be more neutral and natural.

Is it this view—which Swedenborg will not articulate until a good twenty years later in his book on marital love—that he is now presenting and that meets with the bishop's silent approval?

Even more important, the dream can also be seen as still another sign of divine approval and consent regarding the work he is now entering upon. Here, as elsewhere, the woman may represent his intellectual pursuits, for which he burns and eagerly penetrates.

These disparate renderings may all be true. This time Swedenborg does not provide us with a key.

284

I left Oelreich. On the way, there was deep water; but, at the side, there was just a little, a walkway, where I went at the side, I did not think I ought to go in the deep water.

285

I thought that a firework burst above me, shedding a shower of sparks of beautiful fire: love of the high, maybe.

Appropriately, the last entry of the Swedish diary ends in divine fireworks.

12

FINANCIAL AFFAIRS AND
THE DAMSELS OF WISDOM

286

For Anthon and Johan Grill af Hultman on account of Petter Hultman's bill for Johan Spieker in London.

                                                    Guilder

1744, Jan. 20: received bill of exchange in Balairet
    at the Hague, at exchange rate 42-½ and 42-¾ 500
For contribution ....640 daler
To the estate of the diseased Celsing ....327 —
May 30, 1744, took out in London: 15 Pounds,
    15 Shillings at 43-¼ ....684 —
July 23, 1744, from Johan Spieker 60 Pounds
    Sterling, at the proposed rate of 45-¼...............2715 —
                  Balance: 6516
October 11: 5 Pounds, 5 Shilling at 46   241-½
Muillman & Sons, No. 13 through Frantz Jenningz:
1743 September 2, 13, withdrew Florins.....................500
November 12, renewal bill/turned into cash 500
1744, December 21: from Mr. Mackei in London
    60 Pounds Sterling, should be 46 daler
    per Pound Sterling..2760

Swedenborg's notes on his money transactions for 1743–1744 cover two openings in the notebook, pages 104–107. His floating assets are in Swedish Riksdaler copper coins. We get a feel for the amounts in question if we consider that Swedenborg's yearly salary during his leave of absence was 1800 Riksdaler, in the same currency. His income from interests was about 3,000 Riksdaler, according to his own calculation. For his property in Stockholm, bought in 1743, he paid 6,000 Riksdaler, as we can see from extant documents. Before that real-estate purchase, his fortune was 55,000 Riksdaler, as stated in his own capital tax return of 1742. (Our knowledge of the latter figure is due to the war tax of that year.)

To sum up:

(1) The first transaction took place in September 1743, shortly after Swedenborg arrived in Holland. As we see, he paid a firm of bankers, Muillman & Sons, 500 florins, through Frans Jennings. Mr. Jennings was an Irish immigrant in Sweden, who through talent and an advantageous marriage, was able to establish a trading house. Together with an English immigrant, one of his sons founded the company Jennings & Finlay. Swedenborg had considerable exchange dealings with that company.

The transaction in question amounted to about 2150 daler. We suggest that the transaction took place in Amsterdam, the financial center of Holland.

(2) On November 12 of the same year, there is another transaction involving 500 florins. The abridgment *oms.* in the original does not tell us whether it is a withdrawal, an expense, a renewal bill, or a bill of exchange. Even here we can determine the sum to about 2,150 Riksdaler copper.

(3) On January 20, Swedenborg once again got out 500 *gyllen* or guilder, another name for florins, since it was stamped in gold in the Netherlands. This took place at The Hague. His Swedish partner in that transaction was the businessman Petter Hultman in Stockholm. During Swedenborg's many years abroad, Mr. Hultman seems to have acted on his behalf in financial affairs. We should recall that the wealthy Petter Hultman's daughter married Count Fredrik Gyllenborg's son Gustaf Adolf; and, in this way, Hultman

was introduced to the Gyllenborg circle in Stockholm, to which Swedenborg was connected.

The other disbursements mentioned in the same Dutch note are a tax payment and a settlement on account of the estate of Chancellor of Court Gustaf Celsing, both affairs directed by Hultman in Stockholm. The Balair (Balairet) was a mercantile firm in the capital of the Netherlands.

(4) During the eight months after he moved to London in early May 1744, Swedenborg bought English currency four times. Three of these instances were money channeled through Hultman's London connection, John Spieker, while the fourth occurred through a contact named Mackei. In all, this amounts to some 6,400 Riksdaler, a huge amount of money.

If we disregard the unclear transaction mentioned under (2), we conclude that Swedenborg withdraw 11,667 Riksdaler in sixteen months, from September 1743 to January 1744. No doubt, most of this money has been spent on printing costs. The 1,000 florins drawn in Amsterdam, as I have posited, and at The Hague in September 1743 and January 1744 may refer to the printing of the two first volumes of *The Animal Kingdom*, printed at The Hague late in the winter of 1744.

During the next year, in London, from February–March 1745, Swedenborg printed two books: the third volume of *The Animal Kingdom* and the unfinished *The Worship and Love of God*. Apart from two minor cash withdrawals, which almost certainly refer to private needs, on two separate occasions, he drew 5,475 Riksdaler in total. Considering that the English printing costs must have been lower than the expenses for the tomes published at The Hague, volumes that had an extensive apparatus of notes, the London transactions are difficult to explain, even more so if the dates are taken into account.

Still more remarkable is the fact that Swedenborg's fortune does not seem to have been changed by these expenses, which adds up to more than two of his total annual incomes. The Swedish lawyer Frans G. Lindh, a New Churchman who took great pains to scrutinize Swedenborg's private accounts—leaving not one slip of paper unturned—launched a hypothesis: some exalted patron secretly sponsored Swedenborg's works of 1744–1745 and even the later theological writings. Lindh's hypothesis is reasonable, but to lay down documentary evidence here would bring us too far. I hope to approach this enigma in another book.

After these cashbook pages, one last dream entry appears on page 108. It is undated, and in contrast to all other texts in this note book it is written in Latin:

287

Verities or virgins of this genius think it ignominious to offer themselves for sale. They esteem themselves so precious, so dear to their admirers, that they show indignation if anyone take liberty to suggest an affair, and even more if anyone attempts to purchase them. To others, who think they are bad, they lift their eyebrows.

Rather than being undervalued by the former and lay themselves open to the contempt of the latter, they accordingly offer themselves gratuitously [*gratis*] to their lovers [*amatoribus*].

For a last time, we get a glimpse of the Virgin-Woman imago, the persistent figure concealing the stuff the dreamer is dreaming of. All through the dream diary, the question has been whether these loves are right or wrong, if he is on the right track or lost. Now, finally, Swedenborg adopts a more general view. This entry may be clarified by comparing it to the preface of a small work, written some time between 1741 and 1743, *The Intercourse between the Soul and Body*. In a language tinged by Ovid, Swedenborg described his mission:

> *By now, Nature has almost nothing to cover herself with. She is waiting for a gifted man of our time who is experienced by experiment, disciplined by science and studies, trained to find causes and able to reason with the aid of connections and*

analogies, and skillful in presenting proofs based on the interre-
lations of facts in series and degrees. To that man she longs to
get betrothed. She is determined to become a willing target for
the arrows of his love, and with him she will unite in wedlock,
and share his bed and house. Oh, if only I might strew the nuts
and be the first to carry the wedding torch.

Consequently, the admirer of truth, the lover of those synonymous verities and virgins, will reach his goal if he is well-informed and experienced enough and has the required ardor. The same confidence of the writer is intimated in the prologue of *The Animal Kingdom*. Enthusiastically, Swedenborg encourages the reader to follow him on his exploration expedition: "Let us gird up our loins for the work! The Nine Virgins are on our side, adorned and ready to go since almost two thousand years! They are the sciences, the treasures and powers, the protectresses which make this work possible."

Then, God would be proved scientifically. The note of the virgins is the last station on a line of retreat that the diary delineates. The truth of the Divine cannot be analyzed, will not let itself be the subject of earthly bargaining or blather, dissection or discourse. The proficiency of the lover and his practical attainments are of no value. Swedenborg has become the faithful servant of the hidden, the *famulus* of his beloved damsels. They know him well, and willingly they lift the veil on their secrets.

NOTES

—————◆➤❁◀◆—————

The note numbers below refer to the diary entry numbers which they concern. The notes may not refer to the actual entry but the analysis of that dream.

1

Magnus Julius De la Gardie (1669?–1741) and Hedvig Catharina (1695–1745), see: *Biographiskt lexicon öfver namnkunnige svenske män*, 1837–57; and Gustaf Elgenstierna, *Svenska adelns ättartavlor*, 1925–1936.

Concerning the Gyllenborg-Broman circle, see: Oswald Kuylenstierna, *Svensk rokoko: Människor, dagligt liv* (Stockholm, 1923), 61 ff. Catharina De la Gardie sold (presumably immediately before her departure) her property Rosersberg outside Stockholm to Erland Broman. Later, in 1748, Broman and Pontus Fredrik De la Gardie, Catharina's son, both married sisters of Hedvig Taube, the royal mistress; cf. Kuylenstierna, 185; and in Elgenstierna, the article on De la Gardie.

The episode on the posthumous marriage is found in Swedenborg's *Spiritual Diary* §6027 and is also reported in *Swedenborgs drömmar*, 1859, 66 ff.

On horseradish: *Samling af Correspondenser af Emanuel Swedenborg*, manuscript, The Royal Library, Stockholm.

The facts on the Counts von Fersen, on Jakob Albrecht von Lantingshausen (1699–1769), and on Johan Stenflycht (1681–1758) are found in *Biographiskt lexicon*.

On the fate of Börke Filip Skeckta (1699–1770), see: Carl von Linné, *Nemesis Divina*, (Stockholm, 1968), 179.

Carl Klingenberg (1708–1757) was to become a member of the circle around the poetess Hedvig Charlotta Nordenflycht. After Klingenberg's death, Mrs. Nordenflycht, brokenhearted by sorrow, sought refuge with the sister of Hedvig Taube who had married Pontus Fredrik De la Gardie. Cf. Torkel Stålmarck, *Tankebyggare*. Stockholm Studies in History of Literature, Acta Universitatis (Stockholm, 1986), 23 f. On the motto of Klingenberg: op. cit., 24.

3

"Francken, Stripsser" in the original a misspelling of Franken-Triebseer was, along with Knieperthor (misspelled *Kniper-thore*), citadels erected to the defense of the city.

Johan August Meijerfeldt (1664–1749) was one of King Charles XII's generals, governor of Swedish Pomerania from 1713 to 1747.

Claus Philip von Schwerin (1689–1748). Carl Jesper Benzelius (1714–1793).

Double Archimedean screws supplied the waterworks Swedenborg noted with characteristic interest.

4

"Rimits" in the original is a misspelling of Rimitz.

5

"Gadebusk" in the original is a misspelling of Gadebusch.

6

Carl Fredrik Hamilton (1705–1753) was marshal of the court, and Esbjörn Christian Reuterholm (1710–1773) was chamberlain.

Mårten Triewald (1691–1747), along with Christopher Polhem, was the most renowned and proficient Swedish *mecanicus* (engineer) of the time and a famous inventor as well, particularly active in the mining industry. Mårten Triewald had an older brother, Samuel (b.1688), a writer and an official, who, in his later years, served as governor with Prince August, the younger brother of Prince-Bishop and successor to the throne Adolf Fredrik (see below). Samuel died in January 1743, however, so the Triewald (spelled *Trivalt*) mentioned in the diary is probably Mårten.

Johan Fredrik König (1690–1759) was director of the Swedish post in Hamburg, where he was a consular agent and, from 1747, the Swedish consul.

Prince August (1711–1785) succeeded his brother Adolf Fredrik as Prince-Bishop in Lübeck in 1751. See Tafel, vol. II:2, p.1066.

Adolf Fredrik (1710–1771) was elected successor to the throne in 1743 and was crowned in 1751, following the death of Fredrik I. He is often characterized as a somewhat phlegmatic, quiet gentleman, influenced by his powerful wife Louisa Ulrika (1720–1782), the sister of King Fredrik II of Pomerania. The royal couple seems to have felt kindly toward Swedenborg. The queen appears in one of the anecdotes that are often adduced as proofs of Swedenborg's communications with the dead (Tafel, I, p. 612, note 11).

9

"Treckscheut" is a misspelling of *trekschuit*, a horse-drawn canal boat: see further entry 191.

10

Concerning the money transactions, compare entry 286.

11

The "Gustavian family" refers to the older royal family. The monarchs of Holstein-Gottorp, the last of that line being Charles XII and his sister Ulrika Eleonora, were related to the Vasa dynasty. The word "Gustavian" in Swedenborg's peculiar usage thus denotes the heirs of the founder of the Swedish nation-state, King Gustav Vasa (1496–1560).

Anders Hallengren has pointed out that the Swedish word *keden* in dream entry 5 might possibly be interpreted "kid" instead of "chain," according to seventeenth-century and dialectal usage (*ked, kelling* = "kid," used even in biblical language of that time), and that an unfortunate goatherd might be involved in this rustic drama, which is also implied by dreams 6 and 7, Hallengren argues. Support for that translation he found in the *Glossarium öfver föråldrade eller ovanliga ord och talesätt i svenska språket: fån och med 1500-talets andra årtionde* (Lund: Gleerup 1914–1916). F. A. Dahlgren, the linguist who deciphered Swedenborg's dream diary in the Royal Library and who particularly drew upon the literature of Jesper Swedberg's time for his dictionary, wrote the *Glossarium*.

12

The original reads *porterad för Sexen*, which means "drawn to the sexual."

"*Exstasibus vigilibus*" implies "wakeful raptures."

The quote on "revelations . . . " is from *The Word Explained* §1351 and §1353.

13

On the combination of analysis and intuitive synthesis, see Swedenborg's *The Infinite and Final Cause of Creation* §§56, 191–192; and the *Economy of the Animal Kingdom* II, §§208–213.

On the faulty outcomes of intellectual analysis, see further *The Animal Kingdom* §463 (g): "We develop and combine clear ideas, and perspicaciously consider analyses with our reason, and yet they are all mere figments of the brain, unclear images of truth."

Concerning Swedenborg's application for leave of absence, see *Letters and Memorials 1709–1748*, p. 497.

14

For J. C. Cuno's account, see Tafel II, doc. 256, p 497 f.

17

On the guardian angel, see Jesper Swedberg, *Lefwernes beskrifnin.*(Lund, 1941), 23. Concerning temptations on mountains as a biblical paradigm, see Luke 4:5–8 and Matthew 4:8–10. For the term *mountain* being an image of self-conceit and love of the worldly, see Swedenborg's *Arcana Coelestia* §1691.

Temptation as an affliction, *afflictio*, is treated in *Arcana Coelestia* §1846, and "bodily fires" in §263 (g–h).

21

Carl Broman (1703–1784) was governor of Älvsborg County, later in the administrative province of Stockholm. He also served as master of ceremonies in the court of King Adolf Fredrik.

Baron Erland Broman (1704–1757) was court marshal in 1741 and president of the National Board of Trade in 1747. Erland Broman was skillful in real estate business and speculative currency transactions; he earned a fortune on the deprecation of the value of money, a capital soon enough gambled away, however. Erland Broman served as a front when the king of Sweden borrowed money from the Bank of Sweden.

On Carl Tersmeden, see *Memoarer*, ed. Nils Erdmann (Stockholm, 1916). This work contains accounts of society life in Stockholm during the 1730s and 1740s.

Concerning Fredrik Gyllenborg and Elisabeth Stierncrona, see note 60 in the introduction, "Social Circles."

22

Ulrika Eleonora (1688–1741), Charles XII's sister, was married to Prince Fredrik of Hessen. After Charles XII's death in 1718, she was elected Queen Regent in 1719 but abdicated next year on behalf of her husband, who assumed the name of Fredrik I.

Hedvig Taube (1714–1744), a daughter of Councilor Count Evert Didrik Taube, an admiral during the Russian war, 1741–1743. From the age of 16 and until her death, she was the mistress of King Fredrik and was known for her pecuniary interests.

24

Johan Hesselius (1687–1753) is one of Swedenborg's many relatives mentioned in the dream diary. Swedenborg father's was his uncle through his marriage to Sara Bergia. Hesselius became district medical officer in Skara, and for a long time the bishop housed him. When Swedenborg went on his second trip abroad in 1721, Hesselius accompanied him. According to Swedberg's autobiography, Hesselius was very musical: in the evenings, he played cello for the family. Later, he became assessor of Sundhet-skollegium (the national health board). *Biographiskt lexicon öfver namnkunnige svenske män* (Upsala, 1835–1857); Tafel, I, p. 679.

On "the importance of the lungs and the pulmonary artery," cf. dream entry 18.

25

"This was one of the fundamental problems occupying his mind at this time": cf. *The Fibre* §488 and *Rational Psychology* §476.

27

"and it can finally be determined whether the ideological forms are in unison": *Animal Kingdom* II, §458.

"yellow is the color of the earthly": *Spiritual Diary* §1331.

29

"he may also be referring to his grand plans": cf. *Animal Kingdom* I, preface to photo-offset edition, p. vi; and Tafel II:2, doc. 313, p 944.

"Books written by the leading English thinkers behind the advancement of learning in the era, John Locke and Francis Bacon, were in his library." This is evident from *Förteckning på Aflidne Wälborne Herr Assessor Swedenborgs efterlämnade Boksamling. . . att försäljas på*

Bok-Auctions-Kammaren i Stockholm 23 November 1772. See further Lars Bergquist, *Biblioteket i lusthuset: Tio uppsatser om Swedenborg* (Stockholm: Natur och Kultur, 1996).
"we must master all sciences": *Animal Kingdom* I, §12.

30

"In 1914, a ledger was found among some documents from the old German Lutheran congregation": *New Church Life*, Dec. 1914, 766 f.
"One of the congregation's clergy was Johann Gottlieb Pambo": *Nieuw Nederlandsch. . . Woordenboek*, vol. 5 (Leyden, 1921), 435.

31

"Some time after the king's flight from Stralsund in 1714": on Swedenborg's dealings with Charles XII in Lund, 1716–1718, and in connection with the campaign in Norway, see Cyriel Odhner Sigstedt, *The Swedenborg Epic: The Life and Works of Emanuel Swedenborg* (New York: The Swedenborg Foundation, 1952), 47 ff.
"Festivus Applausus": see Hans Helander, *Em Swedenborg: Festivus Applausus Caroli XII in Pomeraniam suam adventum* (Uppsala, 1985).
"Shortly before the king's death Swedenborg seems to have fallen out of his favor": cf. *Spiritual Diary* §4704.

36

Swedenborg prefers to mention "life" in Latin: *"prima vita . . . altera vita"*: the first life . . . the other life.

38

"In his later writings he often returns to these afflictions": e.g., *Arcana Coelestia* §2334.

39

The original reads *"Pingstdagen "* (on Whitsunday), an obvious slip of pen. Should be *Påskdagen*, on Easter day.

45

"Plato used frequently to say" : *A Philosopher's Note Book*, 6.

49–50

"we hear an echo perhaps of his father's pondering on this same problem": Jesper Swedberg, *Guds Heliga . . . dnalag* (Skara, 1713), 152 ff.

50

Swedenborg uses the word *fallaces* when he considers the reliability of sensory data, contrasting them to the Word of God, which is *ipsa veritas*, truth itself.

52

The word *prosternerad*, "prostrate," repeatedly used by Swedenborg in a passive voice, means lying with face to the ground and is derived from the Latin verb *prosternere*, throw in front, cast down.

51–54

"face to face": 1. Cor. 13:12.

"health certificate . . . unusual Swedish word . . .." See also the well-informed account in Signe Toksvig, chapter 12.

"By no means will anyone who shouts 'Lord! Lord!' enter the kingdom of heaven": Swedberg: *Lefwernes beskrifning*, 62 f.

On the Moravian faith in Stockholm 1742, see Hilding Pleijel, *Svenska kyrkans historia*, vol. 5, 421 ff.; and Nils Jacobsson, *Den svenska herrnhutismens uppkomst*, 38 ff., 135 ff.

On Moravian rituals of solemnizing the Passover, see further Taylor Hamilton, *A History of the Moravian Church* (Bethlehem, Pa.,1900), 43; and cf. also Zinzendorf's *Wundenlitaney* and his *Reden über die Wundenlitaney*.

Concerning Zinzendorf's emphasis on divine suffering, see Gösta Hök: *Herrnhutisk teologi i svensk gestalt*, 57 ff., and *Zinzendorfs Begriff der Religion*, 121 ff.

"worshippers had to activate all their senses": Pleijel, op. cit., 452; and Bernhardt Becker, *Zinzendorf und sein Christentum*, 286.

"all theology is summed up": Becker, op. cit., 287.

Song in Moravian worship: *Vollständige so wohl historisch als theologische Nachricht von der Herrnhutischen Bruderschaft*, 19 ff.

"Prostration formed part of the Moravian ritual": cf. Wesley: *Journal*, 24 May 1738, p. 123 ff.

NOTES TO DREAM DIARY

55

"However, as we are commanded to try the spirits . . .": 1. Epistle of John 4:1.

55–57

"Furthermore, to be bound and drawn are important concepts in Moravian terminology . . . ": Hök: *Herrnhutisk teologi i svensk gestalt*, 36.

"Please now call me, tempt me, draw me": *Sions Sånger*, hymn no. 153:5 (Stockholm,1781). The same theme and wording recurs in the edition of 1743, cf. No. 56:13.

". . . You are still sitting in his bosom . . . ": *On the Worship and Love of God* §56. Compare Inge Jonsson (1961), 164 (Swedish edition); and Martin Lamm, 170 (Swedish edition).

"In February 1746, he was to distinguish between four forms of visions": *The Word Explained* 1351.

"When our home was consumed by the fire. . .". Cf. Tafel, I, doc. 153.

58

"The problem of Swedenborg's estate . . . was a matter of principle": cf. Hamilton Taylor, *A History of the Moravian Church*, 67 ff.; Jacobsson, op. cit., 91; and Arvid Gradin: *A Short History of the Bohemian-Moravian Church*, 48 ff.

"to the indignation of his fellow aristocrats, Count Zinzendorf . . . had himself installed as a bishop." Gradin, *A Short History*, 48. Gradin observes that it was considered unfit for a count to be a bishop and that Zinzendorf's decision to take holy orders raised such suspicion against him that he finally resigned from the see.

". . . the well-known mass weddings . . . ": cf. Hermann Plitt: *Zinzendorfs Theologie*, II, 398 ff.; Henri Rimius: *A Candid Narrative of the Herrnhuters*, 81 ff.; and Gradin., 49.

59

The Stockholm Moravians rapturously sang: "Jesus, Jesus, Sweetest Brother, before your cross I genuflect." *Sions Sånger*, hymn no. 83:9 (Stockholm 1743).

61

". . . the living insight into your own corruption and wretchedness . . .": Hök, *Herrnhutisk teologi i svensk gestalt*, 113.

63

"To use an expression frequent in his later writings . . . ." See, for example, *Arcana Coelestia* §154 and *Spiritual Diary* §318.

68

". . . the pair of scales, an image earlier used . . . ": *Rational Psychology* §504.

69

". . . this mental struggle between a conviction of salvation and a despair of his own sinfulness . . . will run all through his later writings." See, for example, *Spiritual Diary* §199, as well as a kind of dynamic unity between these opposites, *Arcana Coelestia* §§1787 and 2694.

77

". . . he will explore the psychology of melancholy." See further *Arcana Coelestia* §5570.

80

Joakim Fredrik Preis (1667–1759) served as Swedish envoy at The Hague from 1714 and stayed on that post until he died at the age of 93. From extant correspondence, it is evident that Swedenborg regularly met with Preis when he was in The Hague and also sent him his writings asking for his opinion about them. During this stay in The Hague, Swedenborg presented Preis with the first two volumes of *The Animal Kingdom*, which had been printed in that city. The third volume of that work was published next year, as was *On The Worship and Love of God*, and Swedenborg sent these books to Preis from London. Preis' background was a bit unusual. In his youth, he had studied Hebrew and Greek in Riga; during those years, he prepared a new Swedish translation of the Book of Isaiah. After studies in Leyden, Cambridge, and Oxford, in 1695, Preis came to the Swedish embassy in Paris; and in 1703, he was sent to the Swedish mission at The Hague. He was ennobled in 1719, as was Swedenborg. According to the *Biographiskt lexicon*, Preis was "perspicacious and well-informed, and at the same time an easy mixer and flexible in his relations. Although he was very busy, he found time for studies, and preferably moved in good society among eminent men of all estates."

81

"In these veering turns of mind, Swedenborg does not differ from other Christian mystics. . . . ." See, for instance, the *Subida del monte Carmelo* by Saint John of the Cross; and Evelyn Under-hill, *Mysticism*.

82

Anders Swab (1681–1731) was, in a labyrinthine way, related to Swedenborg, being the son of Anton Swab who was married to a sister of Swedenborg's first stepmother, Sara Bergia (Bergius). When that sister, Helena Bergia, died, the widower married Christina Arrhusia (Arrhusius) who, in her turn, after Anton's death became Swedenborg's second stepmother by marrying Bishop Jesper Swedberg. In the marriage between Anton Swab and Helena Bergia, Anders Swab was born, a mine-captain in Dalarna and later a superior colleague of Swedenborg in the Royal College of Mines.

According to Swedenborg's observations in the later *Spiritual Diary*, Anders Swab was a most capricious and spiteful person. Those who were loyal and pleased him were rewarded with money and honors, whereas he maliciously hurt those who were against him (§5042). He loved sexual excesses, fornication, and eagerly enticed others to act likewise (§4843). To Swab, Christians teachings served private goals. A long time after Swab's death, Swedenborg was haunted by his spirit and tormented by genii resembling him. They "block my view" (§4835).

Still another Swab is met with in the *Spiritual Diary*, Anton von Swab (1702–1768) was the half-brother of Anders and, like him, subjected to Swedenborg's deprecation. Anton's cunning efficiency in promoting his malicious intents reminded Swedenborg of an animal-head spitting out its venom (§4627). That image can be compared to the dog in entry 41 of the dream diary.

"His intercession days may thus be another instance of Moravian influence." Hamilton Taylor, 43.

85

". . . he uses the opening words of the 'confession of sin' in the Swedish liturgy. . . .": *Evangelia och Epistlar på alla Söndagar, Högtider och Helgedagar* (1739), 291 f.

87

The original phrase reads, *huru alt abouterade*, which means that Swedenborg momentarily beheld "how everything reached its goal" or was fulfilled. Swedenborg describes a cyclic motion in helical space.

"In his prologue of the *Economy of the Animal Kingdom*, . . . he described how . . . he at times felt he was the innermost center of all being": *The Economy of the Animal Kingdom* I, §19.

". . . 'paradise play' of *The Worship and Love of God* . . .": Swedenborg §57, §121f. Cf. Inge Jonsson, . . . *De cultu et amore Dei*, 142.

88

"Swedenborg's tangibly erotic manner of describing . . . ": Evelyn Underhill, 373 f.

". . . rays of the 'light of spiritual power'. . . ": *Animal Kingdom* II, §463 g.

89

"The matter had been carefully stipulated in the Swedish canon of 1686. . .": Chap. 8: 2, 11: 1 of the Canon.

"Beforetime I consoled myself . . . ": *Sions Sånger* (Stockholm 1743), hymn no. 6:4, 5.

90

". . . 'to be a sinner' and even 'to wish to become a sinner' was synonymous with . . .": Nils Jacobsson, 165.

91

On Moravian *pedilavium*, see Hermann Plitt, I, 32; II, 382 f, 516 f.

Concerning *pedilavium* in Swedenborg's later writings, see *Arcana Coelestia* §§3147, 3148, 7442, and 10047.

"Once a month, we all partake . . . ": Gradin, *A Short History*, 48. See also Gerhard Wauer, 70. In Swedenborg's library, there is another book published by James Hutton, a handbook on Moravian teachings translated from the Dutch: *A Manual of Doctrine, or a Second Essay to bring into the form of Question and Answer the Fundamental Doctrines . . . of the Brethren* (London 1742). This book contains a number of elements needed to understand Swedenborg's thought. James Hutton was also the English publisher and printer of the Moravian collections of hymns, 1739–1748.

93

"Not touchy or self-sufficient, but kind, polite . . . ": *Tessin och Tessiniana* (Stockholm 1819), 357.

96

". . . the rain of Grace . . ": Swedberg: "De obotfärdigas förhinder," *Then Swenska PsalmBoken*, 589.

100

On the "hypnagogic" state, see Ernst Arbman, *Ecstasy or Religious Trance*, I, 62. "For what constitutes one's own man (*proprium*) . . . ": *Apocalypse Explained* §318.

101–102

". . . St. Paul's famous words . . .": "For we know that the whole creation groaneth and travaileth in pain together until now," Romans 8:22.

103

"If the loves of the Animus . . . ": *Rational Psychology* §368.

105

". . . he wrote about these organs and their purificatory functions . . .": *The Animal Kingdom* I, §§288–291.

106

"Caisa" refers to his younger sister Catharina Swedenborg (1693–1770), who married Jonas Unge, Dean of Linköping.

109

"Like my fathers I have time and again sinned . . .": *Evangelier och Epistlar* . . . (1739), 291–292.

112

"According to the *Spiritual Diary*, he had already in his childhood . . .": *Spiritual Diary* §3464.

113–116

On Zinzendorf's interest in alchemy and on the attempts to make gold in Herrnhut, see: *Vollständige so wohl historisch als theologische Nachricht von der Herrnhutischen Bruderschaft*, 105 ff. Cf. also

Richard Wilhelm, *The Secret of the Golden Flower;* and Underhill, 140 f.

119

Lars Benzelstierna (1680–1755) was a mineralogist. In 1722, he was appointed assessor in the Royal Board of Mining and, in 1744, promoted to be a councilor of that ministry. Benzelstierna married Hedvig Swedenborg.

Swedenborg seems to have felt a real loathing for Benzelstierna. His brother-in-law was undependable in financial matters and tried to cheat Emanuel and his brother Jesper in a dispute about an inheritance. According to the *Spiritual Diary,* after death, Benzelstierna pursued all that had not belonged to his closest friends. Swedenborg did not belong to that narrow circle of friends and was accordingly attacked by thousands of spirits under the command of Benzelstierna in the nether regions (§5052).

120

Johan Arckenholtz (1695–1777), government official and historian, early on became convinced that good relations with Russia was momentous to Swedish security policy and turned against the intense Swedish–French relations, which largely aimed at strengthening the position against St. Petersburg. During the war with Russia, he was imprisoned but was released when peace was concluded in 1743. Then Arckenholtz became royal librarian in Hessen; among other things, he published documents concerning the Swedish Queen Kristina. It is quite likely that Swedenborg had met Arckenholtz or knew of him. As a member of the chancellery staff, Arckenholtz was in communication with Swedenborg's friend, the envoy Preis, at The Hague.

"As early as 1734, he had warned . . . ": Tafel, I, doc 172, p. 483 ff.

122

The hymn is taken from the 1781 edition of *Sions Sånger* (53:4). The main theme also appears in the hymn book of 1743 (in 72:15, 16 and elsewhere), but nowhere in such a dense form as in the quoted verses.

125

Johan Moraeus (1671–1742), a cousin of Swedenborg, was the son of Bishop Jesper Swedberg's sister Barbro in her marriage with an enforcement officer in Falun. After the death of his father, Johan Moraeus was brought up in Swedberg's house in Stockholm, later in Uppsala, where he served as Emanuel's private tutor from 1696 on. He studied medicine in Leyden and Paris, and later became district medical officer in Skara, where he stayed with his maternal uncle. He ended up as a practitioner in Falun, residing at an estate called Sweden, from which the bishop's family derived their name and origin (the property now belongs to the State-owned Nordiska Museet). Swedenborg and Moraeus appear to have remained friends for life. After Moraeus' death, he appeared to Swedenborg as an angel (*Spiritual Diary* §4717; cf. Tafel, I, p. 672).

126 _____

"Probably this refers to the drafts of his work De sensu communi . . . ": cf. §382 of that work. Swedenborg also treated the function and use of muscles in the *Animal Kingdom* II, §§442–453.

127 _____

" . . . one of his father's favorite hymns, *In dulci jubilo* . . . ": Jesper Swedberg, *Lefwernes beskrifning* (Lund, 1941), 719.

130 _____

Henning Adolf Gyllenborg (1713–1775), count, councilor of the state, the nephew of Fredrik Gyllenborg, was a well-known Hat politician and prompter of the war against Russia, 1741–1743. He was appointed marshal in 1751.

134 _____

"the leader of 'the Nicolaitans' . . .": Revelation 2:6.
"Those who separate charity from faith are called 'Nicolaitans'. . .": *The Apocalypse Explained* §107.

135 _____

For facts on Swedenborg's communion, see *New Church Life*, Dec. 1914, 766 ff.
" . . . a clergyman at The Hague": *Spiritual Diary* §6070; cf. also *Divine Providence* §197.

143 _____

"Stand now having your loins girt about with truth . . .": Ephesians 6:14.

144

"The pious hero of the Apocrypha's Book of Tobit, Tobias
. . . ": Tobit 5: 17.

146

"Sanguineous is the dispensary of Soul": *Sions Sånger*, hymn
no. 29:3.

147

"I saw König and Prof. Winbom approaching . . . ": It is not
completely clear to which "König" Swedenborg is referring, cf.
dream entry 6, although J.F. König is a likely candidate. The professor is Anders Winbom (1687–1745), professor of theology at
Uppsala from 1731 on. Winbom studied at the Skara high school
when Swedberg was *eforus* there and probably knew the family.

148–153

"Many early enlightenment scientists appear to have maintained that science and theology are two sides of the same thing":
cf. Ernst Benz, *Emanuel Swedenborg. Naturforscher und Seer*, 119 f.
Concerning Linné, see Sten Lindroth, "Linné—legend och
verklighet," *Lychnos* (1965–66): 23 f.
"The more the world is perfected in the sciences and in learning . . .": Codex 36. Tafel II:2, p. 1114.
" . . . that which drives and leads me . . .": *Animal Kingdom* I,
§22.

156

" . . . he shed his precious blood . . . ": *Then Swenska Psalmboken*,
hymn no. 143:1.

171

Orig.: *en merveille*, in a marvelous and wonderful way.

172

"The very sexual act was accordingly considered an almost liturgical act": Plitt, II, 364, 369. Cf. Rimius, 60 ff., where it is observed
that sexual union may be consummated in the name of the Savior.

173

"The Order of the Mustard Seed": Plitt, I, 108.

180

In a letter to Gabriel Beyer in 1767, Swedenborg responded to a question about his theological studies that he was "forbidden" to read authors of works in dogmatic and systematic theology until heaven was opened to him, because unfounded views and ideas could then easily have "slipped in." Cf., Tafel, II, doc. 234.

". . . the great interest paid to Boehme. . . ": *Vollständige so wohl historisch als theologische Nachricht*, 27, 104 ff.

183

". . . returned two carolines to me. But it was said that he kept thirteen dalers for himself . . ." From 1719–1776, the relation between the different species of Swedish coins was as follows: 1 daler = 3 daler silver coins = 9 daler copper coins = 12 mark silver coins = 36 mark copper coins. A "caroline" was worth 2 mark silver. If we suppose that that the dalers of the gardener were copper—which Swedenborg mostly uses in his accounts (cf. for instance, dream entry 286), it is obvious that the gardener kept the lion's share.

189

Eliezer Swedberg (1689–1716) was married to Elisabeth Brinck, who, after Eliezer's death, married Swedenborg's colleague and superior in the Royal Board of Mining, Anders Swab—who, in his turn, through Jesper Swedberg's third marriage, was related to Swedenborg. We meet Swab in dream entries 82 and 186.

Jesper Swedenborg was Emanuel's youngest brother (1694–1771). According to Jesper Swedberg's autobiography, Jesper was *något yr*, a bit rambunctious in his youth. He was sent to the Swedish colony in North America, New Sweden (Delaware), where he worked as a teacher in a village called Upland, named for the province of Uppsala in Sweden. Young Jesper returned to Sweden in 1724, was promoted to the rank of lieutenant, and, finally, became the owner of the farm Swedendal in Vestrogothica. After all this, he was, quoting his father's autobiography again, "sound, peaceful, sober, and pious." In 1727, Jesper married Christina Silfverswärd, who was also of a noble family. It is from this couple that the present Swedenborg family descends.

191

Marslandzskuten in the original, should be Maaslandsskuiten trekschuit (canal boat driven by draft-horses) from Maasland. This is the same kind of flat-bottomed vessel mentioned in dream entries 9 and 10. Swedenborg might have made a stop in Scheveningen, where he later embarked a ship bound for England.

193

"Stiver," in the original styfwer: unofficial name for 1 öre in silver.

"Pietasteri": "pecuniary piety," if Swedenborg's witty word is derived from the Latin pietas and the Turkish coin piaster (from the Italian piastra, metal plate). A doubtful alloy.

196

Johan Bergenstierna (1668–1748) was an official in the Royal Board of Mining from 1723. In 1735, he married the widow of Eliezer Swedberg and Anders Swab, Elisabeth Brinck, cf. dream entry 188. According to the protocols of the ministry, Swedenborg seems to have undertaken official journeys in Sweden together with Bergenstierna. The better he got acquainted with his colleague this way, the less he liked him. Bergenstierna appeared to be an impious hypocrite only interested in obtaining advantages. His fate after death was as might have been expected, Swedenborg observed in his Spiritual Diary §5133.

198

". . . grace, the opposite of law . . . ": cf. Karin Dovring, Striden kring Sions Sånger . . . , I, 133f.

". . . Christ 'the throne of grace' . . .": cf. the frequency count in Dovring., II, 171.

". . . a Moravian key. Bliss is a state . . .": Dovring., I, 136.

". . . the paradisian state does not constitute heaven . . .": Arcana Coelestia §2603.

199

"Manna": Exodus 16.

200

Niklas von Oelreich (1699–1770) lived in London at this time, serving as tutor of the young counts Axel and Carl von Fersen. He was a professor of the history of ideas, later of philosophy, at Lund

University. In 1746, he became head of the Swedish censorship office. In 1755–1756, Oelreich published the first political journal of Sweden, *En ärlig svensk* (An Honest Swede), where, among other things, he advocated the domination of the estates of the realm.

201
_____

"We should not live as 'prisoners of nature', but . . .": *The Five Senses* §87:7.

204
_____

"*War en söndag*" is inaccurate since June 16 was a Saturday, from which we can conclude that Swedenborg is referring to the night between June 16 and June 17.

206
_____

". . . that what I had written about providence was the finest . . .": In the *Economy of the Animal Kingdom* I, Swedenborg mentions a future work on divine providence. According to Alfred Acton's comment on §561 in *Rational Psychology* (n. 2), the pages that should have contained that work are missing in the preserved manuscript volume.

"After their break with John Wesley . . .": Wesley, 370, n. 2.

". . . their official name became the 'Moravian Brethren of the English Communion' ": Hamilton, 90 f.

". . . holy and undefiled garment of righteousness . . .": Hök, quoted from Arvid Gradin in *Herrnhutisk teologi i svensk gestalt*, 133. Cf. also Karin Dovring, II, 78 ff.

". . . those who have speculated about Swedenborg's mental health . . .": cf. *New Church Magazine* (1914), 80; and Tafel II, doc. 597. See also Acton, 89, n. 2.

208
_____

"Long after Benzelius's death, Swedenborg was to write in his . . .": see *Spiritual Diary* §§4757, 5074, and 5751.

211
_____

"From the following and other things . . .": cf. also dream entry 216.

"He repeatedly mentioned also the obscurity that remained . . .": *The Five Senses* §§586, 588, 590, and elsewhere.

212

On the difficulty of describing the functions of the senses, see *The Five Senses* §§80:7, 589:4, and 615:11.

Concerning the work on the brain, and the sections then in progress, cf. Acton, 83, n. 1.

215

"Swedenborg outlines this sphere as the source . . . ": *The Worship and Love of God* §117.

" . . . the different layers or auras . . . ": *The Five Senses* §263.

". . . 'fly wherever he wants'. . . ": *The Five Senses* §262.

". . . God punishes the one who faces God's glory . . . ": *The Worship and Love of God* §118.

". . . struck by a fit of swoon or lunacy . . . ": *The Worship and Love of God* §117.

Concerning Brockmer's account and Minister Ringwicht, see the introductory chapter on Swedenborg's health.

". . . that divine truths should be confirmed by the Lord . . . ": *Arcana Coelestia* §9166.

216

Brita Behm was born in 1670 and died in 1755. Her husband, Professor Johan Schwede, died in 1697. This maternal aunt, as well as several other relatives, are met with both in the dream diary and later in the *Spiritual Diary*. By distribution of estates and joint ownership of several mining enterprises, the members of the Swedberg–Swedenborg family maintained close contacts, not always on good terms. When Swedenborg's only maternal uncle, Lieutenant-Captain Albrecht de Behm, died in 1700, Swedenborg together with his siblings and his aunt inherited Brita Axmar's mines in Hälsingland. After having bought out his brothers and sisters, Swedenborg owned a fifth of the mining works. During the 1720s, his aunt pursued a lawsuit against him concerning her share.

"The Rosenadlers" probably refers to the sons of Brita Behm's daughter Eva. She was married to Deputy Assistant Johan Rosenadler.

Arvid Horn af Ekebyholm (1664–1742) was one of the most prominent Swedish politicians of the eighteenth century. After having been promoted to major-general during Charles XII's wars, he served as president of the government offices almost continuously from 1710 to 1738. With his cautious and guarded foreign policy against Russia, he was a typical representative of the fraction later called *mössorna*, the Caps. His measured and moderate mercantile policy should have appealed to the mine assessor and foundry proprietor Swedenborg.

219

"... the fact that he thinks of Jan Hus in this context is, as Inge Jonsson has pointed out ...": Jonsson: *Swedenborgs skapelsedrama De cultu et amore Dei*, 192.

"From Arvid Gradin's history of Moravianism ...": Gradin, *A Short History ...*, 1743.

"... the Moravian Brethren, with whom he was apparently still lodging ...": see the introductory section on Swedenborg's health.

221

"... James Hutton, a friend of ... Sven Rosén". This is evident from Rosén's writings: *Skrifter och bref af Sven Rosén*, edited by Emanuel Linderholm, Upsala 1910, 267.

222

"... When Swedenborg ... had written ... regarding the senses in general, he was struck ...": *The Five Senses* §§569, 570.

224

"I got a coat/and a pilgrim's staff ...": *Sions Sånger*, hymn no. 30:3, 4.

227

"... clothed with the sun, and the moon under her feet.": Revelation 12:1.

229

"In the Old Testament, Zechariah had put forth ....": Zechariah 6:1–3.

231

"The editors of the original Swedish text, Klemming and Dahlgren, conjectured that the abbreviation 'As.B.' referred to the Assessor Elias Brenner ...": the miniaturist and deputy of the Archive of Antiquities Elias Brenner (1647–1717). Brenner's wife Sophia, née Weber (1659–1730), was a famous poet, admired by

Swedenborg who called her "a Sappho of our age" (Tafel I, doc. 39, p. 208).

On communion preparations in Herrnhut, see Hamilton, 43; Gradin, 48; ". . . a social routine within the congregation . . . ": Gradin, 46.

"choir": the Moravian congregations consisted of different categories of people (widowers, bachelors, married men, boys, widows, married women, etc.) called choirs; these choirs were divided into classes and the classes into bands, the bands being very small groups. Every class and band had activities of their own.

"In his later works, Swedenborg argues against ritual confession . . . ": *True Christian Religion* §§528 ff., 538.

232

"In the marginal notes to one of his Bibles . . . ": "Swedenborg's marginal notes in the Schmidius Bible. Daniel." Translated from the Latin by E. E. Iungerrich, *New Church Life* (June 1914): 367 ff.

"In the original Hebrew text, it is called the *Jawan*": *Jawan* is an Old Testament name of Ionians of Asia Minor. In late texts, however, *jawan* refers to Greeks in a broader sense.

"As pointed out earlier in the introduction to this book . . . ": On the importance of Hebrew to Swedenborg, see Jonsson, *Swedenborgs korrespondenslära*, 225 ff.

". . . the section of *The Five Senses* that treats the anatomy of the papillae of the skin": Malphigi's discovery is further discussed in *The Animal Kingdom* III, §397 ff.

234

"In his journal of travel for 1738 . . . ": *Swedenborgs Resebeskrifningar under åren 1717–1739*, 93.

237

Johan Fredrik Didron (1686–1747) was a lieutenant-general. During the Russian war, Didron was accused of passivity and was charged with treason in 1743. Swedenborg dreams that Didron has gone to Denmark, possibly fleeing from a more severe penalty. In reality, Didron stayed in Sweden and was released after six months.

241

". . . the first chapter on the sense of touch *sensu tactus*] . . . ":
Animal Kingdom III, §470 ff.

243

Swedenborg is thinking of *The Animal Kingdom* III, §531ff.

246

The quandary contrived by the fact that we tend to prefer the
baneful for the conscientious is treated at length in *The Worship
and Love of God* §68.
On *amor regnans*: cf. Lamm,179 (Swedish edition).

250

"The qualities of faith are determined . . . ": *The Infinite* §127 ff.
"For all that which cometh not of faith . . . ": Romans 14:23; *A
Philosopher's Notebook*, 391.

254

"Paul's image of the Christian warrior . . . ": Ephesians 6:11.

255

Hans Bierchenius was a secretary of the Royal Board of Mining. According to the *Spiritual Diary* §4714, his complexion was
embellished after death, and he is in a paradisiac state.

257

"Vessels will later become . . . ": *Arcana Coelestia* §§1408, 1496
et passim; *Apocalypse Explained* §537.
"The vessel is also . . . an alchemist symbol . . . ": C. G. Jung,
"Individual Dream Symbolism in Relation to Alchemy," *Dreams*,
140 ff.
"Milk and bread were, at least in later years, Swedenborg's favorite food": Carl Robsahm, "Memoirer öfver Swedenborg": "at
home he always had a bun in boiled milk for dinner": *Skandinavisk
Nykyrklig Tidning* (May 1876), 74. See also Anders Hallengren's
annotated critical edition of Robsahm's memorandum, *Anteckningar om Swedenborg* (Stockholm: Skrifter utgivna av Föreningen
Swedenborgs Minne, 1989), 31.

NOTES TO DREAM DIARY

258

Count Sven Lagerberg (1672–1746) was a councilor. As a commissioned officer, he accompanied Charles XII to Turkey. He supported Arvid Horn's foreign policy and was against the Russian war of 1741–1743.

Count Carl Didrick Ehrenpreus was also a councillor. Ehrenpreus belonged to the circle of officials that went to Turkey with Charles XII. He returned via Stralsund in December 1715. He was known as a proficient judge. According to Swedenborg, he held that post even after death: *Tessin och Tessiniana*, 357.

260

". . . the exquisite Bible print he now has no difficulty in reading was probably Castello's edition . . . ": cf. *Messiah About to Come*, introduction by Alfred Acton, iii.

261

". . . love of God, which according to his doctrine of love, never goes unanswered . . . ": cf. Jonsson, *De cultu et amore Dei*, 158.

262

Hedvig Swedenborg (1690–1728) was married to Lars Benzelstierna, an assessor in the Royal Board of Mining and titular county governor in 1747. Benzelstierna was the brother of Eric Benzelius.

Ulrica Adlersten (1694–1757) was a lady-in-waiting of Princess Sofia Albertina. She was married to Swedenborg's relative, Lieutenant-Colonel Albrekt Schönström (1684–1740).

264

"The Brethren were few": according to Wesley's note in his journal of 1742, two years after he and his friends had left, the congregation consisted of some seventy persons. See *The Journal of John Wesley* II, 370.

"Only 'well-tried souls' could get access to the rites . . . ": Jacobsson, 225; Gradin, 122.

"Spangenberg . . . severely criticized . . . " *Brüderkirche in England*, 130.

On lottery as the tool of God's will, cf. Plitt, II, 395 f. On new members elected by drawing of lots, see Jacobsson, 225.

265

". . . he had written some years before the crisis, in his *Rational Psychology* . . .": *Rational Psychology* §372.

267

"Diminutives were encouraged, and a pious simple-minded-ness . . .": Wilhelm Lütjeharms, *Het philadelphisch-oecumenisch streven der Herrnhuters in de Nederlanden* . . . , 36.

271

amores spurios: illegitimate loves, bastards.

272

". . . mind or reason can operate quite separate from the feel-ings of the body and the perceptions of the soul . . .": *The Five Senses* §492.

"None but Jesus our Beloved. . . ": *Then Swenska Psalm-boken* (Stockholm 1695), hymn no. 247:10.

"the dark night . . . ": *"la noche oscura"*, from the *Libro de la noche oscura* by Saint John of the Cross; cf. the *Subida del monte Carmelo* by the same author.

273

". . . to free himself from the roots of sin, can be related to . . . ": *The Five Senses* §569.

277-278

"After the original sin, human love has obviously no longer sufficed": *Arcana Coelestia* §7882.

". . . celebrate God's omnipotence. . .": *Arcana Coelestia* §§7550, 8271.

286

Swedenborg's economy was closely examined by notary Frans G. Lindh in a series of papers published in the *Nya Kyrkans Tid-ning*, 1927–1930. Lindh proposed that King Ludvig XV of France sponsored Swedenborg's works. This is, in a broader context, dis-cussed in Lars Bergquist, *Swedenborgs hemlighet* (Stockholm: Natur och Kultur, 1999).

287

"By now, Nature has almost nothing to cover herself ": see further *Psychological Transactions*, 55.

BIBLIOGRAPHY

Manuscripts

Ringwicht, Casper Joachim. Letters to Kungl Maj:t (his majesty the king) and to kanslipresidenten (president of the government offices). London, July 10, 1744. Riksarkivet (The National Archives of Sweden), coll. Utrikesdepartementet, "Anglica," vols. 325, 328

"Samling af Correspondenser af Emanuel Swedenborg." Copies made by Carl Deléen. 2 vols. The Royal Library (no date).

Swedenborg, Emanuel. [Emanuel] Swedenborgs Drömbok. The Royal Library (The National Library of Sweden), Stockholm, JS 57.

Selected Editions of Swedenborg's Dream Diary

ENGLISH

Emanuel Swedenborg's Journal of Dreams. Trans. C. Th. Odhner. Bryn Athyn, Pa.: The Academy Book Room, 1918.

Swedenborg's Journal of Dreams 1743–1744. Edited from the original Swedish by G. E. Klemming. Trans. J. J. G. Wilkinson (1860). Ed. William Ross Woofenden. New York: Swedenborg Foundation, 1977.

Swedenborg's Journal of Dreams. Trans. J. J. G. Wilkinson. Commentary by Wilson Van Dusen. New York: The Swedenborg Foundation, 1986.

FRENCH

Emanuel Swedenborg: Le livre de reves. Journal des années 1743–44. Trans. and ed. Régis Boyer. Paris, 1979.

SWEDISH

Swedenborgs drömmar 1744 jemte hans andra anteckningar efter original-handskrifter meddelade af G. E. Klemming. Stockholm, 1859 (utg i 99 ex).

Swedenborgs drömmar 1744 jemte andra hans anteckningar efter original-handskrifter. Reflexioner i oktober 1859 öfver de nyligen uppdagade Swedenborgs drömmar 1744 hvilka derjemte oförändrade bifogas. Stockholm, 1860. Cf., Ehrenborg, Anna Fredrika.

Swedenborgs drömmar. Emanuel Swedenborgs dagbok 1743–44 utgiven och kommenterad med förklarande noter samt bibliografiska och biografiska essayer av Knut Barr. Stockholm, 1924.

Emanuel Swedenborg: Drömboken. Journalanteckningar 1743–44. Ed. P. E. Wahlund. Stockholm, 1952.

Other Publications

An Abridged Chronological List of the Works of Emanuel Swedenborg. Published in celebration of the centenary of The Swedenborg Society by The Royal Academy of Sciences. Uppsala and Stockholm, 1910.

Acton, Alfred. *An Introduction to the Word Explained: A Study of the Means by Which Swedenborg the Scientist and Philosopher Became the Theologian and Revelator.* Bryn Athyn, Pa.: Academy of the New Church, 1927

Åkerlund, L. "Trinitetstanken hos Zinzendorf." *Kyrkohistorisk Årsskrift* (1969).

Allen, Edward F. "Swedenborg's Philosophy as a Whole." *The New Philosophy* LXXXIXV, nos. 3 and 4 (July–Dec. 1981): 104 ff.; LXXXIX (July–Sept. 1986): 144.

Almquist, Johan Axel A. *Bergskollegium och bergslagsstaterna* (1637–1857).

Andrae, Tor. *Mystikens psykologi. Besatthet och inspiration.* Stockholm, 1926.

―――. *Swedenborg. Ur De stora filosoferna: deras liv och deras lära.* Ed. William Durant. Stockholm, 1928.

Arbman, Ernst. *Vision and Ecstasy.* Vol. 1, *Ecstasy or Religious Trance.* Uppsala, Sweden: Svenska Bokförlaget, 1963.

Becker, Bernhard. *Zinzendorf und sein Christentum.* 2 vols. Leipzig, 1900.

Benz, Ernst. *Emanuel Swedenborg: Naturforscher und Seer.* Munich: Hermann Rinn, 1948.

Biblia sacra ex interpret. Sebast Castellionis I–IV. London, 1726.

Biographiskt lexicon öfver namnkunnige svenske män. Uppsala, 1835–1857.

[Ehrenborg, Anna Fredrika]. *Reflexioner i oktober 1859 öfver de nyligen uppdagade Swedenborgs drömmar 1744 hvilka derjemte öfrändrade bifogas.* Stockholm, 1860.

Elgenstierna, Gustaf. *Den introducerade svenska adelns ättartaflor.* 9 vols. Stockholm: Norstedts, 1925–1936.

Evangelia och Epistlar på alla Söndagar, Högtider och Helgedagar; såsom ock ther sig tillböriga Collecter och Böner. 1739.

Freud, Sigmund. *Drömtydning* [Traumdeutung]. Trans. John Landquist. [N.P.], 1987.

Gradin, Arvid: *A Short History of the Bohemian–Moravian Protestant Church.* London, 1743.

Gruhle, Hans W. "Swedenborgs Träume. Ein Beitrag zur Phenomenologie seiner Mystik." *Psychologische Forschung* 5 (1924).

Grund-Lehren der Evangelischen Gemeinen die man seit 300 Jahren Die Brüder nennt, als Ihren übrigen Verstand von der Heil.Schrift, in Frage und Antwort zu fassen . . . Die andere Probe entworffen von dem Verfasser Der Ersten Probe. Büdingen, 1742.

Hamilton, J. Taylor. *A History of the Church Known as the Moravian or Unitas Fratrum or the Unity of the Brethren.* Bethlehem, Pa.: 1900.

Helander, Hans. *Em. Swedenborg: Festivus applausus Caroli XII in Pomeraniam suam adventum.* Uppsala, 1985.

Hök, Gösta. *Herrnhutisk teologi i svensk gestalt. Arvid Gradins dogmatiska och etiska huvudtankar.* (Uppsala universitets årsskrifter 1949:8). Uppsala, Leipzig. Tr. Uppsala 1950.

————. *Zinzendorfs Begriff der Religion*. (Uppsala universitets årsskrift 1946:8). Uppsala, 1948.

Iungerrich, "E E: Swedenborg's Marginal Notes in the Schmidius Bible. Daniel." *New Church Life* (June 1914).

Jacobsson, Nils. *Den svenska herrnhutismens uppkomst*. Uppsala, 1908.

Jarrick, Arne. *Den himmelske älskaren*. Stockholm, 1987.

Johannes av Korset. *Bestigningen av berget Karmel*. Trans. Gudrun Schultz. Helsingborg, 1978.

Jonsson, Inge. *Swedenborg korrespondenslära*. Stockholm: Almquist & Wiksell International, 1969.

————. *Swedenborgs skapelsedrama De cultu et amore Dei. En studie av motiv och intellektuell miljö*. Stockholm: Natur och Kultur, 1961.

Jonsson, Inge, and Olle Hjern. *Swedenborg. Sökaren i naturens och andens världar*. Stockholm: Natur och Kultur, 1976.

Jung, Carl Gustav. *Alchemical Studies*. London: Ark Paperbacks, 1986.

————. *Dreams*. London: Ark Paperbacks, 1986.

————. *Psychology and Alchemy*. London: Ark Paperbacks, 1986.

Jägerskiöld, Olof. *Den svenska utrikespolitikens historia* II:2, 1721–1772. 1957.

Kahl, Achatio. *Narratiunculae de vitis hominum in E. Swedenborgii diario commermoratorum*. Tübingen–London, 1859.

Kleen, E. A. G. *Swedenborg. En lefnadsskildring*. 2 vols. Stockholm: Sandbergs, 1917, 1920.

Kuylenstierna, Oswald. *Svensk rokoko. Människor, dagligt liv*. Stockholm, 1923.

Kyrko-lagen af 1686. Uppsala, 1845.

Lagerroth, Fredrik. *Frihetstidens maktägande ständer 1719–1772* (in *Sveriges riksdag*, parts 5–6). [N.P.], 1934.

Lamm, Martin. *Swedenborg. En studie öfver hans utveckling till mystiker och andeskådare*. Stockholm: Hugo Gebers Förlag, 1915.

————. *Emanuel Swedenborg: The Development of His Thought*. Trans. Tomas Spiers and Anders Hallengren. West Chester, Pa.: The Swedenborg Foundation, 2000.

Lindh, F. G. "Swedenborgs ekonomi." *Nya Kyrkans Tidning* (1927–1930).

Lindholm, Johannes. "Till frågan om den religiösa mystikens väsen." *Svensk Teologisk Kvartalstidskrift* 13:1 (1958).

Lindroth, Sten. "Linné — legend och verklighet." *Lychnos* (1965–1966).

Linné, Carl von. *Nemesis Divina*. Stockholm, 1968.

Lütjeharms, Wilhelm. *Het philadelphisch-oecumenisch streven der Herrnhuters in de Nederlanden in de achttiende eeuw*. Zeist, 1935.

A Manual of Doctrine; or a Second Essay to Bring into the Form of Question and Answer . . . . London, 1742.

Maudsley, Henry. *Em Swedenborg och hans själstillstånd*. Trans. from *The Journal of Mental Science* (July 1869). Stockholm, 1874.

Neiuw Nederlandsch Biographisch Woordenboek. Vol. V. Leyden, 1921.

Odhner, C. T. "Swedenborg's Dreams, or Diary of 1744." *New Church Life* XXIV, no. 7 (July 1914): 390–404.

Olsson, Anders. *Den okända texten. En essä om tolkningsteori från kyrkofäderna till Derrida*. Kristianstad, 1987.

Pleijel, Hilding. *Der schwedische Pietismus in seinen Beziehungen zu Deutschland*. Lund, 1935.

————. *Herrnhutismen i Sydsverige*. Stockholm, 1925.

————. *Karolinsk kyrkofromhet, pietism och herrnhutism 1680–1772* (Svenska Kyrkans historia, vol. V). Stockholm and Uppsala, 1935.

Plitt, Hermann. *Zinzendorfs Theologie*. 2 vols. Gotha, 1869–1871.

Potts, John Faulkner, comp., ed., and trans. *Swedenborg Concordance: A Complete Work of Reference to the Theological Writings of Em. Swedenborg*. 6 vols. London: Swedenborg Society, 1888; rept. 1948.

Rimius, Henri. *A Candid Narrative of the Rise and Progress of the Herrn-huters, Commonly Called Moravians, or Unitas Fratrum*. London, 1752.

Robsahm, Carl. "Memoirer öfver Swedenborg." *Skandinavisk Nykyrklig Tidning* (April–Nov. 1876): 60–171.

――――. *Anteckningar om Swedenborg*. Ed. Anders Hallengren. Stockholm: Skrifter utgivna av Föreningen Swedenborgs Minne, 1989.

Rosén, Sven. *Skrifter och bref af Sven Rosén samlade och utgifna af Emanuel Linderholm*. Uppsala, 1910.

――――. *Sven Roséns dagbok*. Ed. N. Odenvik. Stockholm, 1948.

Sigstedt, Cyriel Odhner. *The Swedenborg Epic: the Life and Works of Emanuel Swedenborg*. New York, 1952.

Sions Sänger. Vol. 1. Stockholm, 1743.

Sions Sänger. 2 vols. Stockholm, 1781.

Stålmarck, Torkel. *Tankebyggare. 1753–1762*. Stockholm Studies in History of Literature 29. Stockholm, 1986.

[Stierncrona, Elisabeth.] *Mariae Bästa Del, eller thet ena nödvändiga Påminnelser angaende den Christna Trons Lärostycken*. 2 vols. Stockholm, 1752–1756.

Stroh, Alfred H., ed. *Catalogus Bibliotecae Emanuelis Swedenborgii*. Stockholm, 1907.

Sundelin, U. R. F. *Den Svenska swedenborgianismens historia*. Uppsala, 1886.

Swedberg, Jesper. *Lefwernes beskrifning*. Ed. Gunnar Wetterberg. Skrifter utgivna av Vetenskapssocieteten i Lund 25:1. Lund, 1941.

――――. *Guds Heliga Ödnalag Wid Menniskiors Timeliga och Ewiga Welferd eller Oferd*. Skara, 1713.

✳

Swedenborg, Emanuel. *Änglavisheten om den Gudomliga Försynen.*
Trans. Björn A. H. Boyesen. Avesta, 1981.

————. *The Animal Kingdom.* Trans. John Garth Wilkinson. 3
vols. London, 1843–1844; rept. by photo-offset, 1960.

————. *The Apocalypse Explained.* 6 vols. Trans. John Whitehead.
2nd edition. West Chester, Pa.: The Swedenborg Foundation,
1993–1997.

————. *Arcana Coelestia.* 12 vols. Trans. J. F. Potts. 2nd edition.
West Chester, Pa.: The Swedenborg Foundation, 1994–1998.

————. [Arcana Coelestia.] *Himmelska Hemligheter som innehållas i
den Heliga Skrift eller Herrens Ord och nu blifvit upptäckta: . . . jämte det
underbara som blifvit sedt i andarnas värld och i änglarnas himmel.* Trans.
J. A. Sevén. Rev. ed. C. J. N. Manby. 17 vols. Stockholm,
1912–1919.

————. *The Brain.* 2 vols. Trans. R. L. Tafel. London: James
Spiers, 1882, 1887.

————. *Concerning the Messiah about to Come and Concerning the Kingdom of God and the Last Judgment.* Trans. Alfred Acton. Bryn Athyn,
Pa.: The Academy of the New Church, 1949.

————. *Den sanna kristna religionen, som innehåller hela läran om Gud
för den Nya Kyrkan, vilken är förutsagd hos Daniel 7:13, 14 och i Uppen-
barelsen 21:1, 2.* Trans. Adolph Theodor Boyesen. Stockholm,
1914.

————. *The Economy of the Animal Kingdom.* Trans. Augustus Clissold. 2 vols. London, 1845–1846; reproduced by photo-offset,
New York, 1955.

————. *The Fibre. The Economy of the Animal Kingdom. Transaction III.*
Trans. Alfred Acton. Philadelphia, 1918; rpt. Bryn Athyn, Pa.:
Swedenborg Scientific Assoc., 1976.

————. *The Five Senses.* Trans. Enoch S. Price. Philadelphia, 1914;
rpt. Bryn Athyn, Pa.: The Swedenborg Scientific Assoc., 1976.

————. *Hieroglyphisk Clav till andeliga och naturliga hemligheter.* 2nd
edition. Wexjö, n. d.

————. *The Infinite and Final Cause of Creation, Also the Intercourse Between the Soul and the Body*. Trans. J. J. G. Wilkinson. 2nd edition with an introduction by L. F. Hite. London, 1908.

————. *Om Guds dyrkan och kärleken till Gud* (De Cultu et Amore Dei). Trans. Ritva Jonsson. Stockholm, 1961.

————. *Om Himlen och dess underbara ting och om Helvetet. På grund av vad som blivit hört och sett*. Trans. Gustaf Baeckström. Stockholm, 1944.

————. *A Philosopher's Note Book*. Trans. and ed. A. Acton. Philadelphia: Swedenborg Scientific Assoc., 1931.

————. *Posthumous Theological Works*, 2 vols. Trans. John Whitehead. 2nd edition. West Chester, Pa.: The Swedenborg Foundation, 1996.

————. *The Principia; or, The First Principles of Natural Things*. 2 vols. Trans. A. Clissold. London, 1846; rpt. Bryn Athyn, Pa.: The Swedenborg Scientific Assoc., 1976.

————. *Psychological Transactions*. Trans. and ed. Alfred Acton. Philadelphia: The Swedenborg Scientific Assoc., 1955.

————. *Rational Psychology*. Trans. Norbert H. Rogers and Alfred Acton. Philadelphia: The Swedenborg Scientific Assoc., 1950.

————. *Resebeskrifningar af Emanuel Swedenborg under åren 1710–1739*. Stockholm: Kungl Vetenskapsakademien (The Royal Academy of Sciences), 1911.

————. *The Spiritual Diary of Emanuel Swedenborg, Being the Record During Twenty Years of His Supernatural Experience*. 5 vols. Trans. George Bush and John N. Smithson. London: The Swedenborg Society, 1883–1902.

————. *The Word of the Old Testament Explained*. 7 vols. Trans. Alfred Acton. Bryn Athyn, Pa.: The Academy of the New Church, 1928–1948.

Swenska Psalm-boken (Then) . . . med koraler. Stockholm, 1695.

Swenska Psalmboken (Then), Med de Stycker som ther til höra, och på följande sida upteknade finnas. Uppå Kongl. Majestäts Nådigste Befallning år MDCXCV öfwersedd och nödtorfteligen förbätrad. Göteborg, 1762.

Svenskt bibliskt uppslagsverk. 1962.

Söderblom, Nathan. *Svenskarnas fromhet.* Stockholm, 1933.

Tafel, R. L., ed. and trans. *Documents Concerning the Life and Character of Emanuel Swedenborg.* 2 vols., 3 parts. London: The Swedenborg Society, 1875–1890.

———. *Swedenborg's Diary for 1743 and 1744.* Repr. from *Morning Light,* no. 112 (1880).

Tersmeden, Carl. *Amiral Carl Tersmedens memoarer.* In *Fredrik I:s Sverige.* Ed. Nils Erdmann. Stockholm, 1916.

Tessin och Tessiniana. Biographie med anecdoter och reflexioner samlade utur framledne riks-rådets m. m. grefve C. G. Tessins egenhändiga manuscripter. Stockholm, 1819.

Toksvig, Signe: *Emanuel Swedenborg: Scientist and Mystic.* New Haven, Conn.: Yale University Press, 1948.

———. *Emanuel Swedenborg: Vetenskapsman och mystiker.* Trans. Daniel Andreae. Stockholm, 1949.

Tottie, H. W. *Jesper Swedbergs lif och verksamhet. Bidrag till svenska kyrkans historia.* 2 vols. Uppsala, 1885–1886.

Underhill, Evelyn. *Mysticism: a Study in the Nature and Development of Man's Spiritual Consciousness.* New York: Dutton, 1961.

Watts, W., trans. *St. Augustine's Confessions.* 2 vols. Loeb Classical Library. London: 1977–1979.

Wauer, Gerhard A. *Die Anfänge der Brüder-Kirche in England.* Leipzig, 1900.

Wesley, John. *The Journal of John Wesley.* Vol. 2. Ed. Nehemiah Curnock. London, 1906–1916.

White, William. *Emanuel Swedenborg: His Life and Writings.* 2 vols. London, 1867.

Wilhelm, Richard. *The Secret of the Golden Flower: A Chinese Book of Life.* With foreword and commentary by C G Jung. Reading, 1984.

Vollständige sowohl historisch als theologische Nachricht von der Herrnhutischen Bruderschaft. 1735–1736.

Zinzendorf, Ludwig Nicolaus, von. *Berliner Reden 1738.* Leizig und Altona, 1749.

———. *34 Homilien über die Wundenlitaney.* 1747.

———. *Sendschreiben an Ihro Königl. Majest. von Schweden von Grafen und Herrn Ludewig von Zinzendorff, betreffende sein und seiner Gemeinde Glauben und Bekänntnis.* 1735.

INDEX